CHARLIE'S CHARTS PUBLICATIONS:

CHARLIE'S CHARTS of the Western Coast of MEXICO by Charles and Margo Wood
CHARLIE'S CHARTS of POLYNESIA by Charles and Margo Wood
CHARLIE'S CHARTS NORTH to ALASKA by Charles and Margo Wood
CHARLIE'S CHARTS of the HAWAIIAN ISLANDS by Charles E. Wood
CHARLIE'S CHARTS of the U.S. PACIFIC COAST by Charles and Margo Wood
CHARLIE'S CHARTS of COSTA RICA by Margo Wood
 A PRAIRIE CHICKEN GOES TO SEA by Margo Wood

Also written by Charles E. Wood:
BUILDING YOUR DREAM BOAT, published by Cornell Maritime Press

Canadian Cataloguing in Publication Data
Wood, Charles E. (Charles Edward), 1928 - 1987
  Charlie's charts north to Alaska
  Includes index.
  ISBN 0-9686370-5-1
1. Pilot guides - Pacific Coast (B.C.) 2. Pilot guides - Pacific Coast
(Alaska) 3. Boats and boating - Pacific Coast (B.C.) 4. Boats and
boating - Pacific Coast (Alaska) 5. Pacific Coast (B.C.) - Description
and travel. 6. Pacific Coast (Alaska) - Description and travel. I. Title.
G1171.P55W66   623.89'28711   C95-910392-9

Copyright © 1986, 1995, 2001, 2004 Charles and Margo Wood
First published 1986, reprinted 1989, revised 1995, 2001, 2005

Updated and enlarged by Margo Wood
Sketches and drawings by Charles Wood
Photographs by Charles and Margo Wood

PRINTED IN CANADA   ISBN 0-9686370-5-1

Charlie's Charts

Twenty-fifth Anniversary
1982 - 2007

This guide belongs to _____

Skipper of _____

(Photo or sketch of your boat)

First mate _____

Crew _____

_____

Home Port _____

Portage Bay reflections

To Albert,
Wishing you many
memorable cruises on
this beautiful coast.
Margo Wood
Feb 07

Glacier Bay vista

ACKNOWLEDGMENTS

Although my late husband, Charles, passed away in 1987 and I continue to revise and update *Charlie's Charts* as needed, he is the original author and creator of these guides. It is his artistry and descriptions that make the guides valuable aids when cruising. I as the caretaker simply continue to update and expand the area covered as I continue to explore this beautiful coast.

There are several people who have been generous with their knowledge and time in the preparation of this updated and enlarged edition and I wish to acknowledge their contributions. Fellow sailors have shared their knowledge of this coast with me and have been most helpful during some of my adventures while sailing single-handed as well as with crew. Among them are the following who deserve special recognition:

Commander Michael Marquardt and Karin Steinkamp of S/V *Innoey* made several suggestions for making the guide more user-friendly and provided current information about facilities and anchorages they visited during a recent cruise to Glacier Bay,

Captain Laura Tritch, contributed her observations of changes that have occurred since her last visit to Alaska,

Marilyn and William Immanse of S/V *Shaman I* and Colleen and Lorne Shantz of S/V *Shaunsea* gave valuable suggestions and worthwhile information related to various anchorages,

Phil Elder of *Pier Review* made timely editorial suggestions that were pertinent and constructive,

Teri Lydiard whose generous assistance and computer expertise made short work of some tedious tasks,

And a sincere note of appreciation to Maurice Brager whose careful proofreading puts *spell-check* to shame.

Thank you all, very much.

Margo Wood

DISCLAIMER

The word, "CHARTS," in the title of this publication is not intended to imply that these hand-drawn sketches are sufficiently accurate to be used for navigation. They and the accompanying text are meant to act solely as a handy cruising guide to harbors and anchorages in the area discussed.

The use of official Canadian Hydrographic Charts and U.S. National Ocean Service (NOAA) Charts is mandatory for safe boating. The list in Appendix I is presented to assist boaters in choosing charts which cover the areas in which they are interested. Since chart numbers are constantly revised, some data may be outdated soon after publication of this guide. **Do not use any of the drawings in this book for navigation.** *Charlie's Charts* and *Polymath Energy Consultants Ltd.* are in no way responsible for loss or damages resulting from the use of this book.

UPDATING INFORMATION

If you have current information that is worthwhile passing on to cruisers following in your wake please send us an email at info@charliescharts.com For updating material visit our website at www.charliescharts.com

CONTENTS

INTRODUCTION

Blessed with an abundance of harbors, magnificent scenery, fascinating cultures, and colorful history this region vies for the title of the greatest cruising area in the world. It is so indented with coves, fiords and inlets, and sprinkled with islands that 1,000 miles of linear distance contain over 25,000 miles of coastline. The Southeast Alaska portion alone accounts for 250 linear miles and 11,000 coastline miles. There are few other places where inland passages can be followed for hundreds of miles and where the sea's bounty can be harvested so readily in all its variety. No other cruising area has so many glaciers which discharge their bergs directly into the sea.

The area lies within the migratory low pressure system belt around the world, thus lacking a settled, continuously sunny cruising season. The annual movement of summer's North Pacific High and the winter's Aleutian Low cause variations in the pattern of the weather, but do not completely deter the passage of the low pressure systems in summer, resulting in frequently cloudy skies often laced with rain. Although more sunshine may be desirable, it must be remembered that it is precipitation that keeps these areas so heavily forested and its glaciers and rivers continuously fed.

When traversing this coast, travelers move through several different zones. The south is more populated and has islands that are generally low and provided with shallow, well protected harbors. As you move further north the inlets become fiord-like and longer, their walls and shorelines are steeper, and the harbors are correspondingly deeper and fewer in number. At the northernmost section of this guide, the snow line creeps down the steep mountains, and the heavy snow cover gives birth to glaciated mountains close to the sea.

These different zones are separated by some crucial open water passages that must be treated with care and caution. These are not of great length, and the majority of the traveling is done within the "Inside Passage" with protection from the open sea. Vessels of all types and sizes make the passage safely, and commercial fishermen move up and down the coast regularly as different areas open for fishing.

Recent years have seen an unprecedented growth in the number of visitors to the area trveling the coast in everything from small boats to luxurious cruise ships. Beauty alone can commend a visit, but its clean air and waters, and the friendly people in the small towns and villages are equally inviting. In addition, it has all the elements of "cruising foreign:" length, diversity of interest and culture, demands on vessel and crew, and even stormy conditions to be encountered in the open water sections.

DESTINATIONS and the AREA COVERED by THIS GUIDE

This guide covers the Inside Passage to Glacier Bay National Park and returns by way of Sitka. Beyond lie other portions of Alaska: Prince William Sound, the Kenai Peninsula, Cook Inlet and the arc of the remote Aleutian Islands which can be reached from this area, but are outside the scope of this guide. Also not included are the offshore Queen Charlotte Islands of British Columbia and the rugged west coast of Vancouver Island.

This volume covers the route from Victoria, B.C. through the waters between Vancouver Island and the mainland and then behind the skein of islands that make the Inside Passage up to Southeast Alaska. First-time cruisers on this coast may not have the inclination or time to make the entire voyage, and so a number of beautiful and rewarding side-trips are described. These include Princess Louisa Inlet, Fiordland Recreational Area, Kitimat and the Kitlope. In addition there are a sufficient number of suggested anchorages and alternate nearby routes that one could easily follow the basic route suggested for the Inside Passage and visit quite different anchorages on the return trip. It would be impossible in an illustrated guide such as this to include all of the possible anchorages available on the entire coast, but the best and most convenient anchorages are given in a format that has proven to be most helpful for cruising sailors for many years.

The focal destination of this guide is Glacier Bay, Alaska. The route described traverses the main beauties of an area which is growing in reputation and popularity. The criteria used in selecting anchorages and harbors are based on a nominal day's run of 50 nautical miles for a slow-moving vessel such as an auxiliary sail boat. Sources of fuel and water are other factors. However, this is no hard and fast rule, and in several sections the anchorages are more closely spaced when they are of special interest. They also allow for a wider selection of stops for fast vessels making long daily runs. At several places it is possible to make additional routes off the main circuit; to go up around Behm Canal to Misty Fiords National Monument for example, or to go into bays and anchorages not described. On the other hand, in a few cases, longer legs may be necessary due to lack of a suitable intermediate stop. This is usually true of the open water crossings i.e. across the Strait of Georgia, the run across Queen Charlotte Sound past Cape Caution, and for the crossing of Dixon Entrance. These are given special attention in the general notes that follow.

The anchorages described in this guide have been personally visited and evaluated. The sketches are all hand-drawn and it is emphasized that they are NOT TO BE USED FOR NAVIGATION. Proper charts and sailing directions should be used for actual navigation or as a back-up for plotters or other electronic navigational systems. This guide does not relieve a skipper of the responsibility of navigating his/her own vessel safely, for a good sailor is always prudent.

THE TYPE OF VESSEL

Though fuel, water and provisions are easily obtained, any vessel chosen should be sound and able to carry the requirements of those aboard for extended periods of time. The ship must be capable of being lived aboard and of facing weather and sea conditions that may worsen rapidly. The vessel should be arranged so that the dinghy can be stowed on board especially when making passages in open water such as passing Cape Caution or during any trip when rough seas prevail. An inflatable life-raft equipped with emergency supplies gives an additional element of safety.

When cruising this area the weather can be damp and cold or quite balmy, depending on the time of year and weather systems moving along the coast. However in the vicinity of the glaciers air and water temperatures are commonly very cold, an important fact that the skipper should keep in mind when outfitting the vessel.

As a long-time sailor, it is painful for me to admit that perhaps the best type of boat for this trip is a trawler-type vessel capable of at least 8 knots. This is not to say that a sailing vessel cannot be used as all areas described in this guide were visited in a 30-year-old, 10m (34ft.) foot wooden cutter with a cruising speed under power of 5 knots. But the prevailing winds over most of this area are such that one should expect to motor for most of the trip when heading north, and for at least some of the time on the return to the south. Moreover, the negotiation of passes (if they are traversed at slack water) requires a vessel that can make a minimum of 4 knots. Lastly, a dodger or cabin where one can be out of the cold wind is essential, as is a heater to take the chill out of a boat during the cold, rainy days that can be experienced.

Power boats (excluding high speed planing hulls) usually have these advantages along with the benefit of higher cruising speeds as compared with most sailboats. They are particularly suitable on the north-bound trip when head winds and seas of moderate level are usually encountered. However, they are less comfortable with following winds and seas and cannot handle heavy weather on the open water crossings as easily as sailboats. Power boats are constrained to wait for suitable conditions—if comfort is desired—and thus the overall times for the full passage for all types of boats does not differ by more than a few days unless exceptional conditions are experienced.

FUEL, MAINTENANCE, WATER and PROVISIONS

Both diesel oil and gasoline are available fuel stations. Prices vary but are higher in the remote areas while larger centers (where there is commercial fishing traffic) tend to have fairly similar prices. The high taxes on fuel in Canada lead to more expensive fuel when in Canadian waters as compared to U.S. prices. Propane may be obtained from dealers in towns along the route and kerosene can be purchased at most hardware stores.

It is advisable to carry a complete set of spares such as oil and fuel oil filters and water pump impellers as well as sufficient engine and gearbox oil for the entire trip. At least one spare fan belt should be aboard in addition to a supply of duct and electrical tape, miscellaneous electrical connections and a well-stocked tool box. Spare batteries for everything from flashlights to cameras should be labeled and stowed in air-tight containers.

Minor repairs to hull and engine can be undertaken in most towns where haul-out facilities and mechanics are usually to be found. Major repairs can only be done at the large towns having shipbuilding facilities—with parts probably having to be shipped from Vancouver or Seattle. Allow at least 3 days for air delivery of parts from a supplier. A well serviced and maintained engine(s) is highly recommended for a trip in these waters.

Water available at public docks is usually good, fresh, soft water. Fresh water is also available at waterfalls and streams, but one should ascertain that the sources are from unpopulated areas, and the water should be treated. Water-makers are not an essential item of equipment when cruising this coast but they have the advantages of convenience and consistency in quality and taste.

Initial provisioning is best accomplished in Vancouver or Victoria, British Columbia or in any U.S. city in the Puget Sound area. However, there are stores at almost all stops with docks along the route and many small towns have supermarkets. Prices vary with the degree of isolation of the store and tend to be approximately 20% higher in Prince Rupert and Alaskan stores compared to southern outlets. Fresh produce in Alaska is shipped from Washington and the selection may be limited in remote places.

ANCHORING and MOORING FACILITIES

The guide describes the most convenient and protected anchorages along the route. Many more can be found if the scope of travel is wider. If desired, one can anchor during the entire cruise. However, there is moorage at all towns along the passage, and one usually uses these facilities for their convenience.

Moorage

At many places in both B.C. and Alaska, there are government installed wharves and floats that can be used on a first-come, first-served basis by either commercial or pleasure craft. These tend to be heavily used during the fishing season and rafting is a common courtesy. In the larger towns there are also public and private marinas. A section allocated to transient vessels is common in most government marinas and they are indicated on the charts. Crowding of these transient floats is uncommon so that there is normally space available. The harbormasters will sometimes direct you to a berth that is temporarily vacant (hot-berthing) in order to accommodate transient traffic. This is one reason why you should report to the harbormaster as soon as possible on arrival.

Fees are usually moderate at government docks though facilities are sometimes limited for such items as washrooms and showers. Charges at private marinas may be several times those charged at public facilities and services available range from basic to luxurious. As a result of high operating costs and a very short season fees charged are higher than those in more populated, warmer areas of B.C. and U.S. which have competition and a longer business season. Inquire about charges prior to tying up for a stop-over at any marina to avoid costly surprises.

Anchoring

Good, strong tackle and experience in setting your anchor for varying bottom conditions and the type of anchorage is essential for safety and peace of mind. A feature of this area is that valuable experience is gained in the less demanding southern portion before reaching the deeper, sometimes restricted anchorages of the mid and northern sections of the guide.

At least two sets of anchors and rodes are essential, while experienced cruisers normally carry three sets (one of which may be a small "lunch hook"). Rope rodes should always include a section of good-sized chain at the anchor, and an all chain rode has some advantage in deep water anchoring. The larger the gear the more essential is an anchor winch which is a necessity with an all-chain rode. A 45 to 60 m (150- to 200-foot) length of 1.2 cm (1/2") buoyant line is useful as a shore line when swinging is to be restricted. Arrangements for its ready access and systematic stowage avoids time-consuming confusion.

The CQR and Bruce anchors are commonly seen and are satisfactory in most anchorages. The Bruce anchor has gained support in northern waters where its ability to hold with minimum scope helps in the deeper anchorages. The Northill is also used, and is favored by fishermen. Danforth anchors are sometimes used but are easily fouled by kelp and eel grass.

The minimum rode for the main anchor should be 90m (300'). Several of the anchorages in northern areas have depths of 90 feet or more, thus bringing the ratio of scope to depth close to the minimum 3 to 1. In considering the depth of an anchorage, remember that this entire area has a high tidal range. Basic anchoring etiquette involves giving ample clearance to vessels already in an anchorage.

WHEN TO TRAVEL

Glacier Bay records show that the bulk of visitors arrive from mid-May to mid-September. Although temperatures are not high in May or September they are good months for traveling in both B.C. and Alaska, as the weather is clear and fog is least likely. The winter snow gives scenic views and melts to feed innumerable waterfalls. In July and August, the weather can be warm, but fog can become a problem; notably in the area from Dixon Entrance to the northern end of Vancouver Island. By October the winter rains commence, marking the beginning of the stormy part of the year, usually lasting until March.

For a trip to be done in one season it is best to start as early as possible, perhaps by mid-May or early June, certainly no later than early July. This gives one a summer in the north, which can be adjusted or expanded to suit the vessel's capabilities, weather conditions and one's interests.

Some consider spending an extended period cruising this unique area, staying for a winter or two in Alaska. It should be noted, though, that the harsh climate and crowded docks are hard on a vessel in winter, and living aboard to care for your boat is essential.

Another possibility for some sizes and types of boats is to trailer your vessel to a launching destination, use it for as long as possible, and return the same way at the end of the season. Some quite large power boats from inland prairie provinces and western states are transported to Comox, Campbell River or Lund, B.C. to enjoy a spring and summer cruising in these waters. The B.C. and Alaska Ferry system do the same for small pleasure craft, taking care of the long journey up and down the coast in a short time and leaving the best part of the year for exploring your chosen area. Kayakers in increasing numbers are seen paddling along the coast and camping on the beaches in the countless coves dotting the shoreline.

THE CRUCIAL PASSAGES

There are four major passages along the route, though any part can be made very easy or very difficult according to weather and sea conditions.

The Strait of Georgia

You may wish to avoid crossing of Strait of Georgia by staying on the eastern side of the Strait. However, this will not eliminate the discomforts of rough conditions in the Strait, for there remain several long passages which must be made sailing against the winds and seas of the prevailing northwesterlies. Moreover, this eastern route takes a newcomer away from the scenic and attractive Gulf Islands area and numerous attractive anchorages would be missed.

As a rule, sailing vessels and large powered craft may cross the Strait almost any time, though in stormy weather the trip can be very uncomfortable. Small craft are well advised to wait for suitable conditions for an easier and safer crossing.

The weather holds the key to the conditions that will be met on the crossing the Strait. Forecasting the weather is a chancy business but in these waters there are some general conditions that can be expected. Good summer weather has settled northwesterly winds. They tend to be light in the early morning, rise during the day, and die down after about 1700 hours. A heavy dew on the decks at night is a good indicator of such a period. Thus, the early morning or the evening hours are the most suitable for traveling.

If the northwesterlies do not diminish in the evening this is because a high pressure area has stayed in position for two or three days. Crossings can be uncomfortable at this time due to the build up of seas, so it is best to wait out the weather and enjoy the Gulf Islands.

Southeasterly winds presage rain and storms. They vary in intensity and while each storm seldom lasts more than 24 hours, several successive fronts may extend this period over several days. Weather reports can usually give one an estimate of the strength of the disturbance. The lighter winds can allow travel, albeit in rain or overcast conditions, while the heavier storms should be treated with caution. In summer there are generally more good traveling days than bad, and most waiting periods are usually of short duration.

In crossing the Strait of Georgia between Nanaimo or Silva Bay and Welcome Passage a special note should be made regarding the area labeled as "Whiskey-Golf" on the charts. This area is set aside for Canadian and U.S. Navy torpedo test purposes. Its full extent is marked on current charts but may not be indicated on older ones. The direct route across the Strait passes through this zone. If you stray into the area without clearing with Winchelsea Control on VHF Ch. 16, you will be speedily apprised of the error. If permission is granted to cross the area when tests are not scheduled, you may be requested to call again when clear of the zone. Tests are not carried out over much of the summer and are usually limited to between 0700 to 1730, but the zone is reserved and must be cleared for passage. Announcements of the times when torpedo tests are to be carried out in the following 24-hour period are given at the end of weather forecasts.

The route from Silva Bay to Welcome Pass can easily be arranged to avoid this area. You should allow for a slight southerly dog-leg, or proceed about 13 miles north of Nanaimo to south of Ballenas Islands and cross via Lasqueti Island. Another route proceeds north to Comox where one can either visit Campbell River before entering Discovery Passage or cross over to Lund and proceed northward to Desolation Sound and beyond. These routes are the safest way to avoid unnecessary encounters with officialdom, and in fact provide suitable slants for the crossing as well as some attractive anchorages.

Mid-Section Passes

The most direct route into Johnstone Strait from the Strait of Georgia is via Campbell River and Discovery Passage. Timing is crucial, for the tidal stream can run to 15 knots at springs through Seymour Narrows. Further north, Race and Current Passage (where tidal currents may reach 7 knots) must also be passed before Johnstone Strait is entered.

Before entering Seymour Narrows, the influence of the strong tidal currents can be noticeable. With the flood (south-flowing) opposed by southeasterly winds, a heavy race occurs off of Cape Mudge and Willow Point. In fact, with any strong wind opposing either stream, the various races and eddies can become quite dangerous.

Furthermore, local travel between harbors near Discovery Passage (even outside the narrows) can be greatly affected by the strong tidal currents unless the passage is made at or near slack water. The current sweeps past the entrances to Quathiaski Cove and Gowland Harbor at a fast rate; if you have been fishing and not watching the tide tables it can be a chore working back to anchor. This is the voice of experience! The Quadra Island Ferry also gives a reading of these currents, indicated by its attitude as it crosses.

The foregoing aside, the passage can be made without difficulty if done at or near slack water or going in the direction of the turning tide. The 25 miles of Discovery Passage can be done in one run, and a favorable tide often carries right to Alert Bay or Port McNeill.

The favored northbound route for pleasure craft is following a series of passes beginning with Yuculta Rapids, Gillard Passage and Dent Rapids, then proceeding along Cordero Channel. Just before reaching Greene Point Rapids you can proceed in a southerly direction along Blind Channel until reaching Johnstone Strait. Alternatively, after passing through Greene Point Rapids you can either join Johnstone Strait via Chancellor Channel or continue on until reaching Wellbore Channel. This passage includes Whirlpool Rapids beyond which it joins Sunderland Channel where you must then enter the final portion of Johnstone Strait. Though slightly longer, this route is more interesting and scenic than following Discovery Passage to Johnstone Strait. In addition, it avoids both the heavy commercial traffic of cruise ships and log booms in Discovery Passage and the northwest winds which often build in the afternoon, and make northbound travel slow and uncomfortable. Though the various rapids can attain impressive velocities, if the first rapids are entered just before the turn of the tide it is possible to carry an ebbing tide through the entire series unless strong westerly winds slow your progress in east/west channels. If this occurs there are many anchorages indicated in the guide in which to wait until the regular change of the tide when the rapids are again passable.

Queen Charlotte Sound

The passage between the north end of Vancouver Island past Cape Caution to the entrance of Fitz Hugh Sound is perhaps the most crucial of the open water passages. Though often crossed in benign conditions with just an easy northwesterly swell, Queen Charlotte Sound can develop steep and dangerous seas. This is caused by the effects of ebb currents flowing northward, a shallow basin (as little as 20 fathoms), and exposure to northwesterly winds with a long fetch. If possible, time your passage so that you have an ebb tide until reaching Cape Caution so the flood tide gives you a lift for the rest of the passage. It is advisable to leave early in the morning so that maximum mileage can be made before the afternoon northwesterly winds create uncomfortable head seas. Obviously, a good weather forecast is essential before commencing the passage.

During winter storms this body of water is at its worst while in the late spring and summer gales are less frequent. Good anchorages are indicated for waiting out inclement weather conditions until the passage can be resumed comfortably.

Most powered craft find that the crossing from Port McNeill or Port Hardy past Egg Island and Cape Caution to anchorages in Fitz Hugh Sound angles comfortably over the prevailing swell. An alternative route with less exposure to the Sound can be made by crossing Queen Charlotte Strait and keeping on the north side of it, then beginning the passage from Allison Harbor or Miles Inlet. Though this route involves shorter distances, it runs directly into the swell and prevailing northwesterly winds. In addition, this is a lee shore; thus caution is advised.

Weather reports are broadcast from Alert Bay, including observations at Egg Island lighthouse which lies along the route. The observations from lighthouses ahead give an indication of wind and sea conditions at the time the observations are made. They are of great assistance in deciding on the time to travel, but it must be remembered that as lighthouses become automated there will be a 6-hour gap between the reports and changes may occur in that time. The schedule of Canadian Coast Guard weather broadcasts is on the weather map in the Appendices.

The Canadian lighthouse system is good for providing key route markers—not just for assisting night passages. GPS readings should be verified by visual means, as islands and landmarks scattered along the route are good navigational aids. It is wise to mark your position on a chart at least every two hours in the event that your electronic navigational plotter and or GPS fails due to electrical malfunction. By so doing you can then proceed to plot a course and navigate safely to your destination. Poor visibility as a result of haze or fog makes it difficult to identify landmarks against the mass of similar terrain. Without plotters at such times dead reckoning can be assisted with radar and a depth sounder.

Occasionally this can turn out to be a trying passage but the vast majority of trips past Cape Caution become a succession of tiring hours with only a slight sea running. The rewards for making the passage are the availability of countless protected passages, beautiful anchorages with much less congestion and a genuine a sense of accomplishment. Seldom does one have the luxury of being the only vessel in a pristine anchorage south of the Cape, but to the north of this common-looking bit of land it can often happen.

Dixon Entrance

The passage of Dixon Entrance takes one across the border between Canada and the United States. This section is exposed to the full effect of the open Pacific, but with a judicious choice of route and weather, the crossing can be made without difficulty.

The hazards of Dixon Entrance include complex currents as well as fog which is a nuisance from July to September and can be a problem of several days' duration. Swells move into the area from the west and southwest, even on calm days.

Exposure to the swell and weather is reduced by crossing from Prince Rupert into the lee of Dundas Island. Thus, open seas are faced only in the 10-mile passage between Green Island (off the northeastern shore of Dundas Island) and Tree Point Light (past Cape Fox). Powered vessels may find sea conditions more of a problem on the return because following seas will be experienced on the section between Dundas Island and the entrance to Prince Rupert. The swell itself is not a problem, but with any wind the sea state is affected considerably. If the wind or swell is running contrary to the current, races of disturbed water occur at several places, and the crossing of these areas can be uncomfortable. As in other crossings, anchorages are noted where you may wait for the best time for a crossing. In addition, harbors are indicated that provide a refuge if conditions deteriorate during a passage.

By using well marked Venn Passage the distance that a vessel is exposed to wind and seas prevalent in Dixon Entrance is greatly reduced. Careful navigation, precise use of the tide and current tables and meticulous use of Chart 3955 are essential.

Open Water Passages of Lesser Extent

There are short periods of exposure when entering or crossing some of the sounds and passages which are open to the ocean, such as Milbanke Sound. Some routes pass a cape open to the sea, such as Cape Chacon or Cape Decision where weather and sea conditions are usually disturbed. In addition, some of the inner waters such as Chatham Sound and Stephens Passage are sufficiently broad and long as to offer a fetch capable of producing conditions similar to open water crossings. Usually the open water exposure in these smaller crossings is limited and not a problem. This does not mean that they should be treated casually, but the discomfort of any exposure is relatively short. Caution in choosing the time to cross and careful navigation should eliminate or reduce problems related to this open water exposure, or alternate routes may be chosen offering more protection at the expense of longer distances.

WEATHER FORECASTS

North American sailors are fortunate in being provided with weather forecasting services that relate specifically to small craft, both pleasure and commercial. In the area of this guide the remoteness of small communities does affect the overall coverage available. Since the area is also very mountainous, radio reception can be variable and though relay stations are used, there are many areas with spotty or inadequate reception. However, considering the costs and problems involved, the system is admirable.

Because the region covered by a weather forecast is broad, the conditions experienced in a particular area can sometimes vary from the overall prediction. The information provided should be strongly considered allowing for modified conditions in your own immediate area.

Canadian Marine Weather Reports and forecasts are conceded by most sailors to be slightly more elaborate and to provide more data over recognizable zones than do the U.S. forecasts. Conditions reported by the manned lighthouses that lie within the area covered are of the greatest use. This data is regularly updated every few hours. The most useful information is that given by a reporting station nearest the vessel's location and planned route. A map showing the location of Weather Reporting Stations, Weather Buoys, suggested channels and frequencies to use as a vessel travels along the coast and the location of manned lighthouses is shown in Appendix II.

The ship's barometer and the skipper's weather sense are also useful to interpret the signs and data received. Some old and useful observations that are widely applicable are:

– The weather pattern in effect today will usually be in effect tomorrow unless definite signs of change are evident.

– Winds usually pick up in the forenoon and increase in the afternoon, then tend to die down in the evening.

TIDES AND CURRENTS

These are of great significance to anyone traveling the waters within this guide. Tide and current tables are essential items of navigational information, particularly for the times of slack water at narrow passes. The basic tidal pattern is semi-diurnal i.e. two high tides and two low tides per day. However, the moon's declination can result in changes in this pattern so that tides can be almost diurnal. The heights of the two high waters and the two low waters vary greatly for the same reason. The tidal range is high throughout this area, varying from 3 m (10 feet) or more in the southern part to 4 m (15 feet) or more in the northern part.

The most complex tidal stream patterns occur between Vancouver Island and the mainland. The flood enters from both ends—Juan de Fuca Strait in the south, and Queen Charlotte Strait in the north. After passing through the various channels the streams meet below Cape Mudge, in the vicinity of Middlenatch Island. Through these areas the narrowness of certain passages combined with the high sills and deep basins cause the tidal streams to pass through at high velocities. Flood and ebb streams can reach speeds of 8 knots at Gillard Islands, 9 knots at Dent Rapids, and 15 knots at Seymour Narrows in Discovery Passage. Similar speeds are reached in other passes. In the larger channels of the Inside Passage, the tidal streams follow the general direction of the passages, with the flood streams setting in from each end, meeting about the middle. The ebb streams run outwards in both directions from this central point. Examples of these flows occur in Grenville channel, Graham Reach and other similar passages.

If there is a heavy snow pack in the mountains in the spring the amount of run-off can be sufficient to cause a prolonged spell of ebb current in the surface waters of Johnstone Strait, particularly following a spell of warm, sunny weather. Northbound vessels in

Johnstone Strait can find a slightly favoring current on the northern side of the passage and when southbound, a favoring current can be experienced on the southern side.

For the long fiord-like inlets with unobstructed entrances, high and low water occur about the same time throughout the inlet but this does not mean that there is not a considerable current to be expectd. But if the entrances are obstructed and narrow, then strong tidal currents result which will affect the times and conditions of entry and exit. Examples of these are Baker Inlet off Grenville Channel and Fords Terror off Endicott Arm.

It is most important to consider the tidal currents, since the major passes can be safely traversed only at or near slack water. If the weather pipes up an adverse current running against a vessel for long passages extends the traveling time considerably for small craft.

A study of the tide books, and attempts to fit the day's plans in step with the currents will be as beneficial to the voyage as thinking of the wind and weather generally. For B.C. waters, the official Canadian Tide and Current Tables are:

- Volume 5: Juan de Fuca and Georgia Straits

- Volume 6: Discovery Passage to West Coast of Vancouver Island

Volume 7: Queen Charlotte Sound to Dixon Entrance

They can be obtained from any Canadian chart dealer or by writing to:

Canadian Hydrographic Service, Dept. of Fisheries and Oceans

Institute of Ocean Sciences, Patricia Bay

9860 West Saanich Road, P.O. Box 6000

Sidney, BC V8L

The following combined volumes covering the entire coast are carried by some chart dealers:

Ports and Passes, published by Chyna Seas and

Pacific Northwest Tide and Current Guide, published by Shipmaster

Reed's Nautical Almanac, American West Coast

For Alaskan waters, the official tables are:

Tide Tables, West Coast North and South America

Tidal Current Tables, Pacific Coast of North American and Asia –

These may be obtained from any U.S. Chart dealer, or by writing to:

Distribution Branch (N/CG 33)

National Ocean Service

Riverdale, MD 20737

Alternatively, to help determine reasonable times of passage you may also pick up the small, annually published tide tables (Dots Fishing Guides) often given away at marine stores in Ketchikan, Sitka and Juneau. These are strictly tide tables, with corrections for various local points. There is no information regarding current direction or velocity, which is included in nautical charts of the key passes.

NAVIGATIONAL AIDS

Generally speaking, the United States and the Canadian systems of lights and buoys are sufficiently alike that most sailors pass from one country to the other without much difficulty. The waters of the United States are marked by the lateral system of buoyage. In 1983 Canada adopted a buoyage which includes both lateral and cardinal buoys as recommended for use worldwide by the International Association of Lighthouse Authorities. In both cases, the main channels are marked by lateral buoys which we remember by the old stand-by, "RED RIGHT RETURNING", i.e. on proceeding upstream the starboard (right) side of the channel has red buoys. Match your green light to the red lit buoys. Fairway and bifurcation or channel buoys are similar for both countries.

Canada, however, now uses cardinal buoys to indicate the deeper water and the safe side to pass a danger, i.e. one keeps to the safe side of a cardinal buoy. The markings for cardinal buoys are now standardized, and a booklet describing them can be picked up at most chart agents, Coast Guard Stations, or from Hydrographic Departments.

In Southeast Alaska all lighthouses have been converted to automatic stations with the exception of Five Fingers light near Cape Fanshawe in Stephens Passage. Similar plans are in the works for conversion of Canadian lighthouses but fishermen, recreational boaters, and commercial seafarers are attempting to convince the Coast Guard that the safety of those on the water would be compromised by such a decision. In addition to emergency aid from lighthouse keepers, the immediate reporting of radical weather changes, so prevalent along the coast is a vital service which would no longer be available. Lighthouses that continue to be manned (as at the date of printing) are identified with a "happy face" on the weather map on page 236.

CHARTS

Canada and the U.S. have first-class charts and navigational systems, well maintained and constantly updated. Those listed in Appendix I have been found to be essential for safe travel. The number of charts given here can be costly to obtain but this is an expense no rational skipper should neglect. Prudent navigators will keep a set of charts aboard as a back-up in the event of a break-down of electronic plotters.

All charts carried should be the newest edition available, and corrected to include the most recent changes as published in "Notices to Mariners." One should always keep in mind the variation of 20°E when referring to compass bearings.

TIME

The area covered by this guide is in the time zone of Greenwich or Universal Standard Time + 8 hours. Furthermore, the entire area uses Daylight Savings Time, which affects the navigator when reading the times in tide and current tables. Add one hour to the Pacific Standard Time given in the tide tables in order to convert the time to Daylight Savings Time. This is usually in effect from the first Sunday in April to the last Sunday in October.

DANGERS

Aside from the obvious and standard danger of rocks, shoals, and heavy weather, there are some additional dangers peculiar to these waters.

Kelp

There are many shoals in the vast area of this coast. Kelp often grows on rocky bottoms, its tendrils streaming out in line with surface currents. Visible kelp beds usually signify depths of less than 10 fathoms and should be avoided. Detached kelp floating on the surface is dead and does not have the same significance.

Deadheads and Log Debris

This is one of the major logging zones of the world with much of the timber transported by log booms. Thus it is no surprise to find that floating logs, deadheads, and sinkers are present in the inland passages and inlets.

Floating logs can be encountered anywhere but are most prevalent near tide lines or at the entrances to inlets during and after high tides or storms. Though they occur in Alaska as well, they seem to be more in evidence in B.C.

Deadheads are logs stuck at one end into the bottom, the other end hanging at or near the surface. They can be very dangerous to quickly moving vessels because they are not seen until one is almost upon them, and when hit at high speed they can cause serious damage.

Sinkers are the most dangerous of all, being large logs that have become waterlogged and rest vertically in the water, rising and falling with the swell. Since they float just under the surface of the water most of the time, they usually are not seen but if one rises when a vessel passes over it very serious damage can result. Report large logs, deadheads or sinkers to the nearest Coast Guard (Canadian or U.S.) who broadcast their location in the "Notice to Mariners", and take steps to remove them.

Debris includes small logs, wood chunks, branches, etc., which, though it can be a nuisance, is not usually a dangerous problem. It is as well to avoid debris in case the branches seen may be attached to partially submerged trees. Occasionally a small piece of wood may become lodged in or near the propeller causing it to vibrate or the vessel's speed to be reduced. Sometimes the obstacle may be removed by simply putting the engine in reverse for a brief period.

These dangers are not continuous, nor found everywhere. A good lookout when traveling and common sense in avoiding travel at times of low visibility or at night, will allow for a safe voyage in these waters.

Plastic Debris

Plastic bags should be retrieved and burned or deposited in trash bins whenever they are seen to prevent blockage of water intake openings on vessels.

Fishing Nets

Fishing was once as important as lumber production along this coast. Although their numbers have declined you will still share the waterways, harbors, and anchorages with fishing craft of various types since their working season falls in the summer and early autumn. Fishing periods are strictly regulated by the governments of Canada and the U.S. since the early years of uncontrolled over-fishing almost ruined this resource. There are four main types of fishing vessels seen in these waters.

Trollers may be seen working the shores, bays, and banks. They are recognizable by their long pole outriggers extended out from the boat when fishing, troll lines streaming out behind. When passing astern of them one should give them at least a 60 to 90 m (200- to 300-foot) berth in order to pass over their lines without fouling them. Troll caught salmon are the highest quality fish seen in markets.

Gillnetters are identified by the large spool and rollers—either on the stern or the bow — from which the net is let out while being supported by floats. A buoy (red or orange) marks the net's free end. DO NOT PASS BETWEEN THE ORANGE BUOY AND THE GILLNETTER as the net will foul your prop or rudder. The white floats which keep one side of the net at sea level can usually be seen between the gillnetter and the orange float. Net size and depth are regulated. Gill nets are usually strung at right angles to the current flow, with the vessel maintaining a pull on the line; but variable currents may cause the nets to curve or wind about. Openings during the fishing season for gillnetters to fish are tightly controlled by Fisheries Departments. Such openings move up or down the coast with timings determined by the salmon runs arriving at river entrances. Since the gillnetters congregate in the high yield areas of a channel, their overlapping and crowded nets can be a major problem if one is traveling on an open fishing day. They are supposed to leave a clear passage but this is seldom done and pleasure craft must weave a route around and past the ends of their nets. When a gillnetter is fishing, check to see if the net drum is on the stern or on the bow and look beyond for the buoy that marks the end of the net.

Purse Seiners are the largest fishing vessels and are clearly identified by their size, the large boom, and power winch. They are not likely to be a problem for small craft; except that when there is an opening, hordes of them can be met rushing to the site of the opening.

Long-liners fish for halibut. They set long-lines (skates) with baited hooks laid down near the bottom with the ends marked by floats. They do not operate during the summer and early fall. In any case, their lines are not a problem as they are set well underwater.

Magnetic Disturbances

There are several places within the area of this guide where local magnetic disturbances occur near land masses. These areas are marked on navigational charts and are noted in the sketches. The magnetic compass should not be relied on in these areas, for not only is there a variation in the disturbance over any zone, but the change may be unnoticed at the onset and navigational errors may occur. During fair weather and good visibility passage across these zones should be done using visual checks. If visual checks are not possible it is advisable to avoid these magnetically disturbed areas or await clearing.

Tsunamis

This danger would seem a little far-fetched except that earthquakes periodically occur in or near the Southeast. Tsunamis are not a problem to a ship at sea, as they pass harmlessly by. The major danger occurs if the vessel is at or near the epicenter of the quake, where very large waves can be generated; or if the tsunami proves dangerous as it moves into a narrowing inlet. A warning system is in operation, and is broadcast through the Canadian Coast Guard Weather reports, NOAA Weather Radio as well as local radio stations. The probability of this danger is extremely low.

Ice

Ice is a problem only in those areas fed by glaciers such as Glacier Bay, Hobart Bay, Tracy and Endicott Arms, and care and prudence will suffice to take you through safely.

Glacial ice is almost always present in the northern arms of Glacier Bay. In the summer season, the amount of ice varies considerably and some glaciers may be more active than others. However, except for the occasional berg or bergy bits in the main bay, ice will be encountered in quantities mainly as one approaches Muir, Tarr and John Hopkins Inlets. The amount of ice usually lessens as the season advances. The tides and winds move the ice up and down the inlets, tending to pack it together or disperse it. However, the circulation of water near the glacial snouts themselves is erratic, since fresh water is always being discharged and the ice movements are correspondingly unpredictable. DO NOT APPROACH A GLACIAL FACE CLOSER THAN .5 MILE. Treat large icebergs with respect and pass well clear of them, keeping in mind that only 20% is visible. Anyone who has seen an iceberg roll over will easily appreciate the reason for caution.

Glacial ice forms as snow crystals accumulate and are buried by successive falls. The pressure slowly changes the crystals resulting in changes in density and structure (a volume decrease of as much as 9 times occurs). The denser the ice, the bluer it looks, since air has been eliminated and the greater proportion of water molecules present absorb all colors except blue, which is transmitted. The bergy bits that are clear and jewel-like are from the older part of the glacier, whereas those that appear whitish are from the newer, top part. Greenish-black bergs come from near the bottom of the glacier and striped brown bergs show layers of moraine sediments from the side of the glacier.

Ice presents a different and much greater problem in winter, when in addition to glacier ice, certain bays are subject to sea ice, and vessels can be dangerously hampered by the accretion of superstructure icing. The majority of vessels using this guide should be snug in harbor during such times.

Mirages

Mirages are not in themselves dangerous. Glacier Bay provides examples of <u>towering</u>—the vertical elongation of distant objects—and of <u>superior mirage</u>—the appearance of an inverted image above an object. Mirages are a fascinating phenomena, but do not need to cause any concern.

Wind Chill, Clothing, and Hypothermia

When traveling in this area, maintaining body temperature is an important consideration even in summer, and particularly in the vicinity of snowy peaks and glaciers. The summer climate in the northern areas of this guide is temperate and tolerable, with daily mean temperatures in the mid 50's (F), and maximums that can be as high as the 80's and 90's. But when cool winds blow with the temperatures in the 50's and 60's, the wind chill factor renders conditions equivalent to much colder temperatures.

Cool winds can cause a considerable amount of body heat loss and strong cold winds can lower body temperature by causing a loss greater than the replacement rate. As this condition is affected by any barrier to the wind's effect, the value of a good dodger behind which to shelter, and windproof clothing, combined with several layers of under clothing is obvious. Except when the sun's rays beat directly down on calm days, it is worthwhile to wear heavy weather rain gear as an outer windproof covering with several layers consisting of sweaters, flannel shirts, and long johns underneath.

Gloves are necessary at times—wool being the best in cold weather, and rubber fisherman's working gloves best in wet conditions. Scarves, wool toques and/or balaclavas help to reduce major heat loss through the head, and woolen socks in sea boots are also recommended. It is important to put on heavy weather rain gear to prevent getting wet for wet clothing loses much of its insulating value. Similarly, when planned trips ashore may last an hour or so, take a windproof jacket or extra sweater in case weather conditions deteriorate for even a brief rain squall accompanied by wind can cause mild hypothermia.

The mean surface water temperature in these areas in summer is about 60°F (13°C). Glacier meltwater-fed inlets have lower temperatures which become colder with increasing depth. If a person is in the water for even a fairly short period of time, the loss of deep body heat can be crucial to survival. Every effort should be made to stay aboard and safety harness should be used before rough sea conditions develop. If a crew member does go into the water, minutes count in the recovery.

Predicted survival time without a PFD is as little as 1.5 to 2 hours when drown-proofing or treading water up to 4 hours with a PFD when assuming the fetal position, or huddling if two or more people are in the water. It is especially important to realize that a person in cold water goes into shock quickly, and as hypothermia advances, the victim can become disoriented and unable to assist oneself.

When rescued, hypothermia victims should be checked for vital signs: an open airway, respiration and pulse. If there is no pulse or respiration, CPR must be started immediately. Move the victim to warmth, replace all wet clothing with dry clothing and wrap him in blankets or a sleeping bag. A warm water bottle or warm, moist towels placed on the victim's neck, groin or chest can be helpful. If the victim is conscious offer sips of warm, sweet non-alcoholic liquids. In cases of severe hypothermia, skin to skin contact in the areas of the chest and neck is most effective. Try to keep the victim awake, and exhale warm air near the victim's mouth and nose. Keep a continuous watch over the victim and get medical attention as soon as possible.

Fog

From the northern end of Vancouver Island to Alaska the highest occurrence of fog is during the summer period (June to September) when there is an average of 4 to 7 days of fog per month. Visibility is reduced below 2 miles for about 15% of the time, and below .5 mile for about 5% of the time. At any other time of the year fog can occur whenever the air is moist and much warmer than the water, but the average number of days of fog drops well below that of the summer period.

Advection fog plagues the major open water crossings of this section, and sometimes works in along nearby coastal parts of the Inside Passage. Fog is often cyclical over a period of several days if the wind patterns stay in the same quadrant. Considering the rocky coasts and danger of the various approaches, care and caution should be exercised when traveling at these times.

In the southern section of this guide, the regime for fog is slightly different, tending to occur from September to January, though fog is occasionally found in the Strait of Juan de Fuca during the summer. From May to August, the inner waters of the southern area are usually free of fog.

Radar is a valuable aid during passages in fog <u>if</u> a member of the crew has had training to interpret the screen correctly. As long as the power supply remains constant, electronic plotters and GPS positions are reassuring. Remember when traveling toward a waypoint, a vessel may be shown to be "on the highway" but if cross-currents affect the boat's path it may drift into danger unless the bearing remains constant.

Tugs, Tows, and Log Booms

Often seen plying these waters, these are essential economic lifelines for coastal communities. Tugs and their tows are not easily maneuvered so it is the responsibility of the yacht skipper to take avoiding action when meeting them. Unless constrained by space, give them ample room. Though obvious, remember the tow-line is submerged between the tug and its tow. Most tows trail a safety line of about 60 m (200') so do not pass close astern. It is important to remember the light configuration of a tug with a tow is three vertical lights shown from the mast. At night, log booms have red hurricane lanterns lit to mark the outer limits of their tow. Since these are fairly close to sea level and are not very bright, they are often difficult to spot.

FISHING LICENSES

Licenses required for fishing in British Columbia and Alaska may be obtained from most marine service outlets, fuel docks, hardware and sporting goods stores. An Alaska Fish and Game License is required for fishing in National Parks such as Misty Fiords and Glacier Bay. Daily and annual catch limits are described in the regulations for each area.

Sportsfishermen and cruisers have a responsibility to limit their catch to what may be consumed during the cruise. When fishing licenses are obtained a booklet is provided outlining regulations regarding the number and size of fish of various species that a person/boat may have possession of at any time and the size and sex of crabs that may be kept.

Female crabs of any size must be released. Fisheries Officers monitor all vessels regularly to see that regulations are strictly being followed. Sometimes cruisers feel they are being hounded by the authorities, but without limits being regulated the fish and shellfish would be decimated by both commercial fishers and sportsfishers.

The entire coastal area was once a Mecca for salmon and other seafood which could be found in abundance. Unfortunately, destruction of spawning streams by logging, over-fishing and poaching have resulted in a serious degradation of the salmon population. The escape of east coast salmon from fish farms occurs frequently and the unknown long-term consequences are of concern. Recently an drastic increase in sea lice in B.C. wild salmon is a major concern.

ENTRY PROCEDURES

To contact a Port of Entry in Canada call 1-888-226-7277 at any time.

The majority of pleasure boaters cruising waters covered by this guide will be citizens of Canada or United States and there are only a few rules and formalities with which to comply. These are primarily aimed at stopping illegal drug traffic and preventing abuse of the customs and immigration laws of both countries. The major requirements are to check in and clear with Customs and Immigration, and to obtain a Report No. (Canada) or Cruising Permit (US) giving permission to travel in the waters of the country being visited. Vessels and crew who are not Canadian or American can obtain Report Numbers if the country of origin has reciprocal arrangements with Canada. Visas may be needed for the skipper and crew.

In order to streamline entry into Canadian waters pre-approved Canadian and U.S. citizens may enter Canada by calling Canada customs provided their application has been approved by the Citizenship and Immigration Department and a permit has been issued. Application forms for a permit may be obtained by writing to: **CANPASS** Processing Centre, #28 - 176 Street, Surrey, BC V4P 1M7 CANADA. A non-refundable processing fee of Can$40 is charged for each applicant 18 years of age or older. All persons aboard a vessel must be a permit holder. The authorization is valid for five years. Following approval of the application a CANPASS – Private Boat authorization is issued.

Permit holders may call 1-888-226-7277 up to four hours in advance to report their estimated arrival time at a Port of Entry in Canada. They must give the boat's name, registration number of the boat along with the full name, birthday and citizenship for all persons aboard the boat. Each person must have photo identification and proof of citizenship. A Report Number will be given to the skipper or he/she will be told to check in to one of the designated reporting stations below for inspection. If a Customs Officer does not meet the boat at the time of arrival the vessel may then proceed to its final destination.

Victoria: Oak Bay Marina, Customs Dock, RVYC (Cadboro Bay or Tseum Harbor)

Metro Vancouver: White Rock, Crescent Beach, Steveston, Delta River Marina (Richmond)

Welcome Dock in Coal Harbour, Vancouver Harbour

Sidney: Canoe Cove, Port of Sidney, Vancouver Isle Marina

South Pender Island: Bedwell Harbour (only from May 1 to September 30)

Salt Spring Island: Ganges, Public float/Breakwater at the pump out station

Pender Island: Port Browning and on Galiano Island: Montague Harbour Marina

North Coast: Nanaimo: Brechin Point Marina, Nanaimo Harbour Commission Yacht Basin
Campbell River: Discovery Chevron Dock, Discovery Marina Dock
Prince Rupert: Fairview Government Dock, PRYC, Prince Rupert
Government Dock and Rushbrook Government Dock

Vessels without permits are to call 1-888-226-7277 and proceed to one of the above Ports of Entry where only the skipper (or his representative) may go ashore to report to the Customs Office. To expedite entry the skipper should bring a list of all persons on board, their citizenship and date of birth. After the vessel has been inspected and cleared a Clearance Number will be issued and this should be clearly written on a piece of paper and shown from a dockside porthole/window so that it is visible during inspection while the vessel is in Canadian waters. In some southern centers it is possible to make first contact with the Customs Officer by telephone, whereupon he will meet the vessel at the Customs dock to check it in. The person reporting must return aboard immediately after reporting and remain aboard unless clearance is given by telephone. Note that the vessel may not land, anchor or meet with another boat until Customs clearance has been given. Though there are some small variations, the customs and immigration laws of both Canada and the United States require the following:

1. The yacht's registration, documentation or license papers.
2. A letter or statement from the owner allowing the skipper to move the boat if the owner is not aboard.
3. Passports, birth certificates, or acceptable identification of the crew.
4. Visas for crew members, when necessary.
5. Limits to the amount of alcohol, beer, and cigarettes for each person. Certain fruits, vegetables or other agricultural products may be prohibited entry.
6. Pets need a certificate of rabies vaccination not older than 1 year or within the last month.
7. Prescription drugs for personal use should have labels and have copies of the physician's prescription or a letter stating the necessity for their use.
8. Canada prohibits the import of hand guns, automatic firearms, and mace and applies a criminal charge to anyone in violation of this rule. Rifles and shotguns must be declared and a permit costing $50 may be issued. The import of hollow point ammunition is prohibited. In the United States hand gun regulations are a state responsibility. To determine current regulations for Alaska write to: Alaska Dept. of Fish and Game, P.O. Box 3–2000, Juneau, AK 99802.

Random examinations of vessels may be carried out to ensure that visiting vessels have the necessary paper work to conform with requirements for declaration and check-in procedures. Non-compliance with regulations make the vessel subject to seizure and/or fines.

FLAG ETIQUETTE

"There is a certain accepted procedure to which pleasure boats should properly adhere when they cross international boundaries into the waters of another nation," is a quotation worth repeating from Charles F. Chapman's *Piloting, Seamanship and Small Boat Handling (PP 470-472)*. Though the position of the foreign flag varies depending on the type of vessel, the general practice is for it to be flown from the foremost starboard spreader on sailing vessels and from the starboard yardarm on powerboats. If the motor vessel is mastless then the courtesy flag is to be flown alone from the bow staff (thus replacing the club burgee).

GARBAGE DISPOSAL

The increasing number of vessels cruising this coast has placed severe strains on small communities to deal with garbage. Boaters can lessen this impact several ways:

1. Beer, liquor, juice and pop containers purchased in B.C. should be returned to outlets selling similar products, where a refund will be made for the deposit charged.

2. Other glass and tins can be cleaned and returned to recycling depots in your home port. There was sufficient space to stow the full containers on board prior to the start of the cruise, so the same space can accommodate empty containers, plus additions since tins can be flattened.

3. Any garbage left over should be sorted into that which can be burned and 'other,' so that shore facilities can deal with the trash as efficiently as possible.

If boaters make an effort to reduce the amount of garbage left in communities along this coast and refrain from discarding trash in an irresponsible manner we can help to preserve the pristine beauty of this coast for future generations.

WHALE WATCHING

This is a highlight of any cruise in these waters. A small cruising vessel provides many excellent opportunities to observe whales closely. The whales found in these coastal waters include four baleen whales: Gray, Humpback, Minke and Finback and three toothed whales: Orca or Killer Whale, the Dalls and Harbor Porpoises.

Whales will often maintain their course and pass near a small vessel. The chances of collision are unlikely, since not only do whales have good eyesight, but they have a built-in sonar facility. However, it is important to maintain a good lookout and take action to avoid a collision as needed. Never chase whales, steer directly toward them, or corner them in bays or narrow inlets where they might feel threatened.

To assist in identification at a distance, sketch silhouettes of the whale's blow characteristics and surface attitudes are given.

Gray Whale

A stocky whale having no distinct dorsal fin, the Gray whale may grow to 12m (40 feet) and reach 40 tons. It is slate or gray in color with whitish patches of barnacles and whale lice. A few grooves may be seen on the throat. It is a slow swimmer, its normal speed being 5 to 8 knots. It may be seen in the Gulf of Georgia and adjacent bays, or traveling along the outer coasts as it migrates from the Baja Peninsula in Mexico to the Bering Sea each year.

Surfacing & Blowing   Beginning a Dive   Sounding (Diving)

Debris Harms Our Marine Life

Rex Herron

Endangered species also suffer. Sea turtles mistake plastic bags for jelly fish (a major source of food) and choke to death.

Michigan Dept. of Natural Resources

Fishermen and boater safety is jeopardized when debris fouls propellers or causes engines to overheat. Heavy losses of time and money are reported from debris damage to vessels and equipment.

George Antonelis

Brian Lawhead

Some 30,000 Northern Fur seals die yearly from entanglement in netting, a 50% decline in population in 30 years has been noted.

Common items like six-pack rings, fishing line, and strapping bands entangle and kill sea birds, fish and mammals. Plastics can last many hundreds of years, harming even large mammals like the gray whale.

Pierce Harris

This page and the one following marked ϟ have been reprinted (with permission) from a brochure published by the National Marine Fisheries Service, Maine Refuse Disposal Project, Newport, Oregon.

Plastics can last for hundreds of years. A careless moment lasts generations. The best method of disposal is at a recycling depot.

Dale Snow

Frans Lanting

Birds, fish and mammals mistake plastic for food. Some birds even feed it to their young! With plastic-filled stomachs, animals die of starvation or poisoning.

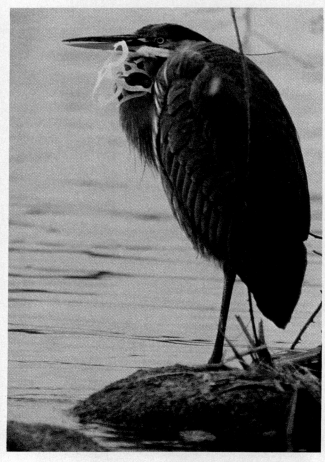
Bill Keay

Six-pack rings can result in starvation and death to seabirds such as this Great Blue Heron and other marine life.

⌇ DON'T TEACH YOUR TRASH TO SWIM!
WGM

Western Canada Wilderness Committee

Oil spills such as the disasters caused by the Exxon Valdez in 1989 (which ran aground in Prince William Sound) and the leaking oil barge (which was deliberately hauled out to sea from near Grays Harbor, Wash. in 1988) caused the deaths of thousands of seabirds and damage to marine habitats along the coasts of Washington, British Columbia, and Alaska.

Public pressure is needed to have a moratorium on offshore drilling, require the transport of oil in double-hulled vessels and establish a Law of the Sea making the owners of oil shipments liable for all clean-up costs and damages anywhere in the world. This would encourage oil companies to act responsibly toward the fragile marine environment.

Jim Boeder

⌇ You can help!
* Make boat policy that no trash is discarded, washed, or blown overboard.
* Minimize the amount of non-degradable products on board. Provision your vessel using bulk-refillable containers.
* Stow trash for disposal in port. Encourage your port to provide convenient refuse disposal facilities.
* Where possible retrieve trash found on the ocean.
* Share your concern with friends, fellow mariners and politicians.
* Participate in beach clean-ups, and leave the beach clean after visits.

Orca or Killer Whale

This striking whale is black, with white patches along the flanks and bottom. It may grow to 9 m (30 feet) and reach 10 tons. Its high, triangular dorsal fin may reach 1.8 m (6 ft.) in mature males but only .9m (3 feet) in females and immature males. Orcas are rarely seen alone as they travel in groups, reaching speeds of 20 knots or faster. Their range includes all areas of the guide but they are most common in waters south of Prince Rupert.

Surfacing and Blowing   Beginning a Dive   Sounding (Diving)

Humpback Whale

Known both for its acrobatics and its haunting songs, this whale is distinguished by its 15-foot slender flippers and the knobs (stove bolts) on its head. It may grow to 15 m (50 feet) in length and reach 45 tons. When sounding, it raises its tail flukes high. Traveling individually or in groups, it usually cruises at 5 knots, but is capable of 10 knots. It can be seen in much of the Southeast Alaskan waters, but is most likely in Lynn Canal, Chatham Strait, and along the outer coast. In Glacier Bay the number of boats is restricted, to reduce disturbances to the Humpback's habitat.

Finback Whale

The second largest of the whale species, these can reach over 21 m (70 feet) and up to 60 or 70 tons. They are fast travelers, swimming at up to 20 knots, and when feeding they can be even speedier. They have a curved dorsal fin and a short ridge about two-thirds of the way along the back. When diving, the back arches deeply but the tail does not break the surface. At close range they can be identified by the asymmetrical color pattern of the head—blue-gray on the left, and white on the right lower jaw.

Minke Whale

Pronounced Min - ke, this small whale reaches only 9 m (30 feet) and about 7 tons in weight. It has a short curved dorsal fin two-thirds of the way along the back with white patches across the flippers. Its blow is low, hardly visible. On the rise, the pointed nose breaks the water first. It may be seen in inlets and bays, and sometimes approaches boats closely. Frederick Sound is a place to look for this whale. It is occasionally seen in northern British Columbian waters.

Surfacing and Blowing   Beginning a Dive   Sounding (Diving)

Dalls Porpoise

Friendly and playful, they will come to cavort in the boat's bow wave. Black with white patches on the belly, throat, and flippers, they could be mistaken for killer whales except that they are small (2 m/7 feet long) and have a small dorsal fin. Porpoises lack the dolphin's beak. They are fast, and traveling in groups, may be found anywhere in South East Alaska waters.

Rising   Blowing   Diving

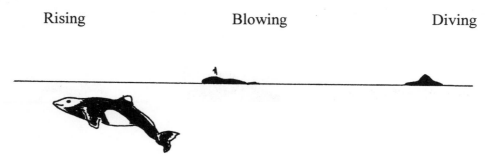

Harbor Porpoise

The smallest of the whales, averaging 1.5m (5.5 feet), they are usually all black or brown. They are more aloof than the Dalls and rarely approach boats closely. A small curved dorsal fin is in the center of the back. Sometimes alone, sometimes in large groups, they can be seen hunting inside small anchorages or passing near their entrances throughout Southeast Alaska.

NATIVE CULTURES

Travel along this coast and visits to any its towns develops a growing interest in the art and culture of the First Nations people. Totem poles are the first and most impressive of the symbols one sees, but almost every object in native life, even the most utilitarian, was decorated with design—as, for example, berry baskets and beautifully carved wooden halibut hooks. This guide can do no more than introduce the tribal areas and point out other sources of information.

From Victoria to about Campbell River, Coast Salish dominate followed by Kwakiutl until north of Bella Bella and the Tsimshian to the Alaska border with an intrusion around Metlakatla. The sea-going Haida inhabit the Queen Charlotte Islands and the southern end of Prince of Wales Island. The Tlinglit tribe are found in the long remaining stretch of the South East. There are similarities as well as marked differences in tribal cultures, and the local museums are a good way of finding out about them; the University of British Columbia Museum of Anthropology is a major source, as are the museums in Campbell River, Alert Bay, Prince Rupert, Juneau and the Sheldon Jackson in Sitka.

BOOKS AND REFERENCES

Duart Snow, Editor. *BC Marine Parks Guide*. Vancouver, BC: Pacific Yachting Magazine (This is an excellent accompaniment to *Charlie's Charts*.)

Blanchet, M. Wylie. *Curve of Time*. Sidney, B.C.: Gray's Publishing.

Chappell, John. *Cruising Beyond Desolation Sound*. Vancouver, B.C.: Naikoon Marine.

Douglass, Don and Reanne Hemingway-Douglass. A series of books *Exploring* selected sections of BC and Alaskan waters. Anacortes, WA: Fine Edge Productions, LLC

Eppenbach, Sarah. *Alaska's Southeast, Touring the Inside Passage*. Seattle, WA: Pacific Search Press.

Flaherty, Chuck. *Whales of the Northwest*. Seattle: Cherry Lane Press.

Hadman, Ballard. *As the Sailor Loves the Sea*. New York: Harper and Brothers

Hale, Robert. *The Waggoneer*. Seattle: Robert Hale Publishing

Halpin, Marjorie J. *Totem Poles - an Illustrated Guide*

Lange, Owen S. *Living with Weather Along the BC Coast*. Ottawa, ON: Environment Canada

State of Alaska, Dept. of Transportation *Southeastern Alaska Harbor and Boating Facility Directory*. Juneau, AK: Southeast Graphics Media.

Wolferstan, Bill. *Cruising Guide to British Columbia: Volume I, II and III*. Vancouver, B.C.: Pacific Yachting.

Woodward, Walt. *How to Cruise to Alaska Without Shaking the Boat Too Much*. Edmonds, WA Nor'Westing Inc.

Yeadon-Jones, Anne and Laurence. *Dreamspeaker Cruising Guides*. Vancouver: Raincoast Books.

PUMPOUT STATIONS (Identified by ⩡ on pages 25, and 71)

It is deplorable to report the non-existent efforts by provincial and federal governments to establish adequate pumpout stations for the thousands of recreational boaters that cruise this beautiful coast. Efforts made by local authorities and private marinas are listed and it is hoped boaters will understand that fees charged are necessary to fund the services provided.

Vancouver Island

Harbourside Marina, Victoria	$10
Port Sidney Marina	$10
Van Isle Marina, Sidney	$10
Tsehum Harbour Authority, Sidney	
Angler's Anchorage Marina, Brentwood Bay (portable caddy available)	
Saltspring Is. Harbour Authority	
Saanich Inlet Protection Society (Mobile Service - Call (250) 480-9292	$10
Port of Nanaimo Eco Barge	$2
Comox Harbour Authority, Comox	$7
Browns Bay Marina, Campbell River	
Campbell River Harbour Authority, Campbell River	20gal. - $10
Coast Discovery Inn, Campbell River	
Deep Bay Harbour Authority, Bowser (Make arrangements in advance)	$7

Lower Mainland

Shelter Islalnd Marine, Richmond	$10
Point Roberts Marina, WA	
Burrard Civic Marina, Vancouver	
Coal Harbour Marina, Vancouver	$15
Heather Civic Marina, Vancouver	
Reed Point Marina, Port Moody	

Bowen Island and Sunshine Coast

Union Steamship Co. Marina, Bowen Island (Portable)
Gibson's Marina, Gibsons
Gibsons Landing Harbour Authority, Gibsons
Porpoise Bay, Sechelt Inlet, (DFO Government Dock)
Madeira ark Public Dock , Madeira Park (Pender Harbour)

North Coast

Sointula, Malcolm Island Harbour Authority	
Port McNeill Harbour Authority, Port McNeill	Nominal
Ocean Falls Public Dock, Ocean Falls	
Sandspit Harbour Marina, Sandspit, Queen Charlotte Islands	

ARTIFICIAL REEFS (Identified by AR on pages 25 and 71)

The Artificial Reef Society of British Columbia has been instrumental in creating six artificial reefs in coastal waters. A far-reaching result of such reefs is the enhancement of an environment that attracts marine life in what was a barren, sandy, undersea lot. Sea squirts are the first to establish a foot-hold followed by showy plumose anemone and feather stars that decorate the metal hulls creating an exotic and enticing environment. Other marine life congregates and an ecosystem is born that becomes a diver's Paradise. With two exceptions the vessels that have become permanent fixtures on the ocean floor were Destroyer Escort ships that served in World War II. The next project planned is to sink a Boeing 737 that is waiting in Comox to be sunk at a location to be determined.

The first artificial reef in B.C. was established in August,1991 when a coastal freighter, *The G.B. Church* was sunk off Portland Island within waters of Princess Margaret Marine (now a part of the Gulf Islands National Park Reserve). The 53m (175 ft.) World War II supply ship built in Goole, England in 1943, is located at 48°43.323'N, 123°21.339'W. About a year later *The Chaudiere* was the first Destroyer Escort ship to be sunk by the Society. This 111m (366 ft.) Restigouche-class vessel was submerged at Kunechin Point, Porpoise Bay in Sechelt Inlet at 49°37.694'N, 123°48.699'W.

In September, 1995 *The Mackenzie,* an anti-submarine destroyer escort ship that saw active service from 1962 to 1972, was sunk 4 miles north of Gooch Island at 48°40.094'N, 123°17.170'W. Less than a year later *The Columbia* was sunk near Maude Island, south of Seymour Narrows. A viewing barge was towed to the site and a piper played "Amazing Grace" as a send-off salute for her tour of duty. She now lies on a rocky bottom at 50° 08.031'N, 125°20.152'W.

In June, 1997 *The Saskatchewan* was the first of two vessels sunk near Snake Island off the city of Nanaimo. Her co-ordinates are 49°12.92'N, 123°53.070'W. She was joined in 2001 by *The Cape Breton*, (originally named the HMC *Flamborough Head),* that served in the Fleet Maintenance Group during World War II. A Victory Ship measuring 134m (440 ft.) 9500 tons, her hull now rests at 49°12.88'N, 123°53.067'W.

To avoid snagging fishing gear, injuring divers and damaging the fragile marine life inhabiting the artificial reefs boaters are encouraged to respect a 250m (300 ft.) no-fishing buffer in the vicinity of the artificial reefs and give plenty of sea-room anywhere you see dive flags.

ORGANIZATIONS PRESERVING THE COAST FOR THE FUTURE

Marine Parks Forever Society is a provincial organization that exists for the purpose of expanding the B.C. Marine Park system. It is an non-profit Society relying on contributions from boaters and yacht clubs in order to purchase land surrounding anchorages before clear-cutting of forests and/or developers proceed to restrict shore access and destroy the pristine beauty of the area. For more information visit their website at www.marinparksforeversociety.ca In addition to many long-standing Marine Parks the success of this society is evident in recently established Marine Parks at Francis Point, Musket Island and Wakes Cove on Valdez Island. If you appreciate access to B.C. Marine Parks and would like to share in their expansion visit their website at www.bcmarineparks.com/society where a donation form and address are provided.

The Nature Conservancy of B.C. focuses on the preservation of environmentally sensitive areas that are the habitat of threatened species. By coordinating various levels of government and industry along with private donations and funding from Marine Parks Forever Society they were instrumental in the preservation of Jedediah Marine Park and the entire Princess Louisa Inlet. For information call toll free, 1-888-404-8428. Donations may be mailed to Nature Conservancy of Canada, #202 – 26 Bastion Square, Victoria, BC V8W 1H9.

HIGH SPEED WIRELESS INTERNET

The latest advance in communication is available in many locations from Victoria to Prince Rupert. Contact the marina for the system that is in use.

SECTION I - Victoria to Campbell River

> **NOTICE:** All marinas in British Columbia monitor VHF Ch. 66A and are to be contacted <u>only</u> on that channel except for Prince Rupert Yacht Club which uses VHF Ch. 73. Do NOT use VHF Ch. 16 to call a marina or harbor authority.

In 2003 the Federal Government established the **Gulf Islands National Park Reserve** by taking over several B.C. Marine Parks such as Cabbage Island, Tumbo Island, Beaumont, Winter Cove on Saturna Island, Portland Island, Wallace Island, D'arcy Island and Sidney Spit. In addition, the Park includes land on Saturna, Prevost and North Pender Islands.

There are many spots in the Gulf Islands where anchorage may be taken in calm, settled weather that are exposd to winds from a certain direction. Each cruiser must pay attention to weather forecasts and move to a more protected anchorage when conditions change that make remaining in a particular moorage unsafe.

Other B.C. Marine Parks and marinas in Section I where moorage is available but may have certain limitations include the following:

Sandy Island (Tree Island) is off the northern tip of Denman Island. Anchorage during good, settled weather may be taken off the south side of the island. The spit connecting Sandy Island and nearby Seal Islets dries at low tide.

Wallace Island, just to the southeast of Secretary Islands, has two anchorages that are approached from Houston Passage. Reefs and rocks in the area make it essential to use a proper chart for navigation when approaching either Conover Cove where there is a public float or Princess Bay, a short distance to the north. Because both bays are narrow, with reefs lining parts of the shorelines, making it necessary to set a bow anchor and tie a stern line ashore.

Sidney Spit at the northern tip of Sidney Island between Miners Channel and Sidney Channel. Enter from Sidney Channel. Fees are charged for the use of mooring buoys and a landing dock is available for easy access to the shore. Several well groomed trails of varying length make shore trips most enjoyable.

Winter Cove at the northern tip of Saturna Island. Enter from Plumper Sound and Navy Channel giving Minx Reef a safe berth. At low tide the anchorage has about 2m (7 feet) of water. Boat Passage joins the cove to the Strait of Georgia and has strong tidal currents; reefs and shoals in the area discourage use of this passage without local knowledge.

Princess Margaret Bay on Portland Island, between Satellite Channel and Prevost Passage provides fair weather, exposed anchorages. Caution must be and a sharp lookout is needed to identify the reefs and shoals surrounding the island. Passable anchorage may be taken in North Bay, with Chads Island providing some protection.

Schooner Cove Resort Hotel and Marina is a major marine center just to the north of Nanoose Harbour. This luxurious facility offers both permanent and transient moorage (look for orange cleats). Guests have complimentary use of showers, pool, spa, sauna, tennis, shuttle to grocery stores and shuttle to Fairwinds Golf Course. For information call 1-800-663-7060.

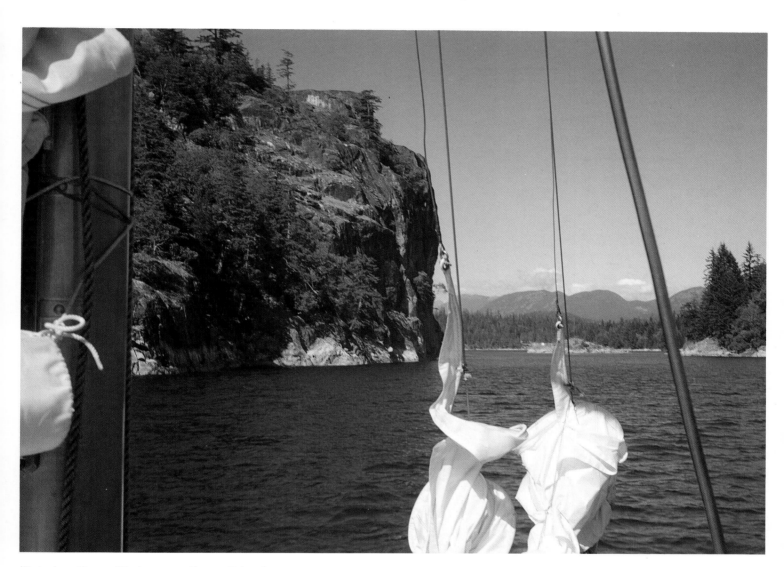

Entering Gorge Harbour on Cortes Island

Looking toward the entrance from within Prideaux Haven

Not to be used for navigation

VICTORIA

Victoria is the capital of the province of British Columbia and is a **Port of Entry**. Promoted for many years as a "bit of Merry Old England," this beautiful city is a unique and attractive blend of turn-of-the-century architecture and modern development. A feature of the harbor is the magnificent view of the Provincial Parliament Buildings and ivy-clad Empress Hotel overlooking the waterfront.

Entry to the busy harbor is clear and simple as is passage to the inner harbor in the heart of the city. A traffic scheme plan maintains a safe distance between pleasure craft and frequent air traffic in the harbor. Vessels less than 20m (65 ft.) are required to keep the yellow buoys close to port when entering and leaving the harbor; those over 20m (65 ft.) should follow the route on the harbor sketch. Upon arrival from abroad vessels must report to the Customs dock to complete entry requirements. Until clearance has been obtained no one may leave the vessel except the skipper. The skipper should phone 1-888-226-7277 to contact a Customs Officer if one is not present on the dock. Flag etiquette requires foreign vessels to fly the Canadian flag while in Canadian waters.

The **Coast Harbourside Hotel and Marina** is a first-class facility that welcomes transient vessels up to 36m (120 ft.). Hotel services such as pool, sauna, and pumpout are free to patrons of the marina. For reservations call (250) 360-1211 or Fax (250) 360-1418. All other moorage in Victoria harbor is administered by the **Greater Victoria Harbour Society** which monitors VHF Ch 66A or you may call them at (250) 383-8326. All docks have power and water with shower and bathroom facilities nearby. Rates charged for moorage are the same in all facilities. The visitors' floats in front of the Empress Hotel, enjoying the best location in the harbor, at the head of the Inner Basin have a 48-hour maximum stay. The Wharf St. floats are also conveniently close to the downtown area though space is limited. During July and August when the fishing fleet is off to the fishing grounds Fisherman's Wharf has transient moorage; a good walk or bus service takes you downtown. Occasionally this facility becomes so congested on holiday weekends that rafting becomes necessary. To make arrangements for moorage skippers are advised to call the Greater Victoria Harbor Society on VHF Ch. 66A when they are about a half hour from entering the harbor.

Victoria has countless interesting shops, ongoing cultural activities and good restaurants featuring international and North American cuisine; many within walking distance of the inner harbor. A visit to the Provincial Museum (next to the Parliament Buildings) introduces visitors to the heritage and resources of B.C. Afternoon tea at the Empress Hotel, though extremely expensive, is considered a "must" provided you are dressed appropriately.

For many visitors, to see Victoria is to see **Butchart Gardens**. These world-famous gardens are easily reached by bus or taxi from all of the moorages described on pages 26 - 29. In addition, cruisers staying at **Angler's Anchorage Marina** in Brentwood Bay may walk to the main entrance or take their boats or dinghies to the water-side entrance where day moorage may be available at a float or overnight at a mooring buoy. See the next page for more details.

When proceeding north from Victoria the first harbor is at **Oak Bay** which can be approached using Chart Book #3313 or Chart 3462. Tide rips, rocks and shoals in the vicinity of Discovery Island demand careful navigation. The entrance to Oak Bay is between the breakwater at Turkey Head and the breakwater projecting south from Mary Tod Island. Buoy "V26" marks the outer end of a reef extending west from Mary Tod Island. Additional cautionary buoys and private buoys lie to the west of the island. The fully modern facility of **Oak Bay Marina** welcomes transient sailors and offers convenient access to both downtown Victoria and Butchart Gardens.

Transport Canada Victoria Harbour Master, Port Operations monitors VHF 18A.

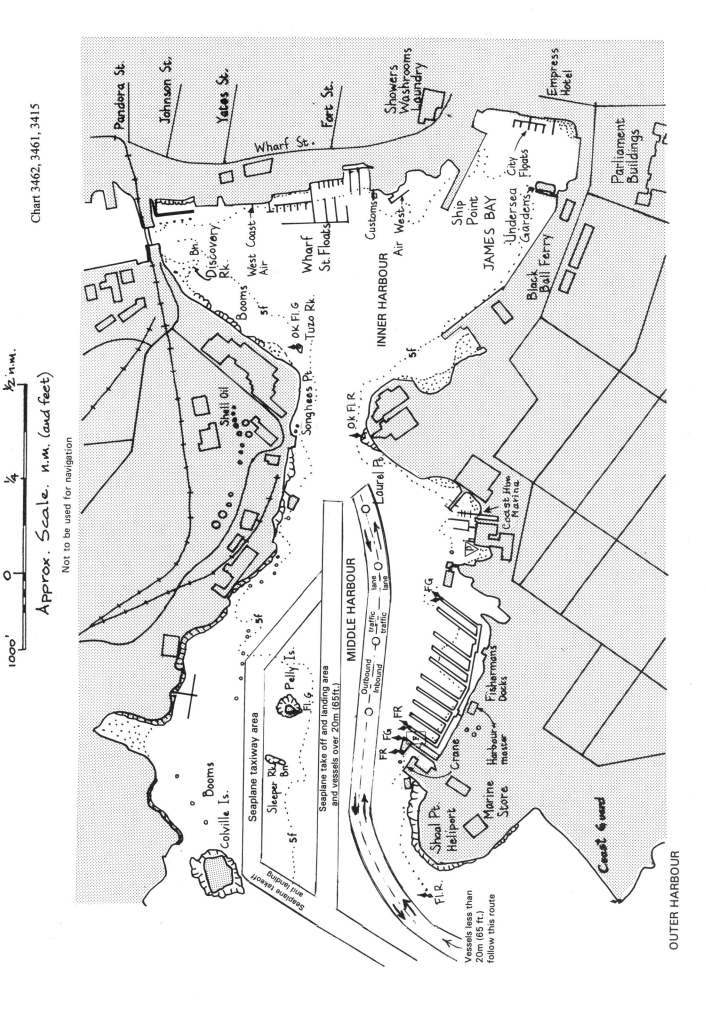

VICTORIA

Chart 3462, 3461, 3415

Approx. Scale. n.m. (and feet)

Not to be used for navigation

1000' 0 ¼ ½ n.m.

Pandora St.

Johnson St.

Yates St.

Fort St.

Wharf St.

Showers
Washrooms
Laundry

Empress
Hotel

City
Floats

Parliament
Buildings

Bn.

Discovery
Rk.

West Coast
Air

Wharf
St. Floats

Customs

Air West

Ship
Point

Undersea
Gardens

JAMES BAY

Booms

5f

Ok Fl.G

Tuzo Rk.

Songhees Pt.

INNER HARBOUR

5f

Black
Ball Ferry

Ok Fl.R

Shell Oil

5f

Laurel Pt.

Coast Hbr.
Marina

MIDDLE HARBOUR

Outbound

Inbound

traffic
lane

traffic
lane

FG

Colville Is.

Booms

Seaplane taxiway area

Sleeper Rk.
Bn.

Pelly Is.
Fl. G

Seaplane take off and landing area
and vessels over 20m (65ft.)

5f

FR FG FR

Crane

Fisherman's
Docks

Shoal Pt.
Heliport

Marine
Store

Harbour
master

Seaplane takeoff
and landing

Fl. R.

Vessels less than
20m (65 ft.)
follow this route

Coast Guard

OUTER HARBOUR

SIDNEY

Sidney is a **Port of Entry** located near the northern end of the Saanich Peninsula. It has two locations from which Customs clearance may be obtained. When approaching the Port of Sidney keep the red buoy to starboard and the black one to port. A breakwater protects the northern floats where pleasure craft may moor while clearing Customs. At the outer end of the public wharf is a telephone with a direct line to Customs. Note: Tidal streams are strong near the wharf making it advisable to berth at slack water, especially during southeasterly weather.

Customs clearance may also be obtained at the Customs float in All Bay in Tsehum Harbor by phoning the Customs House in Sidney at 356-6645 to request clearance. No one may leave the vessel except the skipper until clearance has been obtained. Flag etiquette requires foreign vessels to fly the Canadian flag while in Canadian waters. See page 19 for the proper placement of the courtesy ensign.

Tsehum Harbor has the greatest concentration of boating services and pleasure craft facilities to be found on Vancouver Island. Entry to this beautiful area is between Armstrong Point and Curteis Point; the channel into the harbor is marked by numerous daybeacons. Shoals line the shoreline and patches of kelp are scattered about. Beacons and buoys clearly mark the route to be followed when entering All Bay, Blue Heron Basin, the Royal Victoria Yacht Club facilities and other facilities. This intricate series of bays and coves is lined with docks, yacht clubs, shipyards and repair shops of every kind. Fuel, water, and supplies can be obtained from marinas operating here and hull, engine, and equipment repairs are available in the boatyards and shops clustered about. Haul-out facilities can handle vessels up to 24 m (80').

Brentwood Bay is reached by a short trip around the north end of Saanich Peninsula. Several marinas, fuel docks, and restaurants are in the southeastern part of the bay which is dominated by the huge Port Royal Condos sprawling over the slopes at the southern end. This first-class marina can accommodate vessels up to 45 m (150') and features a marine store, restaurant, and transient moorage. A local ferry runs between Brentwood Bay and Mill Bay which is located on the western shore of Saanich Inlet. Customs clearance can be obtained by calling the Sidney Customs House at 356-6645 from the Customs float at Anglers Anchorage Marina.

Caution: A drying rock located southwest of the ferry landing is marked by buoy U22. Do not approach the marina close south of the ferry wharf between U22 and the day beacon, for drying rocks lie between the buoy and the shore.

Although this is a pretty spot to visit, the main reason for coming here is its close proximity to the world famous **Butchart Gardens**. During July and August out-door stage shows are performed in the amphitheater on week nights and Saturday night fireworks at the Gardens can even be seen (and heard) as they add a festive note to a stop-over in the bay.

VICTORIA & SIDNEY
Ports of Entry

0 1 2 3 4
Approx. Scale n.m.

Not to be used for navigation

Moresby Passage

See detail.

Coal Is.

Swartz Bay
Ferry Term.

Tsehum Hbr.

SIDNEY

Patricia
Bay

Victoria
Int'l
Airport

SAANICH INLET

Brentwood
Bay

Buchart
Gardens

P

Elk L.

Hwy. No. 17

Cordova Bay

VANCOUVER ISLAND

SAANICH

VICTORIA

Hwy. No. 1

Cordova
Channel

Sydney
Channel

James
Is.

Sidney Spit
Marine Park

Miners Channel

Sydney
Is.

Anacortes
Ferry

D'Arcy Is.
Marine Park

N

Cadboro Pt.

Scenic dr.

RVYC

Esquimalt

Esquimalt Hbr.
Naval Base

See detail

Empress Hotel
Parliament Bldgs.

Oak Bay
Marina

Gonzales Pt.

Baynes Channel

Discovery Is.

Royal
Roads

Trial
Is.

Albert Hd.

STRAIT OF JUAN DE FUCA

Chart 3313, 3441, 3462

Ferry

BC Ferry Term.
SWARTZ BAY

Swartz
Hd.

Cardale Passage

Coal
Is.

Ker Is.

RVYC

P

Canoe
Cove

Curteis Pt.

Blue
Heron
Basin

Kelp

Tsehum Hbr.

Van Isle
3f Mar.

F

All Bay

Armstrong Pt.

Roberts Bay

Roberts Pt.

SAANICH

Beacon Ave.

SIDNEY

Wash.
State Fy.

Ferry

Chart 3476

0 ———————— 1 ———————— 2
Approx. Scale - n.m.

shoal

H

G

Customs
F

E

D

C

B

A

Office
Showers
Laundry

N

Fl R

Sidney

BEDWELL HARBOUR*

This **Port of Entry** is tucked in a bay in the northern part of South Pender Island. Two bodies of water, Port Browning and Bedwell Harbour separate North Pender Island from South Pender Island where they meet at Pender Canal. This shallow waterway has a least depth of 2.2m (7 ft.). A bridge with a vertical clearance of 8.5m (28ft.) crosses the canal near its north end. Tidal streams reach a maximum of 4 knots during springs.

Egeria Bay is about midway along the southwestern shore of South Pender Island. A breakwater built out from Richardson Bluff on the northern shore of the bay gives harbor facilities protection from northerly winds. Approach and entry to the harbor pose no difficulties. Connected to the public float located at the head of the bay are the Customs docks where Customs officers clear vessels from May 1 to September 1 from 8 am to 10 pm daily. Vessels entering Canada that have not received a Clearance Number under CANPASS regulations are required to clear Customs at the dock before proceeding elsewhere.

Poet's Cove Marina (formerly known as Bedwell Harbour Marina) has over 60 slips and can accommodate vessels up to 34m (110 ft.). The marina office monitors VHF 66A and can be reached at (866) 888-2683 or Fax (250) 629-2110. Reservations are recommended for week-ends. Shore facilities for the use of cruisers and hotel guests include a restaurant, heated pool, washrooms, showers, spa, an Internet terminal, movies, dog walk, tennis courts, bike rentals, snack bar, playground and grocery store. Wireless internet (BBX) service is available. Ashore, the Poet's Cove Resort features cottages, bungalows and town house style accommodation. A 4 km (2.5 mile) walk along a road leads to an ocean lookout, while another trail leads to the top of Mount Norman where the view is well worth the effort to arrive at the end of the trail.

Since water is scarce here boaters are asked to conserve it and dispense with washing the boat or leaving taps running. The island does not have a landfill site, so trash is not collected and boaters must take their garbage to a community that has collection facilities.

Beaumont Marine Park is a strip of land less than .2 miles wide and about 5 miles long, bordering part of the coast. The steep shores are covered with arbutus, fir and the rare and beautiful Garry oak. About 15 mooring buoys are east of Skull Islet and excellent anchorage can be taken to the south of the buoyed area. Fees for use of the mooring buoys are collected on the honor system at the self-registration stations in the information shelters.

******

Both Pender Island and Bedwell Harbour were named by Captain Richards, commander of the survey ship *Plumper*, after second masters Daniel Pender and Edward Bedwell who surveyed the B.C. coast from 1857 to 1860. Egeria Bay was named after a steam screw sloop *Egeria*, built in 1874 that was used exclusively for survey of the coast until 1902. Port Browning was also named by Captain Richards after George Browning, second master of the survey ship *Hecate*, a paddle wheel sloop..

*The Canadian spelling, <u>harbour</u>, is used in Canadian place names and the U.S. spelling, <u>harbor</u>, is used elsewhere in the guide.

BEDWELL HARBOUR

NORTH PENDER ISLAND

Perry Rk. 2f

PORT BROWNING

Razor Pt.

f u56

PLUMPER

SOUND

0   ½   1
Approx. Scale n.m.

Not to be used for navigation

Chart 3313, 3462, 3477

Mt. Norman

BEAUMONT MARINE PARK

BEDWELL HARBOUR

Skull Pt.

Mooring Buoys

Oaks Bluff

Breakwater

Bedwell Harbour

Hay Pt.

48°45'

Camp Bay

Higgs Pt.

N

Wallace Pt.

Gowlland Pt.

123 15'

Tilly Pt.

Detail –

Poet's Cove Marina

(AKA Bedwell Harbour Marina)

RENTALS   DIESEL
ICE
GAS
GAS

(67-79)

23   22   82

24   93   (27')

Office

(60')

52

66

25

21   4

(60')   3

49

2

(30')

1

51

Canada Customs

Store
Restaurant

50

Bar

Washroom + Showers   Hotel

WHITE ROCK, BRITISH COLUMBIA

White Rock is a **Port of Entry** located on a peninsula in Canada near the eastern end of Semiahmoo Bay, just across the border from Blaine, Washington. An extensive shoal along the coast dries and care should be taken when traveling in the area. A long pier protrudes from the shore with a short breakwater at right angles to the end. Proceed around the breakwater to the small dock on the eastern side. Vessels wishing to clear at this port may tie to the dock while the skipper walks along the pier until reaching a telephone booth on shore. To call for Customs clearance telephone 1-888-226-7277 and await instructions. Have a pen and paper handy to write down your Clearance Number which will show proper entrance has been completed. This number should be visible from a dockside window/port when visiting vessels are checked.

BLAINE, WASHINGTON

Semiahmoo Spit helps to enclose the protected area known as Drayton Harbor. On the eastern side of the harbor lies Blaine, a **U.S. Port of Entry.** A protective dike and breakwater encloses the port of Blaine, which is entered through an opening opposite the end of Semiahmoo Spit.

The eastern end of Blaine harbor (a subsidiary of the Port of Bellingham, which is operated by Whatcom County) has a series of long docks forming a boat haven. The western portion of these floats is for commercial fishing vessels; the eastern floats are for yachts in **Blaine Harbor** where transients can usually find moorage. The harbormaster monitors VHF Ch. 16; working channels are 9 and 68. The Harbor Office is in the one-story building at the head of the gangway.

The western end of Blaine harbor is commercial and includes a repair yard with haul-out facilities and fish unloading docks. A fuel dock is opposite the main entrance to the harbor. The main part of the town is about .25 mile to the east.

Semiahmoo Yacht Basin is an alternative which can be entered through an opening in the floating breakwater behind Semiahmoo Spit. Immediately to starboard on the inside of the breakwater is a fuel station, where temporary moorage can be taken while the harbormaster is being contacted. His office is in the large building beyond the head of the wharf. Moorage is usually available for transient vessels. Facilities are very clean and include a laundromat, shower, and a store handling marine supplies, groceries, and sundry items. Any major shopping will have to be done in Blaine, which though less than .25 mile away by water, is about 7 miles by road.

Anchorage can be taken in **Drayton Harbor** west of Semiahmoo Yacht Basin. The sketch shows the extensive shoal area. Southerly or southeasterly winds can kick up a nasty chop in the harbor. Entry into the U.S. can be easily made from either marina. Call U.S. Customs at (306) 332-6318 from telephone booths ashore; clearance may be obtained either by phone or an inspector will come out to check the vessel and crew. After 5 p.m. or on Sundays and holidays, call 1-800-562-5943.

Blaine is a small border town, so if any major refitting is needed a wider selection and better prices may be obtained in Bellingham or Seattle (a short trip by bus) or across the border in Vancouver.

BLAINE, WASH.; WHITE ROCK, B.C.
Ports of Entry

Chart 3313, 3463

WHITE ROCK

0 ½ 1 1½
Approx. Scale: n.m.

Hwy 99 to Vancouver.

SURREY

Not to be used for navigation

SEMIAHMOO BAY

Semi·ah·moo Marina

Private Dock

Breakwater

Transient mooring

CAN. U.S.A.

Light on conc. str.

Dries

Hwy 15

Can. Customs   Can. Customs
CAN.
U.S. Customs   USA
                U.S. Customs

Store

Police

Public Marina

Dockmaster
Pump-out

Buoy

Light on frame str.   Resort Semiahmoo

Red Buoy

Green water tower

Fuel

Brkwtr.

BLAINE

Hwy 5 to Seattle

Mall

Travel lift
Floating Breakwater

Dries

Semiahmoo Spit

Dries

Semiahmoo Marina

Piles

Park

Shoal

Dries

Drayton Harbor

Shoal

Dries

Dries

3f

Work Yard + Dry Storage

F Fuel + Pump-out
P

Travelift

Marina Office, Marina Supplies + Gifts

Restrooms Showers Laundry

www.semiahmoo.com
email: marina@semiahmoo.com

Shoal

Marina Office

Restrooms Showers Laundry

Pump out

R.R.

P-out

Pump out P Launch Ramp

Restaurant

Marina Store

Comm Fish Facilities

Fuel
F

Boat House

Dock F

4 Kt.

Blaine Harbor

www.blaineharbor@portofbellingham.com

NORTHERN GULF ISLANDS

This is an overview for planning. Many rocks and reefs are not indicated.

Not to be used for navigation

Flat Top Islands

Silva Bay
(See Detail)

Gabriola Pass
(See Details)
KENDRICK I.

Degnen
Bay

GABRIOLA ISLAND

Pylades Channel   VALDES

Pirates Cove   ISLAND

Porlier Pass
(See Details)

Northumberland Channel

Dodd Narrows
(See Detail)

De Courcy Group

NANAIMO
(See Detail)

Secretary
Group.

Clam Bay
THETIS   Houston Passage
ISLAND   KUPER ISLAND

Telegraph
Harbour

Stuart Channel

DUNSMUIR I.
Ladysmith Harbour

LADYSMITH

VANCOUVER ISLAND

Marinas in the Gulf Islands provide moorage, power, water and other services as listed. Use VHF Ch 66A when calling a marina to arrange moorage.

Fulford Marina, Saltspring Island: fuel, showers, washrooms ferries to Sidney, restaurants, grocery and arts and craft shops. Phone: (250) 653-4467, Fax: (250) 653-4457. Email: fulfordmarina@saltspring.com

Ganges Marina, Saltspring Island: fuel, showers, laundry, ice, bait, shopping center galleries, and restaurants. Phone: (250) 537-5242, Fax: (250) 537-4322. Email: info@dganges-marina.com

Lyall Harbour Wharfs, Saturna Island: fuel, outboard mix, restaurant, ice, propane nearby. Phone (250) 539-5725, Fax (250) 539-2229. Caution: watch for ferry traffic.

Montague Harbour Marina, Galiano Island: Fuel, groceries, clothing, lunches, coffee bar, books, gifts. Phone (250) 539-5733 Fax (250) 539-2010 Email: montaguemarina@gulfislands.com Details on p. 36.

Otter Bay Marina, Pender Island: showers, laundry, ice, close to restaurants and golf. Phone: (250) 629-3579 or Fax (250) 629-3589:

Page's Marina, Gabriola Island: Fuel, dive shop, air fills, showers, laundry, cottages, store. Details p. 40.

Poet's Cove Marina and Resort at Bedwell Harbour, South Pender Island: See details on page 30.

Port Browning Marine Resort, North Pender Island: Showers, laundry, pub, restaurant, tennis, nearby post office, bank, bakery liquor store and golf. Fax (250) 629-6552

Salts Spring Marina, Saltspring Island: showers, laundry, chandlery, scuba air refills, haulouts, towing, ramp, restaurant and pub. Phone (250) 537-5810, Fax: (250) 537-9100, Toll free 1-800-334-6629, Pub (250) 537-5559.

Saltspring Island Harbour Authority, Saltspring Island: showers, liquor store, rampk, hospital, pharmacy and nearby shopping. Phone/Fax (250) 537-5711 Email: ssha@saltspring.com

Silva Bay Boatel, Gabriola Island: laundromat, groceries, bait, suites. Phone (250) 247-9351.

Silva Bay Resort & Marina, Gabriola Island: showers, garbage service ice, fuel, groceries, pub and restaurant. Phone (250) 247-8662 Fax (250) 247-8663 Email: silvabay@canada.com

Telegraph Harbour Marina, Thetis Island: laundry, showers, fuel, charts, bait, ice, light meals, store. Phone: (250) 246-9511 Fax: 246-2668 Email: boating@telegraphharbour.com

SOUTHERN GULF ISLANDS

0 1 2 3 4 5

Approximate scale, n.m.

Not to be used for navigation

STRAIT OF GEORGIA

Cabbage Island
Marine Park

Whaler
Bay Sturdies
Bay
Campbell Bay
Belle Chain Isles
Boat Passage
SATURNA
ISLAND
MAYNE
ISLAND
Samuel I.
Winter
Cove
GALIANO ISLAND
Montague
Harbour
(See Detail)
Miner's Bay
Active
Pass
(See Detail)
Boat
Cove
Plumper Sound

Retreat Cove
Parker I.
Wallace Island
Trincomali Channel
Prevost
Island
NORTH PENDER
ISLAND
Port Browning
SOUTH
PENDER
Bedwell
Harbour
(See Details)
Boundary
Pass

Otter
Bay
Beaumont
Marine Park

Long Harbour
Captain Passage
Swanson Channel

Ganges
Ganges Harbour

Vesuvius
Bay
SALTSPRING ISLAND
Fulford Harbour
Moresby Passage
Moresby
Island
Prevost Passage
Stuart Island

CANADA-U.S. BOUNDARY

Crofton
Portland
I.
Princess Margaret
Marine Park

Maple
Bay
Burgoyne Bay
Sansum
Bird's Eye
Cove
Piers
Swartz
Bay
Coal
Canoe
Cove
Sidney Spit
Marine Park
Sidney
Island

Genoa Bay
Narrows
Satellite Channel
Tsehum Harbour
(See Detail)
Sidney
Sidney Channel

Cowichan
Bay
Cowichan
Deep
Cove
Patricia
Bay
Cordova Channel

Sannich Inlet
SAANICH
PENINSULA
Cordova
Bay

Mill Bay
Brentwood
Bay

| F | Float | MF | Marine Park |
| Anchorage | | M | Marina | | Mud Flats |

GOVERNMENT DOCKS

Bedwell Harbour	Browning Harbour	Burgoyne Bay
Degnen Bay	Fernwood	Fulford Harbour
Ganges	Hope Bay	Horton Bay
Kuper Island	Lyall Harbour	Miners Bay
Musgrave	Montague Harbour	North Galiano
Retreat Cove	Port Washington	Sturdies Bay
Thetis Island	Vesuvius Bay	Whalers Bay

ACTIVE PASS

Of the four passes of the Gulf Islands, this is the longest and the busiest. Not only is it used by many yachts, but swarms of small sports-fishermen frequent each end and the B.C. Ferries vessels meet each other every hour within the pass on their routes connecting Swartz Bay on Vancouver Island with Tsawwassen on the British Columbia mainland

During the springs, the tides set through the pass at 7 to 8 knots. Small vessels, particularly deep draft power and sail boats should use the pass at or near slack water. Though it is possible to use the pass for an hour on either side of slack water, it is better to do so going with the tide. But during these periods of use near slack water the concentration of vessels, requires careful and alert seamanship. The pass is crooked and after dark, well lit, and can be used by skippers familiar with it at any time. First-time visitors should use the pass only during daylight hours. One of the greatest advantages of Active Pass is that it has anchorages available on either side, as well as within the pass.

The pass is deep and clear except for a well marked and lighted area at Gossip Shoal near the eastern entrance and a drying patch with a light near Collinson Point at the western end. These are more of a hindrance for large vessels than for small ones, for the pass is quite wide. On any passage, favor the starboard side and allow for plenty of room if a ferry is being passed or met. They kick up a considerable wash which, when combined with current boils and swells, can be most unsettling for small craft. Provided care is taken and the pass is used near slack water, the passage through Active Pass is relatively easy.

On the eastern side of the Pass, anchorages are available in **Whalers Bay** or **Sturdies Bay**. The former has the larger area, with drying shoals at its ends and several rocky reefs along its perimeter. Enter in mid-channel. Sturdies Bay has a terminal for the inter-islands ferry, and there is a small resort alongside where moorage is available. Beware of the reef that projects slightly across the direct passage to the wharf.

Within the pass itself, you can find anchorage in **Miners Bay** to the east of the wharf at the village of Mayne. The anchor should be well set as there is a back current and some wash is created by ferries and large vessels transiting the pass, but the anchorage is otherwise adequate.

Montague Harbour is at the western end of Active Pass and its relation to the pass is shown on the sketch. This Marine Park is one of the most popular anchorages in the Gulf Islands and is part of the Gulf Islands National Park. In addition to cruising families who arrive by pleasure craft there are many who come by ferry to stay at the public campground nestled among the trees. Pleasant walks through the trees give you a chance to stretch your legs; one trail goes past an abandoned orchard and then to a beach on the other side of the peninsula.

Near the government wharf is a ferry dock which is used intermittently. **Montague Harbour Marina** provides moorage, fuel, groceries and sundry items. It is open May to September daily and Saturdays during the rest of the year. A $10 fee is charged for use of the mooring buoys in the northern part of the bay. Anchorage may be taken anywhere in the bay. A popular stop-over for cruisers nearby is the arts and crafts village of Ganges on Saltspring Island with two marinas and anchorage available nearby in Long Harbour. Do not attempt to pass through the Chain Islands, go around when going from Ganges to Long Harbour. Nearby anchorages are also found at **Fulford Harbour** on Saltspring Island and at **Prevost Island**.

Mayne Is.   Vancouver Is. behind.   Galiano Is.

Active Pass

Georgina Pt. Light   Gossip Shoal

APPROACHING ACTIVE PASS FROM WNW, i.e. from across Strait of Georgia

Gulf Islands
ACTIVE PASS
(& Montague Harbour)

Chart 3313, 3473, 3442

0   ½   1   2

Approx. Scale n.m.

Not to be used for navigation

Strait of Georgia

Lion Its

Pvt. Buoys   Is. w House

House with flag pole

Gossip Is.   Gossip Shoal

Whaler Bay

Pvt. dock
Public dock

Rip Pt.

Fairway Bank

Sturdie's Bay
(Ferry Terminal)

Lthse.
Georgina Pt.

GALIANO   ISLAND

Matthew's Pt.

Laura Pt.

Mary Anne Pt.

ACTIVE   PASS

Miner's Bay

Mayne Village

Whf

MAYNE   ISLAND

Village Bay (Ferry Term.)

Dinner Pt.

Collinson Pt.

Dries

Enterprise Reef

Helen Pt.

Ben Mohr Rk.

Phillimore Pt.

Julia Is.

Parker Is.

Private

See detail below

Clearance 125ft at H.W.

Power Line

Marine Park

Montague Hbr. Village
Wharf. (Ferry)

N

Detail – Montague Harbour

old apple orchard
Trees

Road

Campground

Steep cliff

Buoys

A BC Marine Park

4 to 6f m

Swamp

TRINCOMALI   CHANNEL

Chart 3473

PORLIER PASS

Located between Galiano and Valdes Islands, this is the next pass north of Active Pass. It is much used by cruising vessels bound for the Gulf Islands and by fishermen. No deep sea vessels use this pass as Romulus Rock at its western end limits the apparent opening.

This is the shortest and straightest of the three Gulf Island passes. As such, it would normally be the favored route, except that the underwater dangers of the western side make it less attractive for large vessels, and the lack of immediate anchorages on either side reduce its appeal for small craft awaiting slack water. As a result, there is less traffic here than in Active Pass.

Though short, this pass should be traveled at or near slack water. The current can reach 8 or 9 knots at springs and boils, and small whirlpools can make passage hazardous for an under powered small craft. But taken within an hour of each side of slack water, the pass is relatively straightforward.

Although Romulus Rock, on the western side is more of a hazard for large vessels, for small craft the best route through Porlier Pass is to hold about 225 m (700 feet) off the light at Race Point, and set a course to pass a similar amount off of Alcala Point on Galiano Island. This should take small vessels clear of any effects of Romulus Rock. There are more shoals and rocky patches on the northern side of Porlier, including a drying patch called Black Rock, so it is recommended that vessels favor the southern side in passing either way.

A small niche just to the west of the lighthouse can give shelter, but most vessels passing through Porlier proceed to one of the many anchorages available in the Gulf Islands. A particularly nice little one is **Retreat Cove,** about 6 miles south, on the west coast of Galiano Island. Enter only the southern portion, where the government wharf is built, for the northern section of the cove and behind Retreat Island is shallow and is suitable only for very small boats. Though the cove is small, it has good holding in mud, and there is space at the wharf as well. The road ashore offers a scenic, rural walk with many fine views of the area.

Other anchorages within reasonable reach of Porlier Pass are: **North Cove** and **Telegraph Harbour** on Thetis Island, and **Tent Island Marine Park** which is south of Thetis and Kuper Islands.

Fishing is productive at most passes and Porlier Pass is no exception. The salmon congregate at the downstream ends of passes, changing ends as the tide changes. This results in some congestion of small fishing craft which follow the movement of the tides and the fish. When fishing the passes, mooching with bait and lures seems to be the most successful, followed by trolling.

Mayne Is.   Vancouver Is. behind.   Galiano Is.

Active Pass

Georgina Pt. Light   Gossip Shoal

APPROACHING ACTIVE PASS FROM WNW, i.e. from across Strait of Georgia

Chart 3313, 3473, 3442

Gulf Islands
ACTIVE PASS
(& Montague Harbour)

0   ½   1   2

Approx. Scale n.m.

Not to be used for navigation

see detail below

Clearance 125ft
at H.W.

Power Line

Marine
Park

Lion Its.

Strait of Georgia

Pvt. Buoys   Is. w House

House with flag pole

6f

Montague Hbr. Village
Wharf. (Ferry)

3f   F   5f   3f

10f

3f

Gossip Is.

6f

3f

½f   Gossip Shoal

Whaler Bay

Parker
Is.

Private

Julia Is.   3f

GALIANO   ISLAND

Pvt. dock
Public dock

Rip Pt.

Sturdie's Bay
(Ferry Terminal)   3f

Fairway Bank

Lthse.
Georgina Pt.

Phillimore Pt.

Laura Pt.

Matthew's Pt.

Mary Anne P.   ACTIVE   PASS

Miner's Bay

Collinson Pt.   Dries

Ben Mohr
Rk.

old apple
orchard
Trees

Road

Campground

swamp

Steep
cliff

TRINCOMALI   CHANNEL

Helen Pt.

Mayne
Village

Whf.

Buoys

A BC Marine Park

4 to 6f
m

Enterprise
Reef

MAYNE   ISLAND

Village Bay (Ferry Term.)

Dinner Pt.

Detail – Montague Harbour

Chart 3473

PORLIER PASS

Located between Galiano and Valdes Islands, this is the next pass north of Active Pass. It is much used by cruising vessels bound for the Gulf Islands and by fishermen. No deep sea vessels use this pass as Romulus Rock at its western end limits the apparent opening.

This is the shortest and straightest of the three Gulf Island passes. As such, it would normally be the favored route, except that the underwater dangers of the western side make it less attractive for large vessels, and the lack of immediate anchorages on either side reduce its appeal for small craft awaiting slack water. As a result, there is less traffic here than in Active Pass.

Though short, this pass should be traveled at or near slack water. The current can reach 8 or 9 knots at springs and boils, and small whirlpools can make passage hazardous for an under powered small craft. But taken within an hour of each side of slack water, the pass is relatively straightforward.

Although Romulus Rock, on the western side is more of a hazard for large vessels, for small craft the best route through Porlier Pass is to hold about 225 m (700 feet) off the light at Race Point, and set a course to pass a similar amount off of Alcala Point on Galiano Island. This should take small vessels clear of any effects of Romulus Rock. There are more shoals and rocky patches on the northern side of Porlier, including a drying patch called Black Rock, so it is recommended that vessels favor the southern side in passing either way.

A small niche just to the west of the lighthouse can give shelter, but most vessels passing through Porlier proceed to one of the many anchorages available in the Gulf Islands. A particularly nice little one is **Retreat Cove,** about 6 miles south, on the west coast of Galiano Island. Enter only the southern portion, where the government wharf is built, for the northern section of the cove and behind Retreat Island is shallow and is suitable only for very small boats. Though the cove is small, it has good holding in mud, and there is space at the wharf as well. The road ashore offers a scenic, rural walk with many fine views of the area.

Other anchorages within reasonable reach of Porlier Pass are: **North Cove** and **Telegraph Harbour** on Thetis Island, and **Tent Island Marine Park** which is south of Thetis and Kuper Islands.

Fishing is productive at most passes and Porlier Pass is no exception. The salmon congregate at the downstream ends of passes, changing ends as the tide changes. This results in some congestion of small fishing craft which follow the movement of the tides and the fish. When fishing the passes, mooching with bait and lures seems to be the most successful, followed by trolling.

Gulf Islands
PORLIER PASS
(&Retreat Cove)

Not to be used for navigation

Shah Pt.

Dries

VALDES Is.

Vernaci Pt.

...dale Pt.

Cayetano Pt.

Black Rk.   Dries
            Bn

Romulus Rk.
(Dangerous for large
vessels)

PORLIER PASS
6·7 kts. at Springs

Approx. 6 n.miles
to Retreat Cove

0   ½   1   1½ n.m

Approx. Scale n.m.

Race Pt.

Dionisco Pt.

Bn

Lighthouse Bay

Virago Pt

Bris   49°00'N

Alcala Pt.   GALIANO Is.

123°55'W

N

Chart 3442, 3443, 3473

Steep. high cliffs

GALIANO   ISLAND

Sh.   Shallow

Retreat Is.

Float

Gov't. Wharf

Steep face

15f

48°56'N

123°30'W

Detail - Retreat Cove

0   600'   ¼   ½ n.m.

Approx. Scale n.m.

GABRIOLA PASS

This is the most scenic of the three passes. It has good anchorages on each side of the pass and another one half way through. It is a good location from which to commence crossing the Georgia Strait either to Vancouver or to Welcome Pass.

The eastern end of the pass is fronted by Breakwater Island, which divides the current. The dangers are marked, and a mid-channel course is clear of all problems. The constriction between Josef Point on Gabriola Island, and Cordero Point on Valdes Island, is where the currents are strongest. Boils, swells and occasional whirlpools occur downstream of this area when the current is running. Passage should be made at or near slack water—no more than an hour on either side. Large power boats have been known to fail to make headway against the full current and have had to turn back.

At the proper time, however, the passage is simple and straightforward. Once past Josef Point, the opening to the north is **Degnen Bay** where good anchorage can be taken in its northern end near a public wharf. As you continue through the Pass, effects of the current are less noticeable and once through the next section, you are free to roam the Gulf Islands.

On the Gulf Islands side, a very good anchorage is at **Pirates Cove** Marine Park in the southern part of De Courcy Island. When entering the enclosed harbor, favor the De Courcy Island shore, heading toward the private house, for a reef, marked by a concrete marker, projects underwater from the spit. At low water, there may be less than a fathom over the rocky sill of the entrance, so pass between the marker and a buoy marking a rock. This cove is crowded in summer. The holding is in mud on rock, and with strong winds it will be wise to let out additional scope if space permits.

Silva Bay is one of the nicest anchorages on the Strait of Georgia side of the Gulf Islands. The harbor is formed by the protection of the many Flat Top Islands around a cove of Gabriola Island. Shelter is available from all winds and seas, and there is room for many vessels. Beware of the plastic water pipes laid across the bay from the village to Tugboat Island — vessels anchoring in the northern part of the bay can foul their anchors on these pipes. This is a busy spot during the summer when in addition to being crowded with anchored vessels, seaplanes often land and take off from the bay. A large RVYC outstation is on Tugboat Island. Three commercial docks serve the bay: Silva Bay Boatel (250) 247-9351 has a motel, laundry, convenience store and docks for small boats, Silva Bay Resort has showers, and Pages Marina sells fuel and local charts. It can be reached at (250) 247-8931.

Entrance to Silva Bay is from the east, through Commodore Passage. Note the jog that must be made around the reef that is marked with a concrete pedestal and light. Stay at least 18m (60 ft.) off, as the reef extends beyond the marker. Do not pass between the marker and the south shore.

Local boaters also use the passage between Sear Island and Gabriola Island. At low water, the maximum draft that can be carried through this passage is 2 m (6 feet)—rocks and other dangers show clearly. This passage leads to the entrance of Gabriola Pass behind Breakwater Island.

Thrasher Rock and Gabriola Reefs lie about 1.5 miles northwest of Breakwater Island. Pass north around Thrasher Rock, which is a good departure or destination point to or from the mainland. Good fishing can be had around the reefs and around Breakwater Island.

Gulf Islands
GABRIOLA PASS
(& Silva Bay Anchorage)

ENTERING SILVA BAY

Commodore Passage

Reef

Approx. Scale n.m.

0   600'   1800'   ½   1   1½

Not to be used for navigation

N

Approx. 19 n.m. to Pt. Grey buoy, Vancouver.

Gaviola Is.

Lily Is.

Vance Is.

3f

Acorn

FLAT TOP Is.

3f

Note: Water pipes are laid across the harbor under-water.

Silva Bay

Dock

Fuel

Floats

1½f

Tugboat Is. RVYC

Sear Is.

Dries

1f

Commodore Passage

Bath Is.

Saturnina Is.

GABRIOLA Is.

Only vessels drawing less than 6ft. can use this passage

Thrasher Rock Light

Dries

Local knowledge needed for passage.

Dries

Gabriola Reefs

Good trolling

Wharf

2f

4f   3f

Degnen Bay

Breakwater Is.

8

3f

Cliffs

Josef Pt.

Bn

Cordero Pt.

3f

3f

VALDES IS.

Steep Cliffs

Gabriola Pass.
Currents 6-8 kt at springs
Travel at slack.

Red Buoys (2) Pvt.

Vancouver Is.

Valdes Is

Beacon

Silva Bay

Breakwater Is. behind.

Bath Is

To Gabriola Pass

Commodore Passage

Acorn Is.

APPROACHING THE FLAT TOP IS. FROM NNE, distant about 2 miles.

NANAIMO

As the second largest city on Vancouver Island, Nanaimo acts as a hub for much of the activity in the central part of the island. It is the second major terminal of the B.C. Ferry Corporation that links the island and Vancouver. It is also the home of the zany annual Bathtub Race held in July, when hundreds of dedicated entrants take off in their souped-up, uniquely designed and decorated "bath tubs" to race across the Strait of Georgia to Vancouver.

Nanaimo lies north of the Gulf Islands area and can be approached from the Strait of Georgia or from the inside waters via Dodd Narrows, which is north of Gabriola Passage, and between Mudge Island and Vancouver Island. As with other passes in the Gulf Islands, Dodd Narrows should be traversed only at or near slack water. The harbor of Nanaimo lies ahead up Northumberland Channel.

False Narrows, to the east of Dodd Narrows, leads from Pylades Channel. In addition to being narrow and complex it has depths of less than 1.2m (5 ft.) and is clogged with kelp during the summer. It is occasionally used by shoal draft, local vessels at high water.

Newcastle and Protection Islands lie in front of the main small craft facilities in Nanaimo harbor. Approach from the north around Newcastle, or from the south around Protection Island. Do not attempt the channel between these islands, as it is shoal and encumbered by kelp. Mark Bay, part of **Newcastle Island Marine Park**. The anchorage in the bay is in soft mud, and requires care and persistence in order to set the anchor securely. A small passenger ferry makes frequent runs connecting the island to downtown Nanaimo.

Several small craft facilities are located along the Newcastle Passage shore of Nanaimo. Favor the Newcastle Island side of the passage to avoid the marked rocks, particularly Rowans Rock which has bent many a propeller. The harbor has a 5-knot speed limit.

The yacht club station and the Nanaimo harbor basin near the southern part of the harbor, opposite the end of Protection Island are easily identified by a turquoise-roofed large building. Once a prominent landmark, the old octagonal harbor bastion is now hidden by buildings in front of it. There are many berths in the basin, controlled by the harbormaster. As fishing vessels moor here in winter and are out during the summer, space may be available. Showers and restrooms are provided, while across the street is the Harbour Park Mall, with supermarkets, restaurants, a laundromat and other facilities. Fuel floats are moored along the harbor front and repair yards are available. Marine supplies are available at Harbour Chandler on Esplanade St. and West Marine on Island Hwy. N. An excellent marine bookstore that also sells charts is Nanaimo Maps located at 8 Church St. Just a block or two down the hill is Scottish Bakery, known for its bread and sticky buns.

A B.C. Ferry Terminal is Departure Bay, in the northern part of the harbor. The large ferries run every hour (sometimes more frequently in the summer) to Horseshoe Bay in West Vancouver. A second B.C. Ferry Terminal is south of Nanaimo at Duke Point and it runs to Tsawwassen in Delta. As the ferries have a sizable wash, care should be taken when encountering them.

When leaving Departure Bay the grassy hump of Snake Island and (when bound for Vancouver) the barren sandstone Entrance Island are both passed on their north side. A lighthouse and fog signal are located on Entrance Island. If crossing to Welcome Pass, note the comment on page 6 of the Introduction regarding the restricted area designated as "Whiskey-Golf."

VANCOUVER ISLAND

Chart 3443, 3475, 3458, 3447

Jesse Is.

Ferry to Vancouver (Horseshoe Bay)

Snake Is.

Departure Bay Rd

DEPARTURE BAY

Nares Pt.

McKay Pt.

N

STRAIT OF GEORGIA

Townsite Marina

Shaft Pt.

Pimbury Pt.

NEWCASTLE ISLAND MARINE PARK

B.C. Ferry Terminal

Bowen Rd

NANAIMO

Island Hwy

Stewart Ave.

Newcastle Passage

Mark Bay

No passage

Townsite Rd

Bate Pt.

Floats

PROTECTION Is.

For Ferry

Good Pt.

Comox

See detail Over

Satellite Reef.

Alt. W.R.

Ferry to Gabriola Is.

Breakwater

Carpenter Rk.

Seaplanes

Beacon Rk.

F Fuel

P

Commercial Inlet

Harbor

Details

Milton St.

Pine St.

B.C. Ferries

Harbour Park Mall

Victoria Rd

NANAIMO

Not to be used for navigation

0   ½   1

Approx. Scale n.m.

Booms

Bns

8 - 9 Knot Currents

Percy Anchorage

Booms

Joan Pt.

Purvis Pt.

Y.C.

Dodd Narrows

Mudge Is.

VANCOUVER ISLAND

Round

De Courcy Group

Stuart Channel

5f

DODD NARROWS

0   1   2

Approx. Scale n.m.

Not to be used for navigation

VANCOUVER

Vancouver is the principal city of British Columbia and is a **Port of Entry**. Including the surrounding municipalities, Greater Vancouver has over 2 million people, almost half that of the entire province of British Columbia and this is the largest city in the area covered by this guide. It has its own special attractions as well as the disadvantages of big cities anywhere. When Sir Francis Drake explored the coast in 1579 followed by Captain Vancouver who sailed past First Narrows into Burrard Inlet in 1792, who could have imagined that a city such as this would grow from these densely wooded shores.

This city enjoys one of the most beautiful natural harbors in the world. The surrounding mountains offer a scenic backdrop, as well as good skiing in season. The mild Pacific coast climate allows year-round sailing (though winter's cooler weather needs to be taken into consideration with layers of clothes and a source of heat aboard).

Beginning from the south and proceeding northward the centers of population—Delta, Richmond, Vancouver, North Vancouver, and West Vancouver—will be described.

Deriving its name from being part of the delta of the Fraser River, Delta is a sprawling district on the south side of the Fraser River. Significant landmarks seen as one sails northward are the B.C. Ferries Terminal at Tsawwassen and a container terminal adjacent to the huge Roberts Bank Coal Port facility. The silt of the Fraser River has laid two large shallow banks— Roberts Bank off of Delta and Sturgeon Bank off of Richmond. Both banks are well buoyed and courses past them should pass clear of the extensive areas of shoal water.

The South Arm of the Fraser River exits through a buoyed channel protected by a breakwater which ends at Sand Heads Light at the edge of the bank. This route is navigable by deep sea vessels as far as the Port of New Westminster, about 20 miles upstream. Cruising yachts can enter the small town of Steveston for fuel, moorage and provisions, though this is mainly a commercial fishing vessel center. **Captain's Cove Marina** is 9.5 miles up the river from Sand Heads; transient moorage is available and facilities include a travel-lift, restaurant, showers and laundromat. From April till July the melting snows that feed the Fraser cause freshet currents that can run to 5 knots. Upstream travel is affected by these currents and the state of the tide.

Richmond extends between the North and South Arms of the Fraser River. It is one of the largest residential suburbs of Vancouver, and includes the expanse of Sea Island on which Vancouver International Airport is located. Depending on the prevailing winds the jets land from either inland or over the Strait of Georgia. Entrance to Richmond marinas is through the North Arm which exits just south of Point Grey. There are several marinas at the southeastern end of Sea Island. The Arthur Lang bridge has clearance of 19 m (65 feet) and the airport swing bridge beyond it has only 5.5 m (18 feet). Many of the marinas are southwest of this bridge.

The high bluff of Point Grey marks the tip of the peninsula on which Vancouver proper is located. Immediately behind it are the extensive lands and buildings of the University of British Columbia. High-rise towers of the city center can be seen from some distance before Lion's Gate Bridge comes into view.

E. Side, Str. of Georgia

VANCOUVER AREA

MARINAS — DOCKS, FUEL, ETC.

C   Fisherman's Cove   WYYC, EHYC, Thunderbird Marina, fuel
I   Coal Harbour   RVYC, VRC, Commercial docks, fuel, see next map
M   Burrard Bridge   Civic Marina, fuel, boat launch
N   Jericho   Royal Vancouver Yacht Club docks
R   False Creek   Marinas, fuel, and marine services of every kind
V   Richmond   Marinas, fuel, and marine services
X   Steveston   Fishboat docks, fuel and marine services
Y   Fraser River   Captain's Cove Marina, fuel, boat launching

PARKS & ATTRACTIONS

A   Horseshoe Bay   BC Ferry Terminal, docks, fuel, great view
B   Whytecliff Park   Walks, diving, views
D   Lighthouse Park   Pt. Atkinson Light, walks, large trees, views
E   Grouse Mountain   Skyride, view, restaurant, skiing
F   Cleveland Dam   Canyon Park, walks, views, tourist attractions
H   Ambleside Park   Beach, view
I   Stanley Park   1,000 acre (404 Ha) park, walks and aquarium
J   Gastown   Shops, curios, restaurants, tourist attraction
K   Chinatown   North America's 2nd largest Chinatown, shops
L   False Creek North Shore   B.C. Place Stadium
M   Kitsilano   Maritime Museum, Planetarium, Museum, beach
O   Spanish Banks   Beaches, views
P   University of B.C.   Museum of Anthropology, Nitobe Japanese Garden
Q   Granville Island   Public Market, restaurants, marine equipment
S   VanDusen Bot. Gardens   Acres of manicured gardens, restaurant
T   Queen Elizabeth Park   Gardens and conservatory for tropical plants
Z   Tsawwassen   BC Ferry terminal, nearby town with services

SHOPPING CENTRES

(The four major centres easily accessible by bus, car or walking are shown.)

G   Park Royal Centre   Marine Drive in West Vancouver
J   Downtown Vancouver   Several malls and large stores
U   Oakridge Centre   41st and Oak St.
W   Richmond, Lansdowne Ctr.   No. 3 Rd., Richmond

For tourist information about greater Vancouver
call (604) 682-2222 or visit their website at
www.tourismvancouver

Not to be used for navigation

Chart 3463, 3490, 3491,
3492

Point Grey, and Point Atkinson, to the north mark the 3.5 mile wide entrance to Vancouver Harbour. Spanish Banks extend out for .5 mile; a light and bell mark the northwestern edge of this bank that is covered at high water. The outer harbor includes English Bay which is used as an anchorage for freighters as well as by pleasure boaters from the city for recreational use. The Royal Vancouver Yacht Club Station, protected by breakwaters, lies midway along English Bay.

Most Vancouver marinas are in False Creek (between the downtown city center and the residential area of Kitsilano) and Coal Harbour (east of First Narrows, tucked behind Stanley Park). There are other marinas in Burrard Inlet and Indian Arm, but they are less convenient for the transient boater.

The Burrard Street bridge marks the boundary between False Creek and English Bay. The distinctive buildings of the Maritime Museum (large A-frame) and the McMillan-Bloedel Planetarium and Museum complex (onion-shaped) are easily identified on the south shore west of the bridge. Both the Burrard and Granville Street Bridges (to the east) have a clearance of 27 m (90 feet). The north bank of False Creek was the site of EXPO 86, a world's fair with a transportation and communication theme held.

The Burrard Civic Marina, a Coast Guard Station and a fuel barge are to starboard just before passing under the Burrard Street bridge (westernmost of the two bridges). Strong tidal currents flow through this passage. Transient moorage is not available at this marina.

Fisherman's Wharf lies between the two bridges. A harbormaster's office is located near the gate at the south side of the complex. Several other marinas lie within False Creek but space is usually taken by local boats. Anchorage may sometimes be available in False Creek for a limited number of days though this cannot be relied on as local regulations are under review.

The entrance to Vancouver Harbor is through First Narrows and under Lions Gate Bridge which has a clearance of 60m (200 feet). Tidal currents of up to 6 knots run through First Narrows where Marine Traffic Regulations restrict the central section to large deep-sea vessels which have the right of way because of their limited maneuverability. Pleasure craft must stay well to the outer edges of the entrance and maintain a safe distance from cruise ships and all commercial craft.

Vancouver is a **Port of Entry** and foreign vessels are required to report to the **Customs Dock** located at the welcome station. Keep to starboard of the orange buoy after passing the fuel docks as shown on the sketch.

The magnificent green expanse of Stanley Park with its 1,000 acres of woodland and park facilities, is well worth visiting. A lighthouse at Brockton Point marks the eastern tip of the Park. After rounding the buoy which marks Burnaby Shoal turn southwest to enter Coal Harbour where fuel barges are anchored on the eastern side of Stanley Park. On the Stanley Park side are the Royal Vancouver Yacht Club Station and the Vancouver Rowing Club facilities, both private clubs where prior reciprocal club arrangements may allow guest moorage. Two first-class marinas in the heart of downtown Vancouver are: **Coal Harbour Marina**, Tel. (604) 681-2628, Fax (604) 681-4666, often has space for vessels up to 100m (330 ft.) with pump-out facilities for guests and **Bayshore West Marina** (Thunderbird), email: franka@thunderbirdmarine.com or Tel. (604) 689-5331, Fax (604) 689-5332, with transient moorage for vessels up to 40m (100 ft.). Enquire at Barbary Coast Yacht Basin, Tel (604) 669-0088 for transient moorage. In West Vancouver transient moorage can sometimes be obtained at Thunderbird Marina by calling (604) 921-7434. Their website also gives information regarding Bayshore West Marina: www.thunderbirdmarina.com.

DETAIL - VANCOUVER HBRS.

Not to be used for navigation

ENGLISH BAY

Chart 3481, 3493

KEATS ISLAND and GIBSONS

Howe Sound is a popular sailing area, not only because of its protected waters but also because of its proximity to Vancouver. Across from West Vancouver on Bowen Island are two marinas and a public dock in Snug Cove. As you enter the cove, **Bowen Island Marina** is the first marina seen on the north side. It consists of a 100m (340')dock with a least depth of 2.3 fathoms on the outer side. Further into the cove, beyond the prominent government dock is **Union Steamship Marina** which monitors VHF Ch 68. Both marinas have slips for transient cruisers. Stores and a post office are found nearby and a local ferry links the island to Horseshoe Bay in West Vancouver.

Located at the southwestern entrance to Howe Sound, Shoal Channel lies between Gibsons and Keats Island. The bar that gives the channel its name has only 3m (10 feet) of water at low tide. Opposing wind and currents cause short steep seas in this channel which is often filled with small sportsfishing boats "mooching" for salmon. Depending on the draft of the vessel the channel is normally passable on rising tides—a mid-channel course is best.

Plumper Cove Marine Park is on the western shore of Keats Island, with Shelter Islands to the southwest providing a lee. The islands are joined by a drying ledge. The Park Warden collects a nominal fee for the use of mooring buoys in the cove, or anchorage can be taken nearby. There is a small dock which a few small vessels can use. Beyond the gravel beach is a campground.

Gibsons is a fair-sized town on the Sechelt shore of Howe Sound. Steep Bluff is an easily recognizable point at the southern end of Gibsons. The shoal section of the channel below the bluffs is clearly indicated by somewhat more turbulence particularly when a northwesterly swell meets tidal waters flowing outward from Howe Sound. Some drying rocks extend roughly northeast from the foot of the bluff into Shoal Channel. A breakwater protects the harbor where a government dock, fuel station and **Gibsons Marina** are located. The full-service marina often has moorage for transient vessels and has a convenience store with local charts, books and fishing gear. Shopping involves a good walk up the hill to a wide selection of stores and services.

Transient vessels can usually find moorage at the marina on a hot-berth basis. Fuel, water, charts, and provisions are available in the marina store or you can walk to supermarkets and other stores in this quickly growing town. The highway which commences at the Ferry Terminal at Langdale (about 2 miles north along the shore) passes by Gibsons on its way up the Sechelt Peninsula to Powell River. A local ferry connects Langdale to Vancouver from this terminal.

Other protected anchorages with good holding in Howe Sound include:

Center Bay is a small cove in the western side of Gambier Island midway into the long bay. Good anchorage can be taken here.

Halkett Bay Marine Park is the small, easternmost bay on Gambier Island. It offers a good anchorage although care must be taken to avoid an underwater unmarked rock near the center of the bay at its head.

Point Atkinson Lighthouse is a prominent landmark on the mainland that is the datum for many tidal calculations along this coast, and marks the northwestern boundary of Vancouver Harbour. Fishermans Cove, where a marina, marine supply store, fuel station and the West Vancouver Yacht Club are located, is entered by a channel on the north side of Eagle Island.

Detail – Plumper Cove

KEATS IS. & GIBSONS

HOWE SOUND

Approx. Scale n.m.

Not to be used for navigation

Chart 3526

0   1   2   3   4 n.m.

SHOAL CHANNEL

Observatory Pt.

Park Ranger

Marine Park Facilities

Small craft only

Buoys

Rocky Ledges

Shelter Is.

Plumper Cove

KEATS ISLAND

1000'   ¼ m

Approx. Scale – ft & miles

GAMBIER IS.

Camp Artaban

To Squamish

N

Halkett Bay Marine Park

Hope Pt.

Langdale B.C. Ferry Term:

West Bay

Centre Bay

Port Graves

Grace Is.

Pleasant inner route

Hood Pt.

Cates Bay

Bowyer Is.

49°25'N

HOWE SOUND

See detail above

Marina, Wharf, facilities

Gibsons

Steep Bluff

Hutt Is.

KEATS IS.

Home Is.

Ragged Is.

Hermit Is.

Pasley Is.

Popham Is.

(Mostly privately owned)

Worlcombe Is.

COLLINGWOOD CHANNEL

SHOAL CHANNEL

BOWEN ISLAND

Mannion Bay (Deep Bay)

Snug Cove Ferry

Bowen Is. and Union Steamship Marinas + Gov't Dock

Horseshoe Bay B.C. Ferry Term.

Heavy ferry & small craft traffic

West Van. Y.C. Fisherman's Cove Eagle Is.

WEST VANCOUVER

Micro Twrs

C. Roger Curtis

Cowan Pt.

Passage Is (private)

Pt. Atkinson Lighthouse Fl (2). 5s. Fog Sig.

Alternate route

123°30'W

STRAIT OF GEORGIA

VANCOUVER HBR.

SMUGGLER and SECRET COVES

Though passage up the Strait of Georgia can be accomplished on either side, the more popular route is along the mainland coast. For this route, cross from Nanaimo or Silva Bay to either Howe Sound or the Sechelt Peninsula (known as the Sunshine Coast). Merry Island makes a good reference point as it is marked by a light and is close to Smuggler and Secret Coves. Beyond Merry Island is Welcome Passage is straightforward and clear of dangers except for occasional log debris.

Smuggler Cove Marine Park, on the mainland, comes very shortly after exiting from the northern end of Welcome Passage. The opening is about 21 m (70 feet) wide and is marked by a Marine Park sign on the northern side of the passage. Favor the north or port side when entering, staying fairly close to the rocky cliffs where the water is deeper. While popular, this anchorage has no facilities.

Once you are through this passage the cove opens up. Protected anchorage is available in the outer basin. Ahead lies a small island with a home built on it. By continuing on between this island and the north shore (still favoring the north side) make a fairly sharp turn to starboard leads to an inner basin. The sharp bend may seem to limit the size of vessel that can enter the inner anchorage but 12 m (40-foot) vessels can enter without difficulty. Here, safe and protected by the hills and islands, quiet anchorage on good holding is available no matter what the weather is in the Strait. The space is not large, but as the depths are about 1.5 fathoms, several vessels can be accommodated. Do not anchor in the small cove opening to the north as it is quite shallow, and only small sportsfishing vessels and multi-hulls can anchor here. In order to accommodate the many vessels which congregate in both anchorages it is common practice for boats to drop a bow anchor and tie a stern line to the trees or rocks ashore.

Just 2.5 miles further up the coast is the popular Sechelt harbor of **Secret Cove**. When entering leave the entrance light (located on a drying ledge) to starboard. The cove is congested, with little space for anchoring. Secret Cove Marina offers transient moorage as well as fuel, groceries, washrooms, showers, marine supplies and liquor. Buccaneer Marine has facilities to haul sailboats up to 9m (32ft.) and powerboats up to 12m (40 ft.) and provides mechanical and electrical repairs. The Jolly Roger Inn is one of the more popular places for dining on this coast. A Royal Vancouver Yacht Club outstation is located here and this is the home of the specially formed Sechelt Yacht Club which was responsible for *CANADA I* and its entry in the 1984 America's Cup Races.

In settled weather anchorage may be taken at **Buccaneer Bay Marine Park,** off the drying shoal between North and South Thormanby Islands but northerly winds make this a poor spot. A better one is in the small cove off the private dock in Water Bay. Care is needed to avoid Tattenham Ledge when approaching the area.

ENTRANCE TO SMUGGLER COVE MARINE PARK

Chart 3512, 3535

E. Side, Str. of Georgia
SMUGGLER COVE
SECRET COVE

Not to be used for navigation

Approx. Scale n.m.

0   1   2   3

Secret Cove Marina

Secret Cove

Buccaneer Marina

Turnagain Is.

Dries Bn

RVYC Outstation

MALASPINA STRAIT

WELCOME PASSAGE

Smuggler Cove
(See detail below)

Halfmoon Bay

N

SOUTH THORMANBY Is.

Marine Park Sign

50'

60'

Outer Anchorage

3f   3f

6f   3f   1½f

Private

⚓ 2f

House Trees

Private
Dries

v. shallow

1½f

⚓ 1½f m

Inner Anchorage

Trail

WELCOME PASSAGE

GRANT Is.

Detail - Smuggler Cove

0   500'   1000'   1500'

Approx. Scale - feet

LASQUETI, JEDEDIAH and MITLENATCH ISLANDS

Sabine Channel separates the southwestern shore of Texada Island from a number of islands, the largest being Lasqueti Island. This heavily wooded and sparsely populated island rises to 99m (326 ft.) at the summit of Trematon Mountain, located almost at the middle of the island. Many islets, isolated rocks, reefs and islands lie off Lasqueti and Jedediah Islands.

The village of Lasqueti is on the eastern shore of False Bay, a convoluted bay on the northwestern side of the island. When entering the bay there are two dangerous rocks to avoid, both covered with less than .6m (2 ft.): Jeffrey Rock, .2 miles south of Olsen Island and an unnamed rock half-way between Olsen Island and Higgins Island. The public wharf has a fuel float connected to it where diesel and gasoline are available. When brisk westerly winds blow moorage on the wharf becomes uncomfortable and it is much better to anchor in the northern part of the bay in 5 – 7 fathoms good holding mud. The village has a post office, store and restaurant.

Scottie Bay is a popular and perfectly protected anchorage on the opposite side of the island, south of Lindbergh Island. When approaching from the north the dark green foliage on a small island just to the north of Lindbergh Island makes an easily identifiable landmark for the location of Scottie Bay. A reef extends off Lindbergh Island, making the entrance appear quite narrow at low tide but the entrance is clear when a mid-channel course is followed. Many vessels can find quiet, all-weather anchorage throughout the bay in 3 – 4 fathoms, good holding mud. Access to a public road leading to the village is in the northern part of the bay; the other docks are private with clear signage to "Keep Off." In northwesterly winds protected anchorage can also be taken south of Lindbergh Island in 4 – 5 fathoms, gravel and mud.

About 2.5 miles to the south is another excellent anchorage southwest of Boho Island where **Boho Bay** is located. This is the most protected spot for anchorage in the area for exploring Jedediah Island just across Bull Passage.

Jedediah Island is a jewel in the B.C. Marine Park system and became a legacy for future generations when the long-time hobby farmer and his family sold the beautiful island. Anchorage with a stern tie to rings in the rocks can be taken in **Deep Bay**, behind Paul Island. A stern tie to shore is also needed when anchoring in the next bay to the south but in both spots if strong westerly winds develop you should move across to Boho Bay since the gusts tend to curl around the entrances creating dangerous lee shores. A clearly marked easy trail from Deep Bay leads to scenic Home Bay on the other side of the island. The remains of various farm buildings, a horse and some sheep can still be seen on the island. The Marine Park sign and an empty house is in Long Bay but this cove is too shallow for overnight anchorage.

Anchorage during settled weather in 4 – 5 fathoms, mud and some gravel patches can also be taken along Jedediah's southwest shore before the channel opens up separating it from Bull Island. A mid-channel course in this remarkable passage passes between towering rocky ne cliffs on the island side and picturesque stone islets.

Mitlenatch Island Nature Park is home to a vast number seabirds as well as various pinnipeds. Tours by a resident naturalist and hikes along the trails make this an interesting stop-over. North of the island is a shoal spit to avoid. Temporary anchorage in calm conditions may be taken in about 2 fathoms, mud and sand but overnight moorage is not recommended.

LASQUETI, JEDEDIAH and MITLENATCH ISLANDS

Chart 3312, 3516

TEXADA IS.

Sabine Channel

LINDBERGH IS.
Scottie Bay

49° 30' N   49° 30' N

False Bay

LASQUETI IS.

JEDEDIAH IS.

124° 20' W   JENKINS IS.

124°10'W

SANGSTER IS.

Squitty Bay

0   1

Approx. Scale - n.m.

N

Not to be used for navigation

Anchorage Details

JERVIS IS.

PAUL IS.   Deep Bay

BOHO IS.

JEDEDIAH IS.

Home Bay

Long Bay
Park Sign

Boho Bay

LASQUETI IS.

BULL IS.

Bull Passage

Not to be used for navigation

Detail: False Bay

124°22' W

LASQUETI ISLAND

3f   5f

5f

HIGGINS IS.

Fuel 8f

Public Wharf

15f

False Bay

Lasqueti

10f Jeffrey
5f Rock

49°29' N

Stephens Passage

5f

0   ½   1m

Approx. Scale n.m.

Mitlenatch Island Nature Park

Chart 3538

3.5f

30f

20f

2f

15f

MITLENATCH ISLAND

49°57' N

25f

80f

0   ¼   ½ n.m.

Approx. Scale n.m.

PENDER HARBOUR

This popular harbor has a narrow entrance opening into an extensive basin with many fingers and small bays. It has been developed into a busy sports fishing center with several marinas and communities scattered along its shores.

The entrance to the harbor looks complicated because of the many islands, but it is not difficult if a mid-channel course is taken between them. The light at the north end of Williams Island marks the south side of the entrance, which is about 120m (400ft.) wide. A speed limit of 5 knots is enforced in the harbor (past the entrance) because of the numerous docks and floats.

There are several marinas offering moorage, fuel, water, showers and laundry services. The first one seen on entry is **Irvines Landing Marina** (604-883-1145) in Joe Bay. After passing four small coves the sizable bight of Hospital Bay is seen where a Government Wharf is found near its eastern end. Other Government Wharves, located in Garden Bay and Welbourne Cove, can also be identified by their distinctive red railings. Off the western tip of Garden Peninsula is **Fisherman's Resort and Marina** (604-883-2336) where transient moorage is available and facilities include showers and laundry. Next door to the east is **John Henry's Marina** (604-883-2253) where fuel groceries, liquor, propane and post office facilities are located.

East of Garden Peninsula is Garden Bay where a small area on the waterfront has been reserved as the **Garden Bay Marine Park**. When anchoring in Garden Bay be sure to set your anchor well, for gusty winds sometimes sweep the bay, creating havoc when anchors drag or insufficient space has been left between anchored vessels. At the western end of the bay is the Royal Vancouver Yacht Club outstation consisting of docks and a club house. Next door are the floats of the Garden Bay Hotel and Marina where a pub is located. To the east is a Seattle Yacht Club outstation.

Gerrans Bay is a large bight in the southern part of the harbour where good, all-weather protected anchorage can be taken in the southwestern part of the bay in 2 – 3 fathoms, mud. When entering the bay favor the Mary Islet side of the entrance to avoid Griffin Ledge with 2.2m (7 ft.) of water. Markers indicate rocks to avoid in the bay.

Madeira Marina (604-883-2266) in Welbourne Cove has haul-out facilities which can accommodate vessels up to 50 ft. Engine servicing and fiberglass repairs can be done at this facility. Their marine supply store has a fairly good inventory, mainly for power boats.

From Pender Harbor a side trip via 8-mile long Agamemnon Channel leads to Jervis Inlet. This 44-mile fiord with high mountains on each side leads to beautiful Princess Louisa Inlet (6 miles from its head). For details see the following page.

APPROACHING PENDER HARBOR FROM ENE, i.e. coming down Malaspina Str.

APPROACHING PENDER HARBOR FROM W, distant about 2 miles.

Hodson Is.
Carney Pt.
Agamemnon Channel.
Hodgson's Is.
Irving's Landing
Entr. to Pender Harbor
Pearson Is.
Martin Is.

E. Side, Str. of Georgia

PENDER HARBOUR

Not to be used for navigation

0   ½   1   2 n.m.

Approx. Scale n.m.

NELSON ISLAND

Quarry Bay

Fearny Pt.

AGAMEMNON CHANNEL
To Jervis Inlet & Princess
Louisa Inlet.

Nelson Rk.

Daniel Pt.

Pender Hill

Hospital Bay

Mt. Daniel

Hodgsons Its.

3f

Irvings Landing
Duncan Cove

Fishermans
Garden

Marina

Henry Pt.

Fuel

Farrington Cove

Fuel

Bay

Martin Pt.

Jacob Rk.

Nares Rk
Bn

Bn

Pwr line
3f   4f

Pearson Is.

Williams Is.

8f

Skardom Is.

8f

John Henry's Mn.
6f

3f

Temple Rk.

Griffin Ledge
1f

Public
D

Shoal   Gunboat Bay

Martin Is.

124° 05' W

Charles Is.

Power line   3f 5f

Welbourne Cove
Madeira Park

49° 37' N

Gerrans
Bay

Cecil Hill

Beaver Is.

5f

Chart 3512, 3535

4f

3f

N

Bargain Bay

Francis Pt.

Whitestone Is.

APPROACHING PENDER HARBOR FROM S, distant about 3 miles.

Hodgson's Rocks   Agamemnon Channel   Pender Harbor   Francis Point

PRINCESS LOUISA INLET and ANCHORAGES ENROUTE

One of the most photographed sights in British Columbia is Chatterbox Falls at the head of Princess Louisa Inlet. To arrive at this site you must travel for 44 miles up deep and winding Jervis Inlet which penetrates the Coastal Range. A number of beautiful anchorages are available soon after leaving Malaspina Strait which shouldn't be missed even though your destination is Princess Louisa Inlet. During unsettled weather the winds in Jervis Inlet can be quite gusty and during rainy weather the cloud level can be so low as to obliterate the opposite shore.

On the south side of the entrance to Jervis Inlet is Hardy Island and Fox Island is south of it. Between these two islands is **Musket Island Marine Park.** This secure anchorage can accommodate many vessels (with stern ties ashore) in the double-lobed basin. There is easy access to the shore where large rocks make safe scrambling for all ages. In addition to picnic spots, from here you can view sea conditions in Malaspina Strait.

Just around the corner to the south, on the north side of Nelson Island is a magical little cove where several vessels can anchor in **Ballet Bay.** Though the approach channel south of Nocturne and Clio Islands ends with a reef on the starboard side that seems to extend much further than the chart indicates, and signs ashore announcing private property prohibit shore trips, this is a lovely spot. A host of rocky islets outside the bay can provide hours of delightful exploration by dinghy.

When leaving the bay some excitement can be added by entering Jervis Inlet via narrow **Telescope Passage** which separates Hardy Island from the NW corner of Nelson Island. Avoid the rock in the narrowest part of the passage by favoring the Nelson Island side of the passage.

The next available anchorage is at **Harmony Islands Marine Park** on the east side of 7-mile long Hotham Sound, south of Syren Point. Avoid the rock (covered 1 m/3 ft.) at the entrance to the basin. The water here is surprisingly warm, and snorkeling and diving can be enjoyed.

Jervis Inlet can also be reached via Agamemnon Channel and near its northern end is the village of **Earl's Cove.** Regular ferry service to Saltery Bay on the north shore of Jervis Inlet carries road traffic from Powell River and Lund southward to the Sechelt Peninsula and beyond to Gibsons. A public dock is located here as well as a cafe and small grocery store. To the southeast is Skookumchuck Narrows at the north end of Sechelt Inlet. It is worth stopping over to take a hike to view Sechelt Rapids at the peak of the tidal flow. The turbulent waters can be seen from ledges along the shore and the dramatic display makes one a believer in the use of tide tables!

When proceeding up Jervis Inlet, take advantage of a rising tide and plan your arrival at **Malibu Rapids** near slack water for currents in the restricted entrance can reach 9 knots at springs and the turbulence even at half tide is impressive. Slack water occurs about 24 minutes after high water at Point Atkinson and 36 minutes after low water. The actual time is seen by the cessation of white overfalls in the channel. Malibu Lodge, overlooking the rapids, is a Young Life Summer Camp site where several groups of teen-agers from US and Canada congregate for a week or so.

Precipitous mountains reaching 2,450 m (8,000 ft.) streaked with lacy waterfalls (especially after a rain) line the shores of **Princess Louisa Inlet,** (a designated Marine Park). Chatterbox Falls are at the head of the 4-mile inlet where a 120 m (400 ft.) float is located. Because of its popularity, space at the dock is at a premium especially during the summer months, and rafting is normal. When walking ashore care must be taken to stay on the trails and watch your step for the footing is extremely slippery.

PRINCESS LOUISA INLET and Approach

Chart 3512, 3514

Approx. Scale n.m.

Not to be used for navigation

0   5   10

**Top map (rotated):**

Chatterbox Falls
Princess
Louisa
Inlet

Malibu

Queens Reach

JERVIS INLET

Princess Royal Reach

Prince of Wales Reach

Harmony Is.

Skookumchuck Narrows
Egmont Pub. Wharf
Sechelt Rapids

SECHELT INLET

JERVIS INLET

Hotham Sound

Telescope Passage

Ballet Bay

Scotch Fir Pt.

Musket Is.

Sealters Bay

Cape Cockburn

MALASPINA STRAIT

CR.

Pender Harbour

Francis Point

TEXADA ISLAND

Left map (Malibu):

MALIBU

Malibu Is.

9 kts. at Springs

Approx. Scale feet

0   1000'

N

HARDY ISLAND

NELSON ISLAND

Telescope Pass.

Blind Bay

Musket Is.

Ballet Bay

Hidden Basin

JERVIS INLET

MALASPINA STRAIT

Scotch Fir Pt.

49°43.8'

124°10'

Approx. Scale n.m.

0   1

POWELL RIVER, WESTVIEW and LUND

The town of Powell River is next to the mill that is conspicuous because of the tall power plant stack constantly belching dark smoke. The basin near the mill, behind the breakwater and some half-sunken ships and barges, is a log booming ground.

The city harbor is at **Westview**, a suburb of Powell River, south of the mill site. A large rock breakwater extends on either side of the B.C. Ferry Dock. Tanks and long buildings on shore are visible as identifying features as you approach the harbor. The northern basin is a pleasure craft basin filled with local vessels. The southern basin is public, its wide floats shared by fishing vessels and transient yachts. Enter at the southern end where a fuel barge is moored in a tight little spot at the end of the harbor. When mooring in the basin it is required that you reverse into the appointed slip. The harbormaster's office and Harbor Marine (open Mon.- Sat.) are shown on the sketch.

Stores and restaurants are just up the hill and supermarkets and larger shops are a taxi ride away. Ferry service links Powell River to Little River (Comox) on Vancouver Island and Blubber Bay on Texada Island. Buses and airlines link Powell River (Westview) to Vancouver.

Grief Point is the low sandy point about two miles south of Powell River, backed by many residential houses. The point marks the turn from Malaspina Strait (which can be quite windy) into the more open water of the Strait of Georgia. On the south side of the point is **Beach Gardens Resort and Marina** behind a rock breakwater. Moorage and accommodation are available where one can find refuge if winds in Malaspina Strait become boisterous. Turning space at the marina entrance is quite limited, so enter slowly, bearing to starboard.

Lund is a small town at the end of the coastal road from Vancouver. Entrance is around either side of the breakwater, through narrow openings. A concrete breakwater protects a small niche in the rocky coast where moorage is available. Note the green buoy marking a rock between the dock and the north shore of the basin. A launch ramp allows small power boats towed from southern areas to cruise waters in the northern part of the Strait of Georgia, Desolation Sound and beyond. The harbor has a fuel dock and government wharf.

Lund Hotel has one long dock where moorage is available on a first-come, first-served basis. For information call (604) 414-0474. A grocery and liquor store, post office, laundromat, showers, bar, restaurant and craft store are in the large hotel building. Across the way, Nancy's Bakery is famous for its excellent baked goods and prepared foods. The small dock next to the bakery is used by water taxis to take people back and forth to Savary Island, known for its beautiful sandy beaches.

Detail – Lund

Not to be used for navigation

0   100'   200'   300'
Approx. Scale - feet

Chart 3513, 3538

Texada Is.

Airport

Powell River   Hulks for booming around.   Bkwtrs   Ferry Slip   Grief Pt.
WESTVIEW.

APPROACHING FROM W, distant about 2 miles.

POWELL RIVER - WESTVIEW

Not to be used for navigation

Chart 3513, 3536

0   1   2   3 n.m.
Approx. Scale n.m.

Powell Lake

To Lund

Dam & penstocks

Hospital

Mill with r&w banded stack

Powell River

Airport

124° 30′ W

Fl.G
No transient moorage

Fl.R
Hulks used as bkwtrs.

Town of Westview

WESTVIEW

49° 50′ N

See detail below

Pleasure craft marina (mainly local boats)

Grief Point

Resort with small marina & breakwater.

Mar. Supp.

Garbage

Waste Oil

Marine Inn

Harbormaster

Wharf

Ferry Slip

Public docks (Transient moorage)

Breakwater

Fl G

Fuel Barge

Row of fuel tanks

F   Piling

Fl R

Detail – Westview Harbour

Propane Plant

Powell River   Westview   Grief Point

APPROACHING FROM SE, i.e. up Malaspina Strait

COMOX

Comox makes an excellent stop-over for vessels following the Vancouver Island shore of Georgia Strait. A home base for fishing vessels and pleasure craft, Comox also can provide accommodation for many transient vessels. A scenic backdrop for the town is provided by the Beaufort Mountains and beautiful Comox Glacier. The area is a haven for recreation, with summertime water sports, hiking and camping followed by skiing and snow-boarding during the winter. Comox is a weather reporting station, the communication center for airborne search and rescue and the site of the Canadian Coast Guard radio station monitoring calls as far north as Bella Bella.

The harbor is located four miles southwest of Cape Lazo, a prominent landmark with a flat top and distinctive yellow clay bluffs. When approached from the south the cape resembles an island but seen from north of Hornby Island its connection to Vancouver Island becomes evident. When approaching from the north clear Cape Lazo by at least one mile to avoid the foul ground seaward of the Cape. When crossing Comox Bar use extreme caution and follow the route indicated by the buoys and range. The least depth of the passage is 2.4 m (8 ft.) and strong variable currents tend to push the vessel off the desired route. It is essential to use current nautical charts when traveling in this area.

Comox Harbour is entered between Gartley Point on the south (marked by buoy P47) and Goose Spit on the north (where the end of the spit is marked by a light). Two breakwaters protect the marine facilities, cluster of four marinas offering moorage and associated services to cruisers. Moorage, both transient and permanent, is available at all marinas except the Municipal Marina which has permanent moorage only. Facilities differ and the following summary can help you to choose the facility that best suits your needs. Daily moorage rates for transient vessels start at $.50 per foot.

1. **Black Fin Marina** has a fuel dock and convenience store where ice is available. Sail Pacific Yacht Charters operates from this location.

2. **Comox Bay Marina** has showers, laundromat and garbage collection facilities. Desolation Sound Yacht Charters operates from this location and can be reached at (250) 339-7222.

3. **Harbour Authority/Government Dock** provides garbage collection facilities and has water on the dock. Commercial vessels usually fill the space available.

4. **Municipal Marina** has washrooms, garbage collection and oil disposal facilities and a launch ramp. The maximum size of vessel that can be moored here is 8m (27 ft.). To arrange moorage call (250) 339-2202.

Well protected anchorage can be taken north of Goose spit. A block from the waterfront is a sizable shopping mall which includes a well stocked grocery store, a liquor store and several banks. Charts and marine supplies are available at The Crowsnest; fishing gear and local charts are also sold at Ted's Trolling.

COMOX

0　　　　1　　　　2　　　　3

Approx. Scale, n.m.

N

Microwave
Cape Lazo

Shoal
x

3f

Comox

49°40'　Dries　Comox Hbr. &　Shoal

Goose Spit

1.4f

18f　5f　.4f

Range　3f

49°38'　Shoal

42'

Dries

Hwy. 19

To
Nanaimo

Not to be used for navigation

124°56'　124°52'

Desolation
Sound
Charters　Condor　Parking　Pub

Launch Ramp

Pub

Oil　Garbage

Hydro
Hoist　Black
Fin
Marina　Washrooms

Comox Bay
Marina　Garbage

F
Fuel

Breakwater

Municipal
Marina　Shoal

Rock　Breakwater

Hbr.
office　Garbage

Harbour Authority　Pump-out

Detail -

Comox Harbour

Thulin Passage runs north of Lund and **Copeland Islands Marine Park** is located about half-way along on the west side of the channel. The entrance to the anchorage is marked by a Marine Park sign and once within the basin vessels may tie a stern line ashore or anchor in the middle in 5 – 7 fathoms, mud and rock.. Interesting dinghy trips can be taken following the shore through narrow passages to visit scenic rocky islets along the western side of Copeland Islands.

DESOLATION SOUND MARINE PARK – SOUTHERN SECTION

This pretty and deservedly popular area is worth a slight digression off the direct passage to the north. The most attractive areas are largely dedicated as B.C. Marine Parks, and there is often over-crowding during the summer months when Pacific Northwest yachtsmen congregate during the summer vacation. There is little tidal action in this area, so it is designated a no-discharge zone, and cruisers must use their holding tanks. Boaters should have an adequate supply of drinking water aboard and if any surface water is collected it must be boiled for at least five minutes before use.

With a spectacular back-drop of beautifully sculpted mountains, **Desolation Sound** opens to the northeast as one rounds Sarah Point at the northern tip of Maslaspina Peninsula. On a lovely summer's day it is difficult to reconcile the name that Captain Vancouver gave this unique area.

Separating Malaspina Peninsula from Gifford Peninsula is Malaspina Inlet. When approaching the entrance to the inlet take care to avoid Stacey Rock, a dangerous drying rock. Tidal streams at the entrance range from 2 to 4 knots and a few swirls in the channel are often evident. But once past the narrow section there is little tidal action. Fish farms are prominent along the shores outside of the Marine Park boundary.

Grace Harbor offers an excellent anchorage near the head of the inlet in about 3 fathoms, good holding mud. A pleasant trail leads to a small lake about a half-hour walk from the anchorage. As there is little tidal action within the bay its warm waters attract a crowd of summer cruisers.

Within Lancelot Inlet a popular anchorage is in **Isabel Bay**, west of Madge Island or in the southern part of the bay. Swinging room is limited making a stern line ashore advisable both here and at **Thors Cove**. Sometimes westerly winds in the cove are experienced even though there is a southeasterly wind in Okeover Inlet. Anchorage in the northernmost cove of **Wootton Bay** can be taken in about 6 fathoms, mud. Though exposed to southerly winds it is a calm anchorage in settled northwesterly conditions.

The entrance to Theodosia Inlet has a rock awash on the north side to avoid and a shallow spot of 2.4m (8 ft.). But once within a pleasant anchorage can be found west of **Susan Islets** in 4 fathoms, mud and shells.

A little less than a mile south of Coode Penininsula a public wharf with about 73m (240 ft.) of berthing space and a launch ramp is nearby. This is a popular spot for kayakers to use as their departure point for exploring the protected waters of Desolation Sound. A short road beyond the camp ground leads to Lund where provisions can be obtained and one can take the bus to Vancouver or by proceeding to Powell River, ferry service to Vancouver Island is available. Nearby is **Desolation Resort** with a hotel and restaurant. For reservations call (604) 483-3592.

After passing bold Zephine Head, **Galley Bay** opens up to starboard. Give safe clearance to the drying reefs in the center of the bay and rock covered with 1.3m (4 ft.) in the entrance to the bay in the eastern part. Though the bay is exposed to the north good anchorage can be taken in calm weather conditions. The best spots are in the southwest cove in about 4 fathoms, mud or tucked below the islets in the eastern part of the bay.

DESOLATION SOUND MARINE PARK
(SOUTHERN SECTION)

0 1 2 3

Approx. Scale - n.m.

Charts 3312, 3538, 3559

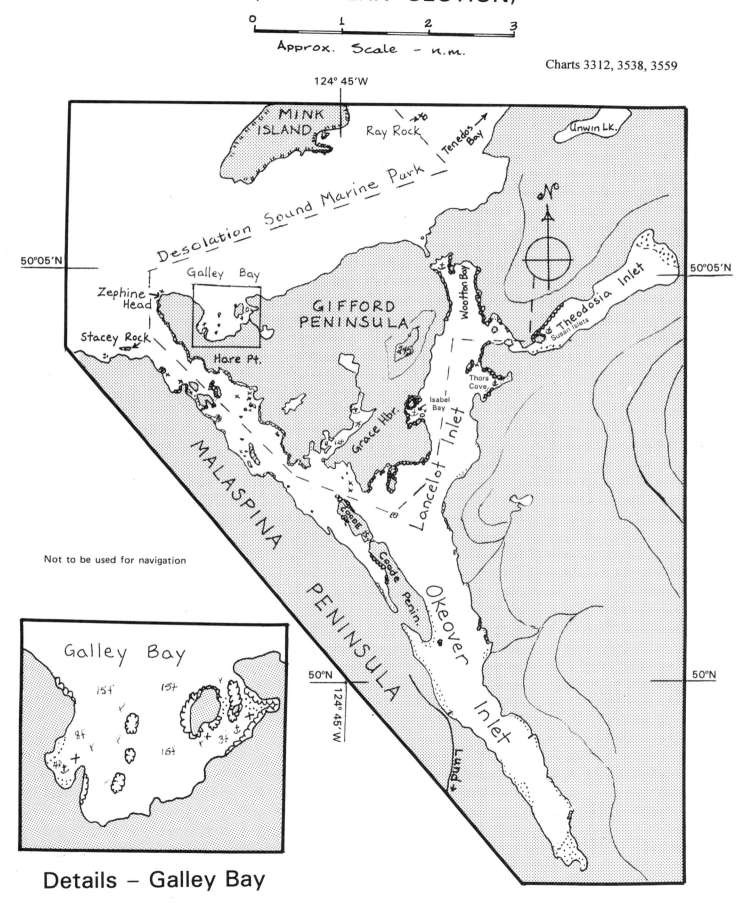

MINK ISLAND

Ray Rock

Tenedos Bay

Unwin Lk.

Desolation Sound Marine Park

50°05'N

Galley Bay

Zephine Head

Stacey Rock

Hare Pt.

GIFFORD PENINSULA

Woottön Bay

N

Theodosia Inlet

Susan Islets

Thors Cove

Isabel Bay

Grace Hbr.

Lancelot Inlet

Not to be used for navigation

MALASPINA

Cobbe Islands

Coode Penin.

Okeover Inlet

PENINSULA

50°N

124° 45' W

124° 45'W

50°05'N

50°N

Galley Bay

15f   15f

8f

15f

3f

Details – Galley Bay

DESOLATION SOUND MARINE PARK – NORTHERN SECTION

When following the coast northeast of Galley Bay the broad opening of **Tenedos Bay** lies ahead. Give Bold Head a wide berth as a dangerous rock lies close to it while Ray Rock and its reef lie offshore. Once into the cliff-edged, deep bay there are three choices for anchorage. On the eastern side is a cove with a beach and a stream descending from Unwin Lake; avoid the rock in the middle of the cove. Other anchorages are on the shelves on either side of the island in the northwest head of the bay. The island is connected to the shore by a drying ledge and anchorages are in the narrow coves on each side. The holding is moderate (rock and mud), stern lines ashore are helpful.

There are some dangerous rocks to avoid when proceeding toward Homfray Channel from the southwest. Several unique anchorages further along Homfray Channel are around the bulk of land forming Bold Head.

Otter Island Anchorage lies between the island and the mainland. It is a narrow, but navigable space allows room for one or two boats. Avoid Sky Pilot Rock (dries) which lies about .25 mile north off the entrance into the channel.

Eveleigh Anchorage is the southwestern cove between Eveleigh Island and the mainland. A drying reef connects the island to the mainland and separates this anchorage from Prideaux Haven on the southwest side.

Prideaux Haven and **Melanie Cove** are entered through the narrow channel between Lucy Point (the east end of Eveleigh Island) and Oriel Rock (part of the William Islands group). The passage is clear in mid-channel. A drying rock is close to Lucy Point and a shelf extends a short distance south of the point. You can spend several hours exploring the rocky coast and interesting passages that lace the area.

Prideaux Haven anchorage lies to the west where it is fairly open and deep. Beyond Melanie Point to the east, **Melanie Cove** is a long, narrow inlet with clear, green water and a stream emptying into the head of the bay. A large area at the head of the cove is shoal and you must avoid large rocky shelves on the southeastern shore. The shores of the cove are deeded to the University of British Columbia and fires are prohibited ashore. Almost hidden in the overhanging trees on the southern shore is a small sign "Tenedos Bay." This is the beginning of a well-marked trail that connects Melanie Cove to Tenedos Bay. Plan on at least a two-hour hike through the woods and up and down the hills separating the coves.

Melanie Cove has become a rendezvous point for groups of power boats that congregate in rafts of 10 or more vessels along the north shore of the bay. Nevertheless there is still plenty of space remaining for sailing vessels and other power boats to find anchorage in the bay.

Laura Cove is entered between Copplestone Point and a rock off the east end of Copplestone Island. Passage should not be taken between the rock and the island. This beautiful anchorage has a rather narrow but easy entrance.

Roffey Island anchorage is entered from the north, off Homfray Channel and is a very snug anchorage for a maximum of two boats. Drying ridges on the sides reduce the available space.

Chart 3538, 3555

Unwin Range Peaks

Copplestone Is William Is Melanie Pt.

Eveleigh Is.

Scobell Is.

APPROACHING THE ENTRANCE TO
PRIDEAUX HAVEN

HOMFRAY CHANNEL

Price Pt.

Roffey Is.

3f

Copplestone Is.

Scobell Is.

Copplestone Pt.

Grass Is.

Mary Is.

William Is.

Laura Cove

Melanie Pt. UBc deeded land.

Melville Is.

3f

3f

Eveleigh Is.

4f ⚓ 3f ⚓

7f ⚓ 6f

Melanie Cove

UNWIN RANGE

Pringle Rk.

Prideaux Haven

Morgan Is.

3f

Eveleigh Anch.

A B.C. Marine Park.

Deep

50°08'N

124°42'

△ 700'

N°

ky Pilot Rk.
(DANGEROUS)

Trail to Unwin Lake

⚓

3f

Not to be used for navigation

Sh. 3f

Otter Is. ⚓

△ 800

Sh.

⚓

Deep

3f

0   ½   1 n.m.

600'   1800'

Approx. Scale n.m.

Tenedos Bay

△ 600

SOLATION
SOUND

Deep

Ray Rk.

Bold Head.
(Do not cut close)

3f

3f

**DESOLATION SOUND
MARINE PARK**

(NORTHERN SECTION)

Tenedos Bay and
Prideaux Haven

CORTES ISLAND ANCHORAGES

This island has a wealth of good harbors that are well worth exploring. The anchorages will be described in a clockwise sequence, beginning from Mary Point on the southeast corner of the island. Mary Point is rocky, with a few stunted trees. To the north are two islands close to shore connected by drying ledges to Cortes Island. About 1 mile east of Mary Point is the first harbor.

Cortes Bay must be approached by steering well clear of the three small, white, rocky islets and the drying rocky ledge near them. At the entrance to the harbor is a rock with a lighted beacon, which should be kept to starboard on entering. A public wharf and float is on the west side of the bay. Anchorage can be taken almost anywhere in about 4 or 5 fathoms, soft mud bottom. Allow plenty of scope for holding is moderate and sometimes winds funnel into the bay. In the southwestern part of the bay is an outstation of the Seattle Yacht Club while on the northwestern shore the Royal Vancouver Yacht Club has their long dock and outstation.

Sutil Point is the southern end of Cortes Island. Using Baker Passage pass outside the lighted red buoy to clear the shoals extending south from Sutil Point. The route turns northward towards other Cortes Island anchorages.

Manson's Landing lies behind some small islands on the shore of Manson's Bay, beyond which lies a drying lagoon. Near the 90m (300 ft.)public wharf is a general store and telephone booth. The floats on the north side of the wharf are occupied by local vessels. Temporary anchorage can be taken in the bay which is exposed to southerly winds..

Gorge Harbour though not a true gorge, has a unique entrance with a spectacular high, rocky buttress guarding its western shore where pictographs can be seen on some flat rocks. The eastern side is much lower with boulders once used as burial caverns. On an approach from the south the two small Guide Islets indicate the entrance. Pass on either side of these islets (not between) then passage through the gorge is taken. The entrance is about .5 mile long, the narrowest part (60 m /200 feet wide) being very short. While currents can be felt which sometimes reach 4 knots, passage is always possible. At the inner end pass between small, bare, rocky Tide Islet and the steep western shore. The government wharf to the south was condemned in 1995 and should not be used until repairs have been completed. Moorage, fuel, a well stocked grocery store, laundry and shower facilities and a good restaurant are available at **Gorge Harbour Marina** which monitors VHF Ch. 73. For reservations call (250) 935-6433. Garbage receptacles require sorting into glass, tins and miscellaneous. Two large anchorage areas with good holding in 5 - 10 fathoms, mud may be taken west or east of the marina.

Uganda Passage is a little pass between Shark Spit on Marina Island and Cortes Island. Although it appears tricky it is quite easy as it is well marked with buoys. Stay within the buoyed channel, keeping the green buoys to port and red buoys to starboard when northbound. Influenced by northern tides, the current floods east and ebbs to the west, with 3-knot currents at springs. Anchorage can be taken behind Shark Spit. Caution: The shallow shelf that runs around Marina Island drops off sharply into deep water.

Marina Is.   Guide Islet   Manson's Ldg   S. end of Cortez Is /
                  Gorge Hbr Entr.   Buoy

CORTES IS. FROM SE, distant about 6 miles, WITH BACKGROUND PEAKS

CORTES ISLAND
ANCHORAGES
Chart 3538

0   1   2   3 n.m.

Approx. Scale n.m.

N°

READ ISLAND

Frederick Pt.

PENN Is.

Evans Bay

HILL Is.

Bullock Bluff

To Yuculta Rapids

LEWIS CHANNEL

SUTIL CHANNEL

Booming Ground

Logging Booms   Waterfall

TEAKERNE ARM

Joyce Pt.   WEST   50°10'N

REDONDA ISLAND

Quartz Bay

Jane It.

Carrington Bay

Dries

Dinghy ent. only

Von Donop Inlet

↕ 4f

Trail

Junction Pt.

Refuge Cove (See detail next page)

Coulter Is.

Coulter Bay

Subtle Its

Plunger Pass

Whaletown

Bns

Trail Using Various Logging Roads

Squirrel Cove

C O R T E S   I S L A N D

Martin Is.

DESOLATION SOUND

Station Is.

Kinghorn Is.

Gorge Harbour

⌂ F 10f   10f

Uganda Pass

Shark Spit

Bns

Guide Its

Tan Is.

Tide Is.

ENTRANCE TO GORGE HBR.

Manson's Landing

To Prideaux Haven Anchorages

MARINA ISLAND

Marina Reef

Buoy △

125°00'W

Smelt Bay

Sutil Pt.

Cortez Bay

Mary Pt.

Three Islets

Central Rk. (Dries)

Little Rk.

TWIN Is.

Echo Bay

Powell Its

Sarah Pt.

MALASPINA PENIN.

Bliss Ldg

Light Buoy

BAKER PASSAGE

Spilsbury Pt.

Not to be used for navigation

COPELAND Is.

50°00'N

Whaletown is in the small indentation of Whaletown Bay. Enter from the south, allowing for shoals and rocks which are marked by beacons. Moorage at the public wharf is often crowded during the summer and the seaplane area must be kept clear. A small grocery store with large ice cream cones makes a visit worthwhile. The tiny church in the village often merits a photograph.

Coulter Bay is the next stop, where good anchorage can be taken in the lee of Coulter Island. Enter as shown on the sketch.

Carrington Bay is a large bay with a drying lagoon. Though anchorage can be tried the rocky bottom has poor holding.

Quartz Bay is smaller than the previous bay but is more acceptable. Enter via the northeastern channel. Good anchorage can be taken in the inner southwestern part of the bay behind the islets, in about 6 fathoms.

Von Donop Inlet is the boater's entrance to **(Ha'Thayim Marine Park)** This 3-mile long narrow entrance inlet provides excellent anchorage with complete protection. The entrance has a rock (covered 1.5m/5'), about mid-channel in the passage at the narrowest part, about .75 mile from the entrance. Enter slowly and favor the south side where overhanging trees mark the rock. Anchorage can be taken almost anywhere either in the widening near the lagoon, where there is little evidence of the out-going current, or further in near the head in 4 fathoms, good holding mud. At the southeast corner of the bay is a short trail leading to the northwestern shore of Squirrel Cove; another trail beyond the islet follows a mixture of tracks and logging roads before joining the paved road linking the village of Squirrel Cove to Manson's Landing.

Squirrel Cove is a popular, pretty and well protected anchorage. Enter the cove through the opening south of Protection Island. The west and northwest arms of the bay are shoal, but anchoring can be done anywhere in the bay and when stern lines are tied ashore over 100 vessels can be accommodated. Fresh baking can be ordered for the following day from **Sandra's Floating Bakery** by calling (250) 935-6497. Off the settlement of Squirrel Cove is a very small government wharf with shoal water close by. A telephone is at the head of the dock.. **Squirrel Cove General Store** has a good variety of groceries, fresh produce, charts, marine supplies and a hardware downstairs.

REFUGE COVE, WEST REDONDA ISLAND

Across Lewis Channel from Squirrel Cove is the busy fueling and provisioning depot of **Refuge Cove**. The cove can be entered on either side of the unnamed island at the entrance, though the south side is usually preferred. Facilities include floats, water, fuel, showers, laundry, ice, and a fast food stand. The store is stocked with groceries, fresh produce and liquor and sundry items. It is open June 1 to September 1. Prior to June 1 the store is open Mon., Wed. and Fri., 1 p.m. to 3 p.m. Showers and laundry facilities are not available before June 1.

ROSCOE BAY MARINE PARK, WEST REDONDA ISLAND

Roscoe Bay is north of Marylebone Point on the east side of the island. Unfortunately, this is such a popular spot from June to September that vessels lining the shore resemble a supermarket parking lot. Enter from Waddington Channel at or just before high water. A drying shoal lies within the entrance channel and care must be taken to avoid rocky outcrops on 5the north side of the narrow passage. A short trail through the forest leads to Black Lake, where large, smooth rocks give easy access to a popular swimming hole.

Detail –

Squirrel Cove

Chart 3538, 3555

Desolation Sound Anch's.

REFUGE COVE

SQUIRREL COVE

0   ½   1 n.m.

Approx. Scale n.m.

Not to be used for navigation

Squirrel Cove detail (top left):

Lagoon

Junction Pt

5f

6f

5f 3f

6f 7f 6f

3f 5f

3f Protection Is.

3f

CORTES Is.

Indian Reserve

3f Boulder Pt.

3f Daymark

3f

Govt. Wharf

Store □

51°07'N   Squirrel Cove Village

124°55'W

Location Plan (bottom left):

To YUCULTA RAPIDS

Redonda Bay Poor anch.

Walsh Cove Prov. Mar. Pk. &

EAST REDONDA Is.

Doctor Bay

WEST REDONDA Is.

LEWIS CHANNEL

WADDINGTON CHAN.

Waterfall

See detail above

Teakerne Arm

Talbot Cove possible ⚓

Squirrel Cove

Refuge Cove

See detail

Gorge Hbr   CORTES Is.

Marina Is.

Reef

DESOLATION SOUND

Sarah Pt

Galley Bay

MALASPINA PENIN.

BAKER PASS.

Hernando Is.

LOCATION PLAN

Refuge Cove detail (bottom right):

Lagoon

WEST REDONDA Is.

Public Mooring

3f

3f

Refuge Cove Village

6f

50°07'N

124°51'W

3f

Detail – Refuge Cove

SECTION 2 - Campbell River to Port Hardy

Cruisers traveling north of Campbell River or Big Bay see a marked decrease in the number of boaters who have the time and inclination to proceed through the various passes in order to visit less populated parts of the coast. After passing this threshold you have the advantage of being in less crowded anchorages and better still, often having the luxury of a spacious and beautiful anchorage to yourself. The numerous inlets reaching into the snow-capped coastal range and countless islands provide a concentrated wealth of spectacular scenery and protected anchorages that is found nowhere else in the world. Cruisers find they can come back for many years in succession and continue to discover new anchorages, trails to ancient trees and even undiscovered pictographs and petroglyphs. There is no need to travel thousands of miles to find great cruising—it's right on our doorstep.

Though the proliferation of Marine Parks is not as concentrated as it is in the southern part of the province there are still a number of spots that have been reserved for present-day and future cruisers. Those that are near the usual route taken by coastal cruisers heading to Alaska are described in the pages that follow but the following are off the beaten path and do warrant mention.

Rebecca Spit is tree-crowned sandy peninsula the east side of Quadra Island off Drew Harbour. Anchorage may be taken off the northwestern end of the spit on hard sand bottom. The anchor must be well set to avoid dragging when northwesterly breezes often pick up in the afternoon.

Walsh Cove on the east side of West Redonda Island is entered from the south via Waddington Channel. Vessels departing Toba Inlet often use this as a well protected stop-over before proceeding to Desolation Sound. Limited anchorage is available in the middle of the cove and most vessels anchor with a stern line ashore.

Broughton Archipelago, at the southern end of Queen Charlotte Strait off the west coast of Gilford Island, includes a number of small islands that are a part of B.C. Marine Parks. This maze of islets is a haven for kayakers and canoeists who pull ashore in countless sandy coves.

* * * * * *

Note: Queen Charlotte Strait may be reached by proceeding west through Johnstone Strait, by following a protected course from Port Harvey to Minstrel Island and west in Knight Inlet, or taking a longer route from Minstrel Island to follow Tribune and Sutlej Channels until exiting Wells Passage to enter the Strait. If prolonged exploration of this area is planned you should have a copy of John Chappell's excellent guide, *Cruising Beyond Desolation Sound.* If your destination is Alaska, a visit to this delightful area might be best postponed until the return trip.

Two spots in Johnstone Strait are worthy of description. **Beaver Cove,** a sizable bight on Vancouver Island is entered between Ellis and Lewis Points. Much of the bay is utilized by logging operations and it is of interest to cruisers only in an emergency. On its east side is **Telegraph Cove** where a **Telegraph Cove Marina** may have space for transient vessels up to 18m (30 ft.). Call (250) 928-3163 for information. Next door, **Telegraph Cove Resort** sells gasoline and can handle boats up the 17m (27 ft.). Call (250) 928-3131 for information. The significance of this area is its fame as a site where orca can often be sighted because they frequent these waters to enjoy conveniently located and comfortably shaped rubbing stones. Campsites dot the overlooking cliffs on the east side of the Strait and whale-watchers in kayaks and tour boats from Port McNeill are a common sight

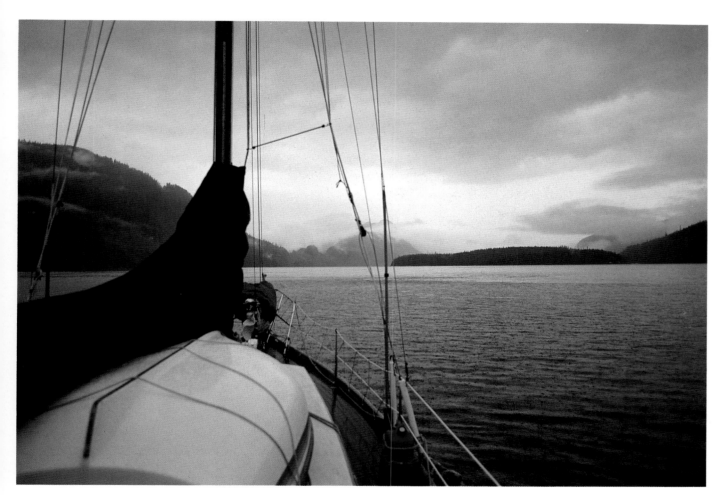

Approaching Dent Rapids from Gillard Passage

Tidal overfalls at Sechelt Rapids, Skookumchuk Narrows

Not to be used for navigation

Rivers Inlet

Knight Inlet

Grappler Sound

Kingcome Inlet

Sullivan Bay

Echo Bay

92 92 92

QUEEN CHARLOTTE STR.

Loughborough Inlet

Gilford Is.

Bute Inlet

Phillip Arm

Minstrel Is

Malcolm Is.

Port Hardy

100 96

Sointula

Port McNeil 98

Alert Bay

94 Beaver Cove

90 90

Port Neville

Forward Hbr.

Greene Pt Rpds

Dent Rpds 82

Yuculta Rpds

88

86 84

Hardwicke Is.

Thurlow Is.

Sonora Is.

78 Kelsey Bay

Helmcken Is.

78

Otter Cove 76

Discovery Passage

80

Quadra Is.

Cortes Is.

VANCOUVER

74

Seymour Narrows

AR1996

Campbell River

72

C. Mudge

Kyuquot Sound

Esperanza Inlet

ISLAND

Nootka Is.

Gold River

Muchalat Inlet

Nootka Sound

JOHNSTONE STRAIT

CAMPBELL RIVER

Campbell River is situated at the south end of Discovery Passage, and lies almost exactly midway along Vancouver Island. This is the center of activity at the north end of Georgia Strait and the largest town in this area. As the importance of marine-related tourism has grown, facilities for cruising vessels of all sizes have been developed. A range of facilities are available, from the basic public wharf to all-service marinas.

Because of the proximity of Discovery Passage to Seymour Narrows the tidal currents are quite noticeable here. They do not pose a particular problem, but one should be aware of the state of the tide when approaching Campbell River and when maneuvering in the area.

Two rock breakwaters angle out from the shore to protect the floats for moorage. The southern basin is the larger one and has **public floats** for both pleasure craft and fishing vessels. The harbormaster's office is in a small building on shore near the walkway leading from the wharves. The docks are often crowded during the summer and rafting may be necessary.

The next basin to the north, adjacent to the Quadra Island Ferry Terminal, is privately owned. A short distance beyond is **Discovery Harbour Marina** where moorage for over 300 vessels is protected by a large breakwater. They monitor VHF Ch 73 and can be reached at (250) 287-4911. This full-service modern marina offers transient moorage and an easily accessible fuel dock. The harbor office is on the second floor of a clearly marked building. Showers and restrooms are in a building to the south. Adjacent to the parking area is a huge shopping mall. In addition, the Harbour Grill restaurant overlooks the waterfront and serves good meals, and several other cafes and pubs are nearby. Three magnificent totem poles carved by Bill Henderson stand before an excellent Native craft shop attached to a theater featuring live performances by Native dancers.

Quathiaski Cove can be entered on either side of Grouse Island. The current stream that sweeps past the entrance and creates tidal rips does not affect the cove. At the south end of the Cove, beside the ferry dock, is a government dock with floats, where rafting is almost always necessary. The ferry can be used for getting to and from Campbell River. A fuel dock and a repair yard are in the harbor.

April Point is the site of a luxurious fishing resort about 1 mile north of Quathiaski Cove. The flagpoles of the lodge are prominent at the point. The landing dock at the lodge is meant for lodge skiffs. The small marina connected with the lodge is about .5 mile southeast along the inner shore of the point. Rates at the marina are high during summer, though you do have access to the lodge and its facilities. Anchorage is good beyond the marina, but the head of the cove is shoal.

Gowlland Harbor can be entered north of Steep Island and Gowlland Island, taking care to avoid Entrance Rock. Anchorage can be found behind Crow and Doe Islands. In the northern end of the harbor good anchorage is possible only on weekends when logging operations are closed. Logs in the booming area make a convenient spot for many seals and sea lions to haul out. Private docks line much of the harbor. Do not attempt the pass south of Gowlland Island leading to the cove at April Point as it is foul.

Rebecca Spit is on the east side of Quadra Island off Drew Harbour. Anchorage may be taken off the northwestern end of the spit on hard sand bottom. Set the anchor securely, for brisk winds can test how well you have set your gear.

Discovery Passage Anch's

-CAMPBELL RIVER
-QUATHIASKI COVE
-GOWLLAND HARBOUR

Not to be used for navigation

Chart 3513, 3539, 3540

Approx. Scale of Detail of Quadra Is. Anchs. below

0   ½   1   2 n.m.

Hyacinthe Bay

QUADRA

Heriot Bay

Store Wharf

Rebecca Spit (Mar. Park)

Drew Harbour

See detail

Gowlland Harbour

ISLAND

DISCOVERY   PASSAGE

Tyee Spit

Quathiaski Cove

50°02'N

Campbell River

LOCATION MAP

0   1   2 n.m.

Yaculta

Francisco Pt.

Fl. 15s 58' 13m

C. Mudge

Wilby Shoal

Sods + Booms

May Is.

Entrance Bank

Entrance Rk.

QUADRA   ISLAND

N

Wren. I.

Crow. I.

Fawn I.

Mouse Is.

Stag Is.

Doe Is.

GOWLLAND HARBOUR

Steep Is. (U) Fl. 12s.

GOWLLAND Is.

Rips at Flood

DISCOVERY   PASSAGE

April Pt.

Lodge

Marina

Rips at Flood

No thru passage

Shopping Mall

Fuel

Discovery Harbour Marina

Harbour Office

Showers + Laundromat

Charter Boat Office

DISCOVERY   PASSAGE

Ferry Dock

Supermarket

Tyee Plaza

Museum

Fuel F

Shallow

Sportfish Centre (Private Marina)

CAMPBELL RIVER

Fuel

Breakwater

Harbormaster

Showers/Restrms

Public Floats

Discovery Pier

Concession (Fishing Lic.)

Grouse Is.

QUATHIASKI COVE

Boat Yard

Gulf Stn. Wharf

Public Floats

Ferry

Rips at Flood

SEYMOUR NARROWS AND DISCOVERY PASSAGE

This famous passage, with its high-velocity tidal currents, appears to be a big obstacle when approached for the first time. However, as the B.C. Coast Pilot points out, navigation through the passage is simple if done at or near slack water. For most of the passage a mid-channel course is all that is needed.

When going north leave Campbell River against the last of the flood, which sets south, planning to reach Seymour Narrows about 8 miles from Campbell River at slack water. At Race Point, on the flood, there are rips and swirls that occur well to the east of it, so give it a wide berth on passing—it is less disturbed on the ebb. If Seymour Narrows is taken at the slack there is little problem in passing through and a favorable stream can be carried all the way through Johnstone Strait. However, if anchorages are needed, several are available.

A similar pattern should be followed when going south, i.e. taking the northern part of Discovery Passage against the last of the ebb to reach Seymour Narrows at Separation Head about slack water. Again, the passage should be simple and the favoring stream will carry one to Campbell River or out past Cape Mudge.

Anchorages are available on either side of Seymour Narrows to allow passage through at slack even if the turn is to an unfavorable direction. Since the velocity of the stream can increase quite rapidly an hour or so past the change, it behooves a slow vessel to reach its anchorage before the current becomes too strong.

The hazards caused by Ripple Rock were eliminated in 1958 when it was destroyed by the largest non-nuclear explosive charge of its time. The rips, whirlpools and swirls associated with the current at full strength are still awe-inspiring. Only large vessels with speeds in excess of 17 knots can attempt the channel at times other than near slack water. Even for them this can be dangerous, and quite large vessels have been swamped when caught in the violent rips and whirlpools. If you are in the passage at other than slack water remember that a vessel going with the current has less control than one going against it. It is strongly recommended that travel through Seymour Narrows be done only at, or near, slack water.

Anchorages on the south side of Seymour Narrows are:

- **Campbell River, Quathiaski Cove**, and **Gowlland Harbour** as described

- **Menzies Bay**, behind Defender Shoal (if anchorage close to the Narrows is needed)

Anchorages on the north side of Seymour Narrows are:

- **Otter Cove** at the end of Discovery Passage, 2.5 miles north of Elk Bay

- **Kanish Bay** and **Small Inlet** on Quadra Island - use Chart 3539

- **Plumper Bay** towards its southeast corner, keeping clear of the shoal area

- **Brown Bay** on the west shore, opposite Plumper Bay, where there is a resort with mooring slips behind a floating tank-car breakwater. Fuel, water and other supplies are available.

Chart 3539

Deepwater Bay

Anch's. on N. side:
- Brown Bay (marina)
- Plumper Bay
- Deepwater Bay

SEYMOUR NARROWS
DISCOVERY PASSAGE

Separation Head

Brown Bay
(Marina, Fuel)

4 to 6 kn   4 to 7 kn

Plumper Bay

6f rocky patch

0   1200'   2400' ½   1   1½

Approx. Scale n.m.

Notes:

Plumper Pt.

Puget Bluff

1. Attempt passage at or near slack water only.

2. Choose the tide so you will leave with a favorable stream.

△ 950'
△ 960'

SEYMOUR
NARROWS
Flood - 15 kt
Ebb - 14 kt Spr.
△ 900'

Mt. Lolo
700'

Lagoon

North Bluff

3. Fresh winds opposing the tidal stream cause dangerous races, rips, and eddies, especially at the Narrows, at Race Point, & Cape Mudge.

Purline Cliffs

Wilfred Pt.

Not to be used for navigation

Stephenson Pt.

Dam

Maud Is
Fl. R

8f
7f

Yellow It.

Defender Shoal

Site of Ripple Rock

N

Menzies Bay

6f

6 to 10 kn

White cliffs

Many piles
3f

Huntingford Pt.

Race Pt.

Anch's. on S. side:
- Campbell River (marina).
- Gowlland Harbour.
- Menzies Bay.

Current arrows are shown as during the main part of the tide.

OTTER COVE (ROCK BAY MARINE PARK)

This cove lies at the north end of Discovery Passage, where the channel turns almost at right angles to become Johnstone Strait. Housing for the lighthouse keeper's are at the point of the turn on Chatham Point, but the light itself is erected on Beaver Rock almost 300m (1,000 feet) to the north. The light is on a white painted steel tank on top of a white polygon-shaped concrete base. The foghorn of this station sounds every 20 seconds in fog, from a small building on the rocky point to the west of the light. This separation of light, houses, and foghorn is notable because if one is approaching Chatham Point in fog without radar, it is important to pass north and east of the light. It is dangerous to hold close to the shore in fog since rocks off the point prevent passage between it and the light where swirls and strong currents occur on the flood.

Immediately south of Chatham Point is a tiny cove with a cable strung across it to moor the keeper's boats. Two small islands, Rocky Islets, lie off the south side of Chatham Point. They are connected by a drying rocky ledge and have other ledges extending around their sides.

Otter Cove can be entered only by passing between Rocky Islets and Limestone Island. This rocky, 18m (60 foot) island has a few shrubs and trees. South of Limestone Island, between it and Slab Point (the southern point of Otter Cove entrance) there are shoal areas with kelp. Do not enter Otter Cove through this southern passage.

Anchorage can be found in the cove well in towards the head, in 5 to 8 fathoms, mud and rock; this area gives good protection from westerly winds. Though strong currents and swirls occur in Discovery Passage off Chatham Point the anchorage is relatively unaffected. This cove is a convenient base either to wait for slack water when southbound in Discovery Passage, to await quiet conditions in Johnstone Strait when northbound.

Several other anchorages in this locality are:

- **Turn Island,** across Johnstone Strait from Chatham Point has an anchorage behind it in a cove on Thurlow Island. Take care on entry from the east to avoid reefs found on both sides. There may be some sunken debris remaining for the logging camp that was located here..

- **Cameleon Harbour** and **Thurston Bay**, around the corner in Nodales Channel, offer several anchoring locations. Thurston Bay is an undeveloped Marine Park where anchorage may be taken behind Block Island.

- Rock Bay on Vancouver Island appears to be a possible anchorage but this is not the case. The government pier does not have a float and currents sweep the bay.

THE JUNCTION OF JOHNSTONE STRAIT, NODALES CHANNEL AND DISCOVERY PASSAGE

Discovery Passage

<u>APPROACHING OTTER COVE FROM NW</u>, i.e. from near Chatham Point

Otter Cove — Light structure

Swirls

JOHNSTONE STRAIT

NODALES CHANNEL

Foghorn + kelp

Light
Fl. 4s.
Fog Sig. ev. 20s

Swirls at flood

50° 20′ N

Rock Bay

Chatham Point — Mast Houses

Rocky Its.

↑ ↓ 3 kts

15

5

3

Limestone Is.

Kelp — Do not enter.

Slab Point

DISCOVERY PASSAGE

125° 27′ W

OTTER COVE
DISCOVERY PASSAGE

Not to be used for navigation

1000′ 0 ½ 1 n.m.

Approx. Scale n.m.

Chart 3539, 3543

Chatham Point
Keeper's Houses
Mast
Light

No entry Kelp Limestone Its. Rocky Its.

<u>OTTER COVE FROM NE, OFF THE ENTRANCE</u>

RACE and CURRENT PASSAGES and KELSEY BAY

The eastern portion of Johnstone Strait from Chatham Point to Kelsey Bay (about 21 miles) has steep mountains along the southern side, with no chance for anchorage The mountainous islands on the north side are not as high, and several large channels open into the Strait joining it to the northern passes. Though the passage has much beautiful scenery it has some drawbacks for small vessels.

This relatively narrow part of the Strait has strong currents, made more turbulent at certain areas such as Ripple Shoal and Race and Current Passages. Strong summer northwesterlies can kick up seas that make it a testing passage. Sometimes, too, summer fog hangs on in this part of the channel long after it has burned away in the other inside waters. In addition, traffic is heavy as cruise ships (often four or five in row) as well as log booms and fishing craft transit this area. Mayne Passage enters Johnstone Strait on the north side, opposite Ripple Point. A short distance west, Knox Bay is deep but can offer some respite from the westerly wind and sea.

Chancellor Channel enters the Strait about 12 miles along, leading to Helmcken Island, with Current and Race Passages on the N and S sides respectively. Favor the shore to avoid the eddies and rips near Ripple Shoal. The 1-mile long shoal lies in the red sector of the Helmcken Island light, about 1 mile east of Helmcken Island.

Large vessels observe a traffic separation pattern, with westbound craft passing north of Helmcken Island in Current Passage and eastbound using Race Passage. Small vessels do not always heed this requirement. The current can run to 6 knots in these passages, and it is always a good feeling to get by them. If an anchorage is needed, **Billy Goat Bay** on the north side of Helmcken Island can be used. Enter with care, for there are several rocks, islets and shoal areas nearby though the entrance is clear. Earl Ledge extends off Hardwicke Island for about .25 miles into the channel. Stay well clear of the light marking its end to avoid the turbulence found here.

As a result of snowmelt from the various inlets pouring into Johnstone Strait the current runs westward for long periods, and the tide and current tables will often show a continuous ebb current even while the water level is rising with the flood tide. This is a curious feature of the basins and sills of the various passages, one that confuses many transient skippers. *The tide and current tables are to be believed.* Since the prevailing westerly winds seem to develop their strongest force through this section seas can build seas against the ebb flow that make this passage lumpy and uncomfortable. Rainy weather or an early start assist in transiting this section during its quietest conditions.

Kelsey Bay is on the Vancouver Island side of the Strait, at the mouth of the Salmon River. The wide, shallow delta of the river has six sunken freighters forming a breakwater for a booming ground. This feature, together with buildings behind at Sayward and numerous tanks identify Kelsey Bay. If strong westerly winds are blowing against a high ebb tide in the Strait, heavy tidal rips will be encountered off Kelsey Bay. Alternate anchorages are justified when the rips are particularly turbulent or when tidal currents make progress in the area difficult.

The small craft floats are behind the rock breakwater west of the prominent ferry slip, where your vessel is protected from the wind and sea. The fuel dock is behind the high pier beyond the breakwater. Facilities are limited and are exposed to wash through the pilings making it unsatisfactory as an overnight stop.

RACE & CURRENT PASSAGES

Chart 3544

0   ½   1   1½ nm
Approx. Scale n.m.

Chart 3544

JOHNSTONE STRAIT

Hardwicke Is P.O.

Earle Ledge
Fl. R.

CURRENT PASSAGE

HELMCKEN

See detail below

Red Sector

Billy Goat Bay

Kelsey Bay
see detail

Floating bkwtr.

Sh

Sh

SALMON BAY

Graveyard Point

Hkusam Bay

RACE

(U) Fl. WR
32 ft. 11 M.

White Sector

PASSAGE

VANCOUVER ISLAND

Fuel dock

Tanks

Store P.O.

Small craft floats

Road to Sayward

JOHNSTONE STRAIT

Rock Breakwater

Hulks

Salmon Bay

Detail - Kelsey Bay

Detail - Billy Goat Bay

0   600'   1200' ¼   ½ n.m.
Approx. Scale.

N

150'

Shoal Dries

Billy Goat Bay

Sh.

160'

4f

5f Dries

10f

Shoal

Dries

3f

HELMCKEN IS.

Old hulks used as a breakwater for the booming ground

Sayward Clearing

Breakwater

High wharf with piling

APPROACHING KELSEY BAY FROM NNW, i.e. down Johnstone Strait abt. 1 mile.

OCTOPUS ISLANDS MARINE PARK

This beautiful marine park is a destination for many families from the Pacific Northwest and southern B.C. who find Desolation Sound and the Gulf Islands to be overcrowded during July and August. If time permits, it is also a side-trip worth taking when cruising the coast to or from Alaska. Located near the northeast tip of Quadra Island, it can be reached by one of three routes: from Okisollo Channel (joining Discovery Passage north of Seymour Narrows), through Hole in the wall (connecting Okisollo Channel to Calm Channel just to the north of Cortes Island) or via Surge Narrows (joining Okisollo Channel to Hoskyn Channel through Beazley Passage). Regardless of the approach taken, strong tidal currents with swirls, eddies and overfalls combined with a profusion of rocks and shoals demand careful timing and precise navigation.

Approaching the park <u>from the west</u> via Okisollo Channel must be timed for slack water in the Upper and Lower Rapids, as tidal currents can reach 9 knots accompanied by heavy overfalls and turbulence. Several anchorages are available while waiting for slack water. **Chonat Bay** on the south shore provides anchorage in the middle of the bay, but don't go too far in as much of the bay is shoal. **Barnes Bay** offers anchorage in the eastern part on a rocky bottom. The entrance to **Owen Bay** is affected by currents and eddies from the Upper Rapids unless entry is made less than an hour before slack. Clearance must be given to the drying reef .1 mile SW of Grant Island and rocks on the SE side of Walters Point. This is a pretty anchorage.

When approaching the park <u>from Hole in the Wall</u> timing of slack water at the western end is essential, for tidal currents can reach 12 knots while those at the eastern end, are only 2 knots. A convenient anchorage to await slack water is on the south shore at **Florence Cove** where a private dock is located. At the western end a mid-channel course must be followed when entering Okisollo Channel to avoid the drying rocks lying close to both the north and south entrance points where a 3.5 fathom band of water reaches across the opening.

The entrance to the Marine Park is through Bodega Anchorage followed by an interesting passage through a narrow channel having depths of 3 - 4 fathoms Anchorage may be taken in the first cove to starboard, taking care to avoid a large underwater rock extending off the shore to port. Further along the channel is another bay to starboard where many vessels find good anchorage. The tidal range must be considered when anchoring in the western bay where extensive shoals line the western and northern shores.

Approaching the park from the south via Surge Narrows is not recommended for first-time visitors. The route is narrow (Beazley Passage is only 60 m/197 feet wide) and many rocks and shoals must be negotiated only at slack water as tidal currents reach 12 knots.

Many pleasant hours can be spent rowing around the islets exploring this peaceful, undeveloped park. During high tide you can row to a little stream which empties into a small niche on the western shore to have a freshwater wash. Cruisers who prefer a less crowded anchorage may proceed further to anchor in **Waiatt Bay** in 4 - 5 fathoms, mud. A trail at the head of the bay leads to Small Inlet on the other side of Quadra Island and beyond to a lovely protected area surrounding Newton Lake where a quiet approach is often rewarded by hearing the melancholy song of loons.

OCTOPUS ISLANDS

Approx. Scale n.m.

Not to be used for navigation

Chart 3537, 3539

Barnes Bay

Hyacinth Lake

Owen Bay

House's Private Access

OKISOLLO

Gov't. Wharf

1735 ft.

To CALM O: CHANNEL + N To YUCULTA
RAPIDS OR S To DESOLATION SOUND

Grant Is

HOLE IN THE WALL

Florence Cove

Lower Rapids

Cooper Pt

Upper Rapids Heavy Overfall at Ebb tide

Springer Pt

Flood 12 kn Sp.
Ebb 10kn Sp

1270 ft.

Upper & Lower Rapids 9 kn Flood & Ebb

Etta Pt

Chasina Is.

OCTOPUS ISLAND'S MARINE PARK

Octopus Is.

CHANNEL

Elephant Mtn

5 f

Waiatt Bay

Barnsley Shoal

Trail to Small Inlet & Newton Lake

Surge Narrows

YUCULTA RAPIDS and DENT RAPIDS

Two routes lead from the north end of Georgia Strait to Johnstone Strait and on to the waters of northern British Columbia. The Seymour Narrows-Discovery Passage route is more direct, although it is influenced throughout its length by currents and at times northwesterly winds funnel down Discovery Passage making northbound travel uncomfortable. It is heavily used by commercial fishermen, tugs and cruise ships. Northbound yachtsmen favor the more interesting, prettier route that involves passes where the high currents are interspersed by stretches of calm water. Vessels planning to use this route usually depart from Refuge Cove, Squirrel Cove or Teakearne Arm. During settled, fair weather, Frances Bay (just to the north of Raza Island) can be used as a departure point. Anchor in 4 – 6 fathoms, gravel bottom near the head of the bay.

The entrance to this northern route is through Calm Channel (between Stuart and Sonora Islands}. The dock in the cove north of Harbott Point is privately owned.

<u>When traveling north</u>, leave Harbott Point about one hour before the tide turns to the ebb. (Remember the flood runs south and the ebb runs north in this channel.) Hold close to the Stuart Island shore till off Kelsey Point, then cross over to take advantage of a back eddy along the Sonora Island shore. Swing clear of Sea Lion Rock. There is a light on the east tip of the largest Gillard Island and the pass is immediately north of the light. One should enter Gillard Pass no more than 20 minutes before high water slack. The current tables are essential for correct timing, for the change in current direction does not always coincide with the tidal change.

Barber Passage lies northeast of Gillard Passage. While free of dangers, it is not as convenient to use. Big Bay is east of these rapids and provides a refuge from nearby currents. A detached shoal, marked by kelp, with a least depth of 4 m (13 ft.) lies in the center of the bay. A 204m (699 ft.) public wharf is protected by a breakwater. ~~Nearby is **Big Bay Resort**, a well known fishing resort with excellent facilities that is a popular stop-over for cruisers. For information call (250) 830-7524.~~ Across the channel is Sonora Resort, a luxury development where patrons arrive by float plane or helicopter. For information call 1-888-576-6672.

Dent Rapids are 2 miles northwest of Gillard Passage along Cordero Channel. The narrowest section is about .25 mile wide. The strong currents at peak flow create a standing wave off the tip of Little Dent Island with a large whirlpool "Devil's Hole," occurring down current. Favor the Sonora Island shore to avoid these turbulent waters. Do not pass close to Little Dent Island for the back eddy draws a vessel toward the whirlpool. <u>When traveling south</u> plan to be at Dent Rapids at low slack. Since this occurs 25 minutes prior to Gillard Passage enter it at the right time to pass through Yuculta Rapids about a half-hour into the flood. Do not attempt Tugboat Passage between Dent Islands as local knowledge is essential. Mermaid Bay is frequently used by log booms and pleasure craft find little space for anchorage.

APPROACHING STUART Is. & YUCULTA RAPIDS

YUCULTA & DENT RAPIDS

Not to be used for navigation

Chart 3539, 3543

0   ½   1   1½ n.m.

Approx. Scale n.m.

Secord Rk. (Dries) ✳
Temp. Anch.
Horn Pt.
Horn Bay (foul)
Burnt Bluff
Tugboat Passage
Little Dent Is.

DENT RAPIDS
Flood   7 to 9 kts
Ebb   6 to 8 kts

Dent Is.
Devil's Hole
Log Booms
Mermaid Bay
Engels Rk.

S O N O R A   I S L A N D

ARRAN RAPIDS
Arran Pt.

Current streams are shown as at the main part of the tide.

Asman Pt.
Bells Bay
Barber Passage
Hesler Pt.
Jimmy Judd Is.
Jimmy Judd Rk.
Gillard Passage
Rt. Resort
Big Bay

Innes Passage (Avoid)
Gillard Is.
SICA DOCK
Whirlpool Pt.

Sea Lion Rocks
Sonora Resort
Helipad

YUCULTA RAPIDS
Flood   5 to 7 kts
Ebb   4 to 6 kts

Proceeding up at the last of the flood

Kellsey Pt.

S T U A R T   I S L A N D

Yuculta

Harbott Pt.

C A L M   C H A N N E L

Bassett Pt.

SICA

~~Big Bay~~ Resort facilities include:

Restaurant

Liquor store

Grocery store

Showers and laundry

~~Fuel~~

Moorage

~~Mechanical repairs~~

GREENE POINT RAPIDS

Cordero Channel continues in a northwesterly direction beyond Dent Rapids. At Hall Point, the northern tip of Sonora Island, Nodales Channel leads off Cordero Channel in a southwesterly direction to join Johnstone Strait near Chatham Point. The northern pass route continues along Cordero Channel.

Branching off on the north side of Cordero Channel is Frederick Arm. Just .75 n.m. NE of Gomer Island is **Oleos** where reservations can be made the for dinner by calling VHF Ch 73. Moorage for four vessels is provided for those patronizing the excellent family restaurant.

Shoal Bay is on the south side of the channel about 2 miles from Nodales junction. A government dock with a long pier is at the southwest corner of the bay, where a boardwalk leads to **Shoal Bay Lodge** where the bar is known for its excellent hamburgers. For information call (250)287-6818. If the small float at the dock is fully occupied you may anchor east of the dock in 3 - 4 fathoms, mud. The head of the bay shoals for a considerable distance.

Two miles further west on the south side of the channel is another large bay. **Bickley Bay** is a convenient anchorage if it is necessary to wait for passage of Greene Point Rapids. If carrying the favoring current from entering Gillard Passage just before high slack, you can plan on transiting these rapids (if the vessel's speed is at least 6 knots). Depending on the vessel's speed they will be commencing to ebb, and though milder than Dent or Gillard they should not be treated lightly.

Greene Point Rapids are a T-shaped meeting of channels. Cordero Channel continues along the head of the T, while Mayne Passage leads southward to join Johnstone Strait. At the junction there are several groups of islands that narrow the passage and which should be passed with care. The ebb shows swirls and small overfalls from south of Cordero Islands for a considerable distance west along Cordero Channel. Slow vessels need to favor the south shore to avoid being pushed towards Griffith Islet, marked by a light. On the flood, going east, swirls and currents extend past Erasmus Island. Here too, a slow vessel should avoid being set towards the island.

About 1.5 miles east of Greene Point Rapids is Lorte Island with light and a prominent "restaurant" sign. In the cove nearby are the floats of an excellent dining room at **Camp Cordero**. Approaching the dock is easy near slack water but at other times strong currents in the cove make mooring the vessel somewhat challenging and care is needed.

Good anchorage can be found in the **Cordero Islands** where most of the effect of currents are blocked by the islands. Crawford Anchorage behind Erasmus Island is not recommended. **Charles Bay**, roughly opposite Blind Channel, offers a safe and beautiful anchorage in 2 fathoms, good holding mud for two or three vessels. Keep clear of shoal areas and allow for slight swinging about as some current effects are experienced in the vicinity of Eclipse Island.

Tide and current effects should be kept in mind when entering or leaving Blind Channel. In the narrow section of Mayne Passage rips and eddies are encountered. A mile south in Mayne Passage, on the west side is **Blind Channel Resort**. This well run resort provides a welcome rest spot with first-class facilities, including fuel, grocery, showers, laundromat and an excellent dining room. For reservations and docking information call (250) 949-1420 or 1-888-329-0475. The government dock is in the southwestern part of the bay with floats on either side. This is a busy spot in summer so rafting may be necessary. A pleasant walk along a forest trail leads to a point of interest—the ancient Thurlow Cedar which is more than 6m (20 ft.) in diameter.

Chart 3543

GREENE POINT RAPIDS

Not to be used for navigation

0   1200'   ½   1   1½ n.m.

Approx. Scale n.m.

C O R D E R O

Pt. Dock

3f·0

See detail

Cordero Its.

C H A N N E L

Tallac Bay

Griffiths ight

Reef across

Lorte Is.

Rest. Dock

Restaurant Sign

2f

WEST THURLOW ISLAND

Greene Pt.

Greene Point Rapids

kelp

Edsall Its.

Private Dock

Mink Is.

Erasmus Is.

Parrott Pt.

(Crawford Anch.)

THURLOW Is.

3

12

15

F

Resort Floats

Seaplane dock

Public Floats

M A Y N E   P A S S A G E

Shell Pt.

Shoal

EAST THURLOW

Charles Bay

ISLAND

Ecllipse It.

Mayne Passage Resort

Dining Rm, cabins P.O.

Blind Channel

F

POWER BOATERS
Please reduce your speed when passing Blind Channel Resort and Cordero Resort to avoid damaging docks and moored vessels.

N

Detail – Blind Channel

Butterfly Bay

M A Y N E   P A S S A G E

Gravel bank

3

Dries 6'

10

7

9

Mayne Pt.

C O R D E R O

ISLAND

3

3

Dries

Edith Pt.

3

Dries

Griffiths Its.

Rips

C O R D E R O   C H A N N E L

JOHNSTONE STRAIT

WELLBORE CHANNEL

Cordero Channel continues west from Greene Point Rapids for 3.5 miles to join Chancellor Channel marked by a light on Lyall Island. North of this junction, Loughborough Inlet* extends 18 miles to the north. The ebb effects of Greene Point Rapids are felt as far as this point. Chancellor Channel leads southwest for about 7 miles to join Johnstone Strait east of Helmcken Island and Race and Current Passages. If the weather is calm this exit into Johnstone Strait can be taken to shorten the distance to be traveled. However when strong westerlies are blowing they create disturbed seas in Chancellor Channel (as well as Johnstone Strait) and the side-step via Wellbore Channel can offer more miles but greater comfort.

For a slow vessel running the northern passes all together, the ebb will be well advanced by the time the entrance to Wellbore Channel is reached. The channel can be taken if the tides and currents (as given in the tables), are not large. But for bigger tides, or if the tide is too far advanced you should wait to enter Wellbore Channel nearer slack water. Small craft can find good anchorage close to shore in the little bays on either side of **Shorter Point,** depending on wind direction.

The effect of the currents are felt throughout Wellbore Channel. The main current effects are at Whirlpool Rapids off Carterer Point. The south-flowing flood effects extend south of Carterer Point, with the strongest back-eddy and whirlpools on the west side. Small floods have lesser effects and a vessel can pass through even at mid flood. Snug anchorage can be taken in a small cove west of Robson Point for one boat.

The north-flowing ebb has a narrow center section with large back-eddies and whirlpools on each side. The eastern back-eddy, together with the effects from Forward Harbour is strong. Entering Forward Harbour when the ebb is strong will require considerable power and it is best avoided. On small ebb flows the current effects are diminished, but swirls and currents sweep out past Althorp Point almost across Bessborough Bay.

Forward Harbour has a clear entrance channel leading to an attractive anchorage. It can be easily negotiated except, as noted when strong ebb currents exit the inlet. Douglas Bay provides good anchorage off the muddy beach. The depths drop off fairly quickly and stern ties to trees or rocks can be helpful. Good protection is provided during westerly winds, but if strong easterly winds are expected the log booms which are sometimes tied along the south shore may offer a more comfortable moorage. A seasonal restaurant operates near the logging camp is at the head of the bay. The operators sometimes offer a launch pick-up/drop-off service to patrons anchored in Douglas Bay or you can make the trip with your outboard in a few minutes. The food is reported to be good although, understandably, the menu is limited.

In Sunderland Channel a small anchorage can be found in the lee of Murray Islet in **Topaze Harbor.** Otherwise, some protection may be obtained behind log booms in Jackson Bay. Strong westerlies in Johnstone Strait also affect Sunderland Channel but the seas are not as heavy due to a shorter fetch. Sunderland Channel enters Johnstone Strait west of Kelsey Bay. Most vessels keep to the north shore, except when avoiding the rips off Gunner Point. If the seas are bad, respite can be found in the bay east of Gunner Point, in **MacLeod Bay, Tuna Point** or **Port Neville**

*If westerly winds pick up and make westbound progress in Cordero Channel slow or uncomfortable, moorage is available a few miles to the north in Loughborough Inlet at Heyden Bay where you can tie to log booms or anchor near the head of Jane Bay in 4 to 5 fathoms, mud.

WELLBORE CHANNEL

Not to be used for navigation

Anch's. on N. side:
- Douglas Bay (Forward Hbr.)
- Jackson Bay (Topaze Hbr.); behind Murray Its. also
- Bessborough Bay (emergencies) (bad in W'lys)

Bessborough Bay

Douglas Bay

FORWARD HARBOUR

To Topaze Hbr.

SUNDERLAND CHANNEL

Thynne Pt.   Trail   Robson Pt.

Louisa R.

MAINLAND

0   1200' 2400'   ½   1   1½ n.m
Approx. Scale n.m.

Althorp Pt.

Midgeham Its.

Do not enter on a strong ebb.

N

Horace Pt.

Jackson Bay

Carterer Pt.

Whirlpool Rapids 5 to 7 kts

Neale Pt.

Exposed Anch'g - May Find Protection Behind Log Booms

Detail

TOPAZE HBR.

WELLBORE CHANNEL

Foul, do not enter or leave this side

HARDWICKE

Murray Is.

Bulkely Is.

Anch's on E. side:
- Shelter Point anch.
- Blind Channel Resort
- see Cordero Channel chart. p.

ISLAND

SUNDERLAND CH.

Termagant Pt.

D'Arcy Pt.

Dickson Shoal

Anch's. on W. side:
- Billy Goat Bay (Helmcken Is.)
- Kelsey Bay
- Vere Cove (emergencies), open to W'lys.
- see Johnstone Straits chart, p.

CHANCELLOR   CHANNEL

Shorter Pt

Joins Cordero Channel

Shelter Pt.

Anchor close inshore.

Joins Johnstone Strait

WEST THURLOW ISLAND

PORT NEVILLE

The central portion of Johnstone Strait is where vessels transiting Seymour Narrows meet those traveling the northern route through the Yuculta, Dent and Greene Point Rapids. Some join Johnstone Strait at the junction of Chancellor Channel, others connect at the western end of Sunderland Channel (probably following a stop-over at Forward Harbour). Because prevailing northwesterlies funnel down Johnston Strait it is often uncomfortable to pass through this section when proceeding up the coast, yet all vessels must pass this way.

Sunderland Channel enters Johnstone Strait west of Kelsey Bay. On its north side the large opening of Blenkinsop Bay looks attractive, and can be used as an anchorage in calm weather, but westerlies tend to blow into the Bay.

Tuna Point anchorage, behind the little point and Mary Island gives relief from turbulent seas and apart from some effect of strong northwesterlies, the waters are calm. The cove has limited space and the middle and east part of the anchorage have some kelp and grass so care is needed to set the anchor securely. McLeod Bay is very small, offering protection to a single boat.

Port Neville, about four miles northwest of Tuna Point, is a popular stop-over for anchorage can be taken if the public wharf is filled. The wide, easily recognized entrance is between Ransom Point and Neville Point. The most noticeable feature marking the point is the nearby steep and rocky Milly Island where a prominent house overlooks the Strait. Kelp beds line much of the entrance channel to the bay but a mid-channel course presents no problems. Because of the large volume of water passing through the entrance, tidal currents can reach three knots. The direction and speed of these currents must be considered when mooring or anchoring in the bay.

Anchorage may be along the western shore of the outer part of the inlet taking care to set the anchor securely and have extra scope to prevent dragging as a result of strong currents or changes in depth with a rising tide. When proceeding further into the inlet you pass over an area with least depths of about 1.5 fathoms where it is easy to thread a way through lengthy tendrils of kelp waving at the surface. Within the inlet, anchorage in 4 to 5 fathoms, mud, may be taken in a wide area during settled weather. However, during easterly winds a considerable chop can develop making this exposed anchorage unsatisfactory and a spot in the lee of Robbers Nob off the shoal can give better protection.

A peaceful walk can be taken along the shore and grounds of Port Neville. The log buildings beyond the public dock have such an interesting history that there has been considerable pressure from cruisers and local inhabitants to have the area declared a Provincial Park. The log buildings date from 1916 when the Hansen family first settled here. For many years when logging and fishing were the economic life-blood of many small operators working the coast this was a center of activity. The small log store which operated from 1924 to 1960 is still standing and the daughter of the original settlers lives here and acts as a postmistress but there are no facilities ashore. Deer are often seen browsing in the open green spaces.

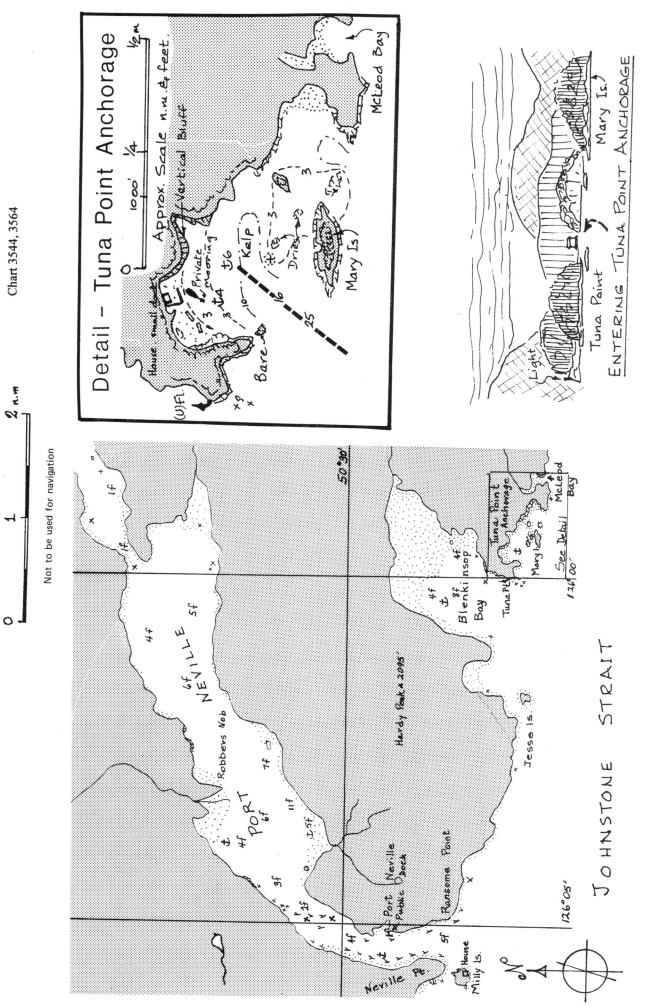

PORT NEVILLE

Chart 3544, 3564

0   1   2 n.m

Not to be used for navigation

Detail – Tuna Point Anchorage

Approx. Scale n.m. & feet.

0   100'   1/4   1/2 n.m

Vertical Bluff

McLeod Bay

Private mooring

Kelp

Dries

Mary Is.

Bare

House small dock

(W.Fl.)

Light

Tuna Point

Mary Is.?

ENTERING TUNA POINT ANCHORAGE

50°30'

PORT NEVILLE

Robbers Nob

Hardy Point ▲ 2085

Blenkinsop Bay

Jesse Is.

Tuna Point Anchorage

See Detail

Mary Is.

Tuna Pt.

McLeod Bay

126°00'

126°05'

Port Neville Public Dock

Ransom Point

Neville Pt.

House Milly Is.

JOHNSTONE STRAIT

PORT HARVEY, LAGOON COVE and other anchorages

This inlet indents the coast for 3 miles off Johnstone Strait, between East and West Cracroft Islands.* The entrance is wide, but there are several dangers that require attention when turning off the Strait. Broken Islands, a group consisting of two large islands, some islets and many rocks, lies to the east of the point where Havannah Channel joins Johnstone Strait. Escape Reef is about .5 miles off the south shore of West Cracroft Is. and 2 miles west of Broken Is. Hull Rock is a detached rock off the southeast shore of West Cracroft Is. and about .75 miles west of Domville Point. Slightly favor the southeast side of the passage to clear all dangers in the area. Fish farms are becoming a common sight in several spots along Havannah Channel

A number of pretty anchorages with good holding are available. **Open Cove** is a small cove on the east side of Port Harvey between Transit and Harvey Points. It can be used as an anchorage during easterly winds, but is open to westerlies and the swell they create in Johnstone Strait.

A few sparsely scattered houses and private docks dot the shoreline of the upper end of **Port Harvey**. Though anchorage may be taken NNW of Mist Island, it is fairly restricted by rocks. A large area where anchorage may be taken is off the large private floats and dolphins, north of Range Island. Northeast winds can affect the anchorage so set your anchor well. Do not anchor northeast of Range Island as the bottom shoals until becoming a marshy area.

Cruisers who wish to top up their fuel or visit a lovely area often take a side trip via Havannah and Chatham Channels to Minstrel Island. From this spot a route can be chosen which reaches Greenway Sound and Sullivan Bay and proceeds to Queen Charlotte Strait. Havannah Channel leads to two attractive anchorages before approaching Chatham Channel. **Boughey Bay** is a spacious anchorage with good holding in 4 - 6 fathoms, mud. It can be affected by southerly winds and you must not anchor too far into the bay as the head is shoal. A few miles to the north is **Burial Cove** where excellent protection can be obtained in 3 – 5 fathoms, mud.

Chatham Channel is best traversed near slack water as 4 to 6-knot currents are found in the narrow, shallow channel where kelp shows at mid-tide. Range markers must be watched carefully and speeds should be kept down so that your wake does not disturb the safe course of other vessels.

Cutter Cove is a long, narrow bay opening off the northeast end of Chatham Channel. The anchorage can become lumpy when winds pick up; anchor on the north shore during westerlies and on the south shore during easterlies. There is excellent crabbing here.

Minstrel Island has moorage, and fuel. Passage through the Blow Hole, a narrow channel separating Minstrel Island from East Cracroft Island, should be made at high water via a mid-channel course, but vessels drawing no more than 1.8 m (6 feet) can pass at any state of the tide. Beyond the Blow Hole is the entrance to **Lagoon Cove** where good anchorage in 4 – 5 fathoms, mud can be taken by many vessels. **Lagoon Cove Marina** is a popular stop-over for fuel, water, moorage and supplies. The evening pot-lucks and Bill Barber's fireside story telling are becoming legendary. About 6 miles to the southwest in Clio Channel is a beautiful refuge in **Potts Lagoon**. There are no facilities but the outer coves and inner lagoon provide fascinating exploration by dinghy.

*When proceeding west in Johnstone Strait the next anchorages are at Boat Bay, .5 mile east of Swaine Point (entering along the shore of W. Cracroft) to gain protection from west winds or 1.5 miles further west to a bight opposite Sophia Islands (avoid offlying rocks) when winds are easterly. Bay traveling on the starboard side of Johnstone Strait favorable currents can be helpful.

PORT HARVEY & VICINITY

0   1   2   3
Approx. Scale n.m.

Not to be used for navigation

Chart 3545, 3564

Vancouver Is.

Cormorant Is.

Pearse Is.

Harmon Is.

West Cracroft Is.

Alert Bay

THE WESTERN EXIT FROM JOHNSTONE STRAIT SEEN NEAR PORT HARVEY

KNIGHT INLET

Minstrel Island

Shacks

Cutter Cove

F

The Blow Hole

Clio Channel

Lagoon Cove

Ft.

Sambo Pt.

CHATHAM CHANNEL

LIGHT RANGES

Ray Point range lights in line bear 88°
East Cracroft Island range lights, WSW of Bowers Islands, in line bear 271°.

Ray Pt.

Bones Bay

EAST CRACROFT IS.

Rbn.

Cracroft Inlet

Root Pt.

Turn Pt.

2060'

WEST CRACROFT IS.

50° 31' N

Pvt. Docks

Dolphins

Burial Cove

Browning Rk.

Mt. Thomas
1765'

Range I

Mist.

Hull Is.

Malone Pt.

N

Port Harvey

Bockett Is.

Boughey Shoal

Boughey Bay

Transit Pt.

Open Cove

HAVANNAH CHANNEL

Hull Rk.

Broken Islands

Escape Reef

Bare Mtn.
1715'

Port Harvey

Light

Logged

West Cracroft Is.

Transit Pt.

Harvey Pt.

Domville Pt.

Broken Is. Group (whitish bases)

To Ministrel Is. via Havannah Channel

APPROACH TO PORT HARVEY & HAVANNAH CHANNEL FROM JOHNSTONE STRAIT

DRURY INLET TO MACKENZIE SOUND

Not to be used for navigation

NUMAS ISLANDS

0 1 2 3 4 5

Approximate scale, n.m.

This is an overview for planning routes. Many rocks and reefs are not indicated.
Not to be used for navigation.

MARINAS are located with a keyed reference on these pages. All marinas offer moorage; other services are listed below. When calling a marina use VHF Ch. 66A.

MEcho - **Echo Bay Resort**:   fuel, kerosene, propane, water, laundry, showers, ice, haul-outs, regular flights. Phone/Fax: (250) 956-2121.

MGreen – **Greenway Sound Marine Resort**: power, water, showers, laundry, garbage service, restaurant, books, clothing, beauty/barber shop, and air service. Phone: (250) 949-2525, Toll free: 1-800-800-2080, Fax (250) 949-4040.   Website: greenwaysound.com

MKwats – **Kwatsi Bay Marina**: water, gift/bookshop, guided hike to waterfall, daily dockside get-together (pot luck etc.), family welcome. Phone (250) 949-1384.

MLagoon – **Lagoon Cove Marina**: fuel, propane, charts, clothes, book exchange, potlucks, marshmallow roasts and fireside stories.

MMins – **Minstrel Island Marina**: fuel, restaurant. Phone (250) 286-8444.

MPierre – **Pierre's Bay Lodge and Marina:** power, water, ice, laundry, fresh baked pies (Di's Pie), lodging and pot-luck dinners. E-mail: pierresbay@direcway.com

MShawl – **Shawl Bay Marina**: power, water, ice, groceries, laundry, tackle, cabins, bakery, complimentary pancake breakfast. Website: shawlbay.perspective-imaging.com

MSulBay – **Sullivan Bay Marine Resort**: fuel, water, power, propane, ice, laundry, showers, groceries, post office, liquor, fishing gear and regular flights. Phone: (250) 949-2550

MWind -- **Windsong Sea Village**: bakery, arts and crafts store, float planes, cabin rentals, trail and park access. Phone (250) 974-5004 Fax (250) 974-5004

Knack - **Knacktik Cultural Tours** - Eco-tourism facility on Harbledown Island open Mondays, July 1 to Sept. 15 featuring Tribal dances, salmon BBQ and walking tours, with free moorage for patrons of events. Special performances any day with reservations for 10 or more. For information call Bill Glendale at (250) 974-2179 or toll free 1-877-207-9797.

KINGCOME INLET TO KNIGHT INLET

Not to be used for navigation

ALERT BAY, CORMORANT ISLAND

Cormorant Island is a comma-shaped island where Johnstone Strait ends and Broughton Strait begins. The town of Alert Bay is the center of much of the cultural activity in northern Vancouver waters. The town and the major Nimpkish Indian village are almost inseparable, and lie along the southern inner curve of Cormorant Island. Colorful homes dot the island's shores and are the first sign of habitation since leaving Campbell River or Lund. Two white microwave towers are prominent on the southern part of the island. On the hill above the town the antenna of Alert Bay Coast Guard VHF Radio is conspicuous.

Southwest of Alert Bay the Nimpkish River estuary is evident on Vancouver Island. A large bank, which dries in some places and is shoal elsewhere, extends a considerable distance out from the Vancouver Island shore. Two beacons mark the edge of these shoals. Vessels should favor the Alert Bay side (away from the beacons) as the currents can be strong and the course should be checked often.

Grizzly bear mask carved by well known local carver, Johnathan Henderson

There are many wharves and docks along the waterfront. Perhaps the simplest way to orient oneself is by referring to the remarkable totem poles near the southern end of the town marking the Nimpkish Burial Grounds. A walk along the road will give you a closer look at these impressive poles. Posted signs ask visitors to stay off the sacred grounds.

A few hundred yards or so to the north is a government wharf and a float. There is seldom much space here as it is in the center of town. The mooring buoys are normally occupied by commercial vessels. A short distance beyond is a fuel dock.

About 1 mile northwest of the Burial Grounds is a tall totem pole on the hill behind the old three-story Indian School. At one time this was the tallest totem pole in the world. About midway between this totem pole and the burial grounds (north of the ferry dock) is a long, angled rock breakwater. The entrance to the small craft floats is around the northern end of the breakwater. When the fishing fleet is out there is plenty of room at the floats. But when the fleet is in port there may not even be sufficient space for rafting.

A strong current runs along the shore which must be taken into account when maneuvering in this harbor. The many facilities include: a supermarket, laundromat, hospital, drug store, post office, hotels, and restaurants. Several craft shops are on the main street. Near the tall totem pole is a Long House where Indian dancers perform in costume when arrangements have been made by 15 or more people. The U'Mista Cultural Center and Museum have an exceptional collection of Native Indian masks and other artifacts and are well worth visiting.

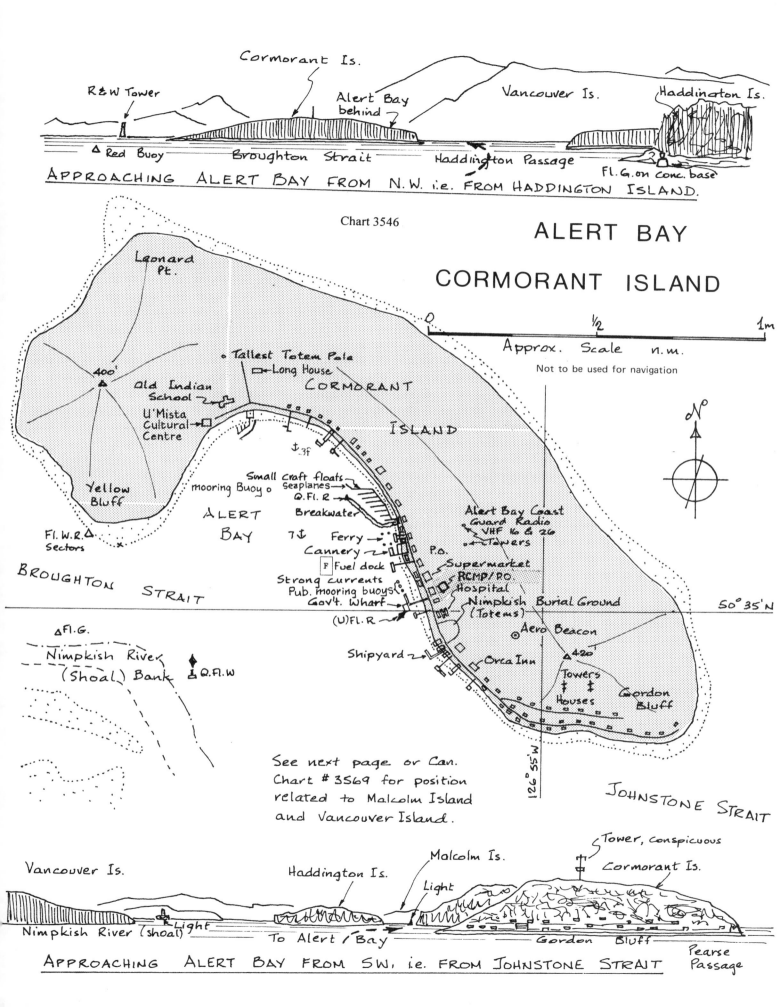

Approaching Alert Bay from N.W. i.e. from Haddington Island.

R&W Tower
Red Buoy
Cormorant Is.
Alert Bay behind
Vancouver Is.
Haddington Is.
Broughton Strait
Haddington Passage
Fl. G. on conc. base

Chart 3546

ALERT BAY
CORMORANT ISLAND

Leonard Pt.
400'
Old Indian School
U'Mista Cultural Centre
Yellow Bluff
Fl. W.R. Sectors
Tallest Totem Pole
Long House
CORMORANT
ISLAND

Approx. Scale n.m.
Not to be used for navigation

N°

mooring Buoy
Small Craft floats
Seaplanes →
Q. Fl. R →
Breakwater
ALERT BAY
Ferry
Cannery
Fuel dock
Strong currents
Pub. mooring buoys
Gov't. Wharf
(U)Fl. R →

Alert Bay Coast
Guard Radio
VHF 16 & 26
Towers
P.O.
Supermarket
RCMP/P.O.
Hospital
Nimpkish Burial Ground
(Totems)
Aero Beacon
Shipyard
Orca Inn
420
Towers
Houses
Gordon Bluff

50° 35' N
126° 55' W

BROUGHTON STRAIT

Fl. G.
Nimpkish River
(Shoal) Bank
Q. Fl. W

JOHNSTONE STRAIT

See next page or Can. Chart #3569 for position related to Malcolm Island and Vancouver Island.

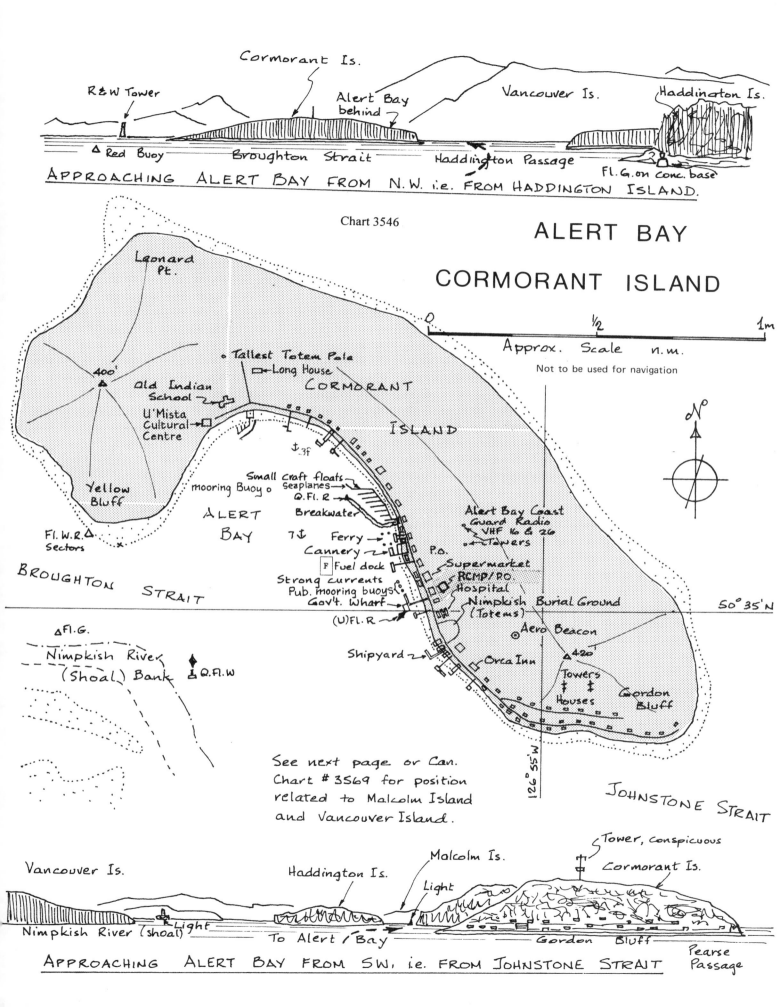

Vancouver Is.
Haddington Is.
Malcolm Is.
Light
Tower, conspicuous
Cormorant Is.
Nimpkish River (shoal)
Light
To Alert Bay
Gordon Bluff
Pearse Passage

Approaching Alert Bay from SW, i.e. from Johnstone Strait

SOINTULA, MALCOLM ISLAND

Malcolm Island was settled by Finnish immigrants of the Kalevan Kansa Colonization Company in 1900 in one of the first attempts at a socialist cooperative commune. The hard working settlers made their living from fishing, farming and logging. Sointula, which means "Place of Harmony," was the site of their main village. Personality conflicts, particularly with the irascible leader, caused a break-up in 1905. Many of the original residents remained and the community survived in a slightly different form. A walk through the cemetery gives proof of the strong family ties of the Finnish forebears.

The calm simplicity of Sointula, the neat cottages with their carefully tended flower gardens and the industrious residents gave this place a feeling of peace, in contrast to the raw, rough land around it. Much of the success was due to the fact that there was no liquor, no religious intolerance and no police force on the island, until the 1960's when the island became popular with hippies.

Malcolm Island and Sointula are connected to the B.C. road system by a three-town ferry that calls at Port McNeill and Alert Bay. The ferry dock is northwest of Dickenson Point. The small craft harbor is about 1 mile further into Rough Bay, behind an L-shaped breakwater.

This is a busy place during the fishing season as many vessels from southern B.C. use Sointula as a base in summer. In addition to the old wharf and four finger floats, a newer wharf and three finger floats have been added to the north. Both sets of floats are approached around the end of the breakwater.

The wharfinger controls all berthing in the small craft harbor and collects government fees. To arrange moorage he may be reached at (250) 973-6544 or report to him on arrival. If you arrive after hours find any berth and check in the next morning. At the head of the wharf and across the road is the marine hardware branch of the Cooperative Store. The main store, post office, hotel, restaurant, and a museum are at the center of town, a pleasant walk from the wharf.

Toward the eastern end of the island Mitchell Bay is a good anchorage in 3 – 4 fathoms, sand and gravel. It provides protection from all except southerly winds. The short public float 10m (39 ft.) on the eastern shore of the bay is often occupied.

Just across Broughton Strait from Sointula, on Vancouver Island is Port McNeill, a modern town, with many facilities described on the following page. The approach from Alert Bay to Sointula or Port McNeill passes Haddington Island. A traffic separation scheme (for cruise ships and large freighters) is established for each side of the island. Lights mark the reefs, ledges, and shoals. The passages are wide enough to cause small vessels few problems if the lights and marks are carefully identified. Continuing west from Sointula through Broughton Strait, the route enters Queen Charlotte Strait after passing Pulteney Point Lighthouse. This lighthouse on the northwest tip of Malcolm Island is an important weather reporting station whose deep fog horn can be very welcome during poor visibility.

QUEEN CHARLOTTE STRAIT

Malcolm Pt.
Grant Sitka Spruce
Bere Pt.
Nice Walk to Bere Park

Lizard Pt.

50° 40'

MALCOLM ISLAND

Rough Bay
See detail below.
Sointula
Dickenson Pt.

Gov't. dock

Mitchell Bay
± 3·4f
Tank

Pulteney Pt.
Lighthouse Fl.R.10s
Fog horn ev. 40s

Ferry Term.

BROUGHTON

Neill Ledge
Ledge Pt.

Haddington Reefs
Leonard Rk.

Cormorant Channel

CORMORANT IS.

Booming Grounds

See Detail Next Page

Haddington Is.

Alert Bay

Pearse Passage

Pearse Is.

Port McNeill
(Ferry, P.O., Stores, docks)

STRAIT

Nimpkish River

Shoals

JOHNSTONE STRAIT

VANCOUVER

Telegraph Cove
(Dock, Store, P.O.)
Lewis Pt.

Beaver Cove

ISLAND

May tie to Log Booms

Englewood

Detail –

Gov't. floats

Harbor-master

Private floats

Transients may tie either side

Bn.

Reserved for seaplanes

Fish Pack Plant

Breakwater

Ways

Co-op Hdware.

Old boathouse

Houses

Sointula Harbour

Road to town. abt. 1 mile.
To ferry, P.O., store, hotel, etc.

SOINTULA

MALCOLM ISLAND

0 ——————————————— 5 m

Approx. Scale n.m.

N

Not to be used for navigation

Chart 3546

Red roofs

PULTENEY POINT LIGHTHOUSE
MALCOLM ISLAND
VIEW FROM EAST

PORT McNEILL

At this bustling logging and tourist town on the south side of Broughton Strait, the municipal floats and floatplane dock are sandwiched between two sets of breakwaters. The high structure of the ferry dock extending northeast from the end of the causeway is prominent from a distance. For a mile or two the coast is lined with neat homes, and a cement block seawall protects the foreshore against winter storm action. From a distance the white rock breakwater stands out clearly beyond the black creosoted pilings of the ferry dock. The breakwater along the northwestern side of the basin backs on to a large dump site where logging trucks unload. The inner part of the northwestern part of the bay is a booming ground.

This busy town has become such a popular provisioning and fueling stop for vessels cruising the coast that sometimes during July and August it is quite overcrowded. Federal Docks, intended for use by commercial fishermen lead off the causeway. Here overflow pleasure craft from the Municipal Floats are often rafted alongside workboats as space permits. Rafting (sometimes as much as three abreast) is often the norm. The alternative is laying at anchor on the north side of the channel. The Port McNeill Harbour Authority administers port activities.

Moorage is under the control of the harbormaster who should be contacted prior to entering the harbor by phoning (250) 956-3881 or calling VHF Ch. 66A which is monitored from 8 a.m. to 7 p.m. Moorage is on a first-come, first-served basis; reservations are not accepted. Water and 15 and 30 amp power are on most docks. Make arrangements at the office for use of the tidal grid and to obtain pump-out services.

Showers and washrooms next to the harbor office are available from 8 a.m. to 9 p.m. A laundromat is located next to Blue Heron Gifts, a gift shop featuring unique items and crafts from local craftsmen. Two telephone booths are along the road next to the harbor. Across the road is McNeill's, a coffee shop that vies with Refuge Cove for serving the largest ice cream cones on the coast. Next door is the post office and then a short walk takes you to the town center where there is a liquor store, marine repair and supply store and several supermarkets that will deliver groceries to the harbor. The friendly shopkeepers and accessible, well stocked stores make this an excellent location for provisioning. Arrangements for purchasing propane can be made at the fuel dock.

The tri-Island ferry route links Port McNeill to Alert Bay on Cormorant Island and Sointula on Malcolm Island. The town is linked by Highway 19 to Port Hardy to the north and southern Vancouver Island and bus and air services operate daily. Airplane and boat charters for fishing nearby waters and inland lakes as well as whale watching trips to nearby Robson Bight and Telegraph Cove (famous for its whale rubbing stone beach) add to tourist activity.

Named after Captain William McNeill who explored this part of the coast in 1825, Port McNeill's first permanent white settlement was established in 1937 by a lumber company. The economy continues to be based on logging as the old steam donkey featured on the shore and a logging museum demonstrate. A Logger Sports Day, held annually in June attracts competitors from far afield to compete in such events as log scaling, log burling and log splitting. Incidentally, the world's largest burl weighing more than 22 tons measures 14 m (45 feet) in circumference can be seen about 2 miles north of the town on Hwy. 19.

Chart 3546

PORT McNEILL

Not to be used for navigation

PORT HARDY

A pleasant, small town situated near the northern end of Vancouver Island, this is the last fuel and provisioning center before sailing to the north. It marks the end of the island highway from the south and is the terminus for the B.C. Ferry, *Queen of the North,* which sails to Prince Rupert. Although many vessels depart from Port McNeill for the Queen Charlotte Sound crossing, some choose to leave from Port Hardy.

Hardy Bay is large, and marked at its eastern end by a light on Masterman Islands about .5 mile off Dillon Point. **Port Hardy** lies at the southern end of the bay, beyond the two shoal bars marked by lighted buoys at their seaward ends. A government wharf lies between the buoys, but the small craft harbor lies beyond the southern shoal buoy. Pass on the east side of the buoy before entering between the two breakwaters. The harbor offers two small craft facilities.

The government wharf is popular with commercial fishing vessels but can be used by cruisers when space is available. Locally called "Fisherman's Wharf, during the fishing season it is extremely busy and rafting may be necessary.

Quarterdeck Marine, in the southern part of the harbor, offers transient moorage, haul-out (40-ton travelift) and repair facilities. Reservations are recommended during July and August when space is at a premium; call on VHF or (250) 949-6332. A marine supply store, showers, laundry, and other facilities are at the head of the dock and a restaurant is nearby. Fuel may be obtained at a Chevron station at Quarterdeck Marine or just outside the breakwaters to the north at the Esso Marine Station which also carries nautical charts. Both stations are very busy in summer, and short waits may be necessary.

Goletas (Schooner) Channel leads WNW from Hardy Bay to the northern end of Vancouver Island at Cape Sutil. Vessels heading for the west coast of Vancouver Island or north to Rose Harbour in the Queen Charlotte Islands use this channel to reach **Bull Harbour** on Hope Island, as the departure point for these destinations.

The route for transiting Queen Charlotte Strait follows Goletas Channel to Noble Islets where a light is located. Here, Christie Passage separates Hurst and Balaklava Islands. Hurst, Bell and adjacent small islets are included in **God's Pocket Marine Park**. Harlequin Bay on the north side of Hurst Island provides sheltered anchorage from south and west winds. God's Pocket Resort is in the indentation on the west side of Hurst Island off Christie Passage. Even though this small is hardly noticeable on regular charts it provides adequate shelter. **God's Pocket Resort** welcomes cruisers, with a small dock where moorage may be arranged and shower facilities are available. For information call (250) 949-9221 or visit their website at www.godspocket.com The two white tire floats in the bay are often used by rafted fishing vessels, leaving little space for anchoring.

Scarlett Point Lighthouse on the northeast tip of Balaklava Island is 2 miles northwest of God's Pocket. This is a good departure or destination point for the crossing of Queen Charlotte Sound. The favored northbound route proceeds northwesterly in Gordon Channel passing west of Pine Island. The course is then changed more to the north to pass Cape Caution and Egg Island across South Passage to Fitz Hugh Sound.

If the weather deteriorates after leaving God's Pocket, refuge may be found in the Walker Group, between Kent and Staples Is. Avoid Nye Rock and Sussex Reefs southeast of Redfern Island.

The routes past Cape Caution and factors to consider when making this passage are described and illustrated on the following page. If northwesterly winds develop and build when a vessel is some distance from Port McNeill or Port Hardy then rather than returning to port it is possible to run for refuge to several locations. Travel can then be resumed when weather and sea conditions moderate and northbound progress can continue from part way up the coast.

EAGLE TOTEM POLE (Kwakiutl)

The **Walker Group** provide a convenient protected anchorage when either Port McNeill or Port Hardy are the departure point. Approach the Islands from the west and good anchorage is available between forest-covered Kent and Staples Islands. Productive fishing can be found off the south and southwest shores of the island group.

Vessels departing from Sullivan Bay and Wells Passage may find that northwesterly weather has produced uncomfortable sea conditions by the time they reach waters of Queen Charlotte Strait. Rather than returning to port they can find protection in all but southerly weather at **Dickson Island** (50°50.50'N 126°56.00'W) at the south end of Wells Passage. Approach from the south between Vincent and Percy Islands, then pass between Broughton and Dickson Islands. On the northeast end of the island is a small cove where anchorage can be taken on the eastern side. Avoid the mud shoals in the western part of the bay which dry at low water.

Blunden Harbour is across Queen Charlotte Strait from both Port McNeill and Port Hardy and is about 22 miles from Sullivan Bay. It is the first mainland spot where anchorage may be taken by cruisers proceeding up the coast. Careful use of Chart #3548 is necessary to thread a route through numerous rocks and dangers near the entrance. Anchorage may be found off the beach in 7 fathoms, mud. The abandoned Indian burial site on Byrnes Island and the shell middens ashore must not be disturbed as they are protected by law.

Allison Harbour is about 13 miles northwest of Blunden Harbour and the multitude of outlying rocks off the coast on the north side of Queen Charlotte Strait demand caution when traveling in this area. Entry to Allison Harbour is between Ray Island and City Point. Depending on the direction of the wind, anchorage may be taken north of the old settlement (8 fathoms), 1 mile north of the 2.4m (8 foot) drying rock, or near the head of the harbor in 4 fathoms. All locations have good holding, mud bottom. Formerly an active logging center, the settlement is now abandoned and there are no facilities ashore. A sketch of Allison Harbour is shown on page 106.

Aptly named **Murray Labyrinth** is in the middle of the extensive group of islands northwest of City Point. The intricate entrance to this magical hideaway demands vigilance, precise navigation and calm nerves. You could spend several days exploring the countless islets and peaceful channels that are a photographer's and painter's sanctuary. As an extra reward, you may be welcomed by the resident grey whale. It is essential to use CHS Chart #3921 when exploring this wonderland.

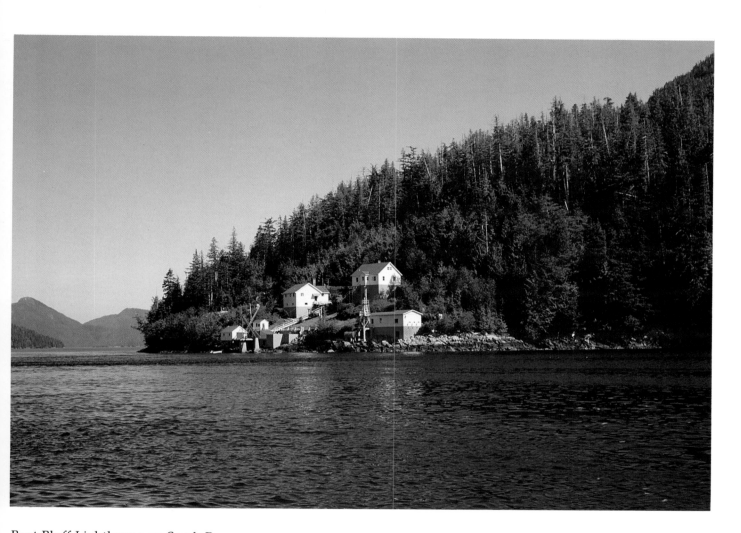

Boat Bluff Lighthouse on Sarah Passage

Peaceful Oliver Cove Marine Park off Reid Passage

Not to be used for navigation

Dean Channel

Roscoe Inlet

Klemtu
122

Price Is.

120

Ocean Falls P

Bella Coola

FINLAYSON CHANNEL

MATHIESON CHANNEL

Yeo Is.

Chatfield Is.

Fisher channel

King Island

Burke Channel

118

Dowager Is.

Milbanke Sound

116

Denny Is.

Campbell Is.

Lama Passage

Hunter Is.

52°   52°

Goose Is.

FITZ HUGH SOUND

Namu
114

Hakai Passage
112

Good Hope Resort

Calvert Is.

Safety Cove

Wadhams

110

110

C. Calvert

108

Rivers

Duncanby Landing

Queen   Charlotte
       Sound

Egg Is.

C. Caution

Allison Hbr.

104

Storm Is.

Blunden Hbr.

51°   51°
106

Hope Is.   Bull Hbr.

Nahwitti Bar

Queen

C. Sutil

Nigei Is.

Charlotte

Scott Is.

Strait

C. Scott

VANCOUVER

100   Port
       Hardy   F

Malcolm Is.

96

ISLAND

Sointula

Alert Bay

Port McNeill   98   94

ROUTES PAST CAPE CAUTION

The crossing of Queen Charlotte Sound past Cape Caution is one of the key passages of the trip. Although the name itself invokes possible trepidation for first-time cruisers transiting the coast the majority of summer crossings are completed with little more than moderate winds and a northwesterly swell. If you are departing from Greenway Sound in a low-powered vessel you will probably be making the crossing in two days with a stop-over along the way. Vessels from Queen Charlotte Strait depart from either Port McNeill or Port Hardy. The route from Port Hardy is detailed on page 100.

The most direct route from Port McNeill uses Pulteney Point as a departure and a course is laid to Echo Island in the Deserters Group. This takes you about .25 miles west of Ewen Rock, where if the weather deteriorates you can seek refuge in anchorages described on page 102 or further along at Miles Inlet, shown on the following page. A course change in the vicinity of Ewen Rock to clear Cape Caution by about a mile will be followed by a further change to clear Egg Island and northward to the desired anchorage.

In clear weather these routes have interest but offer no problems other than those that nature provides in the wind and sea. The entire coast is well marked with lights and lighthouses that provide assurance and useful bearings. Summer fog can be disconcerting but with the help of a professionally swung compass, a depth sounder and fog signals at key lighthouses, navigation of the crossing can be safely made. Of course radar, GPS and electronic plotters assist greatly in reducing navigational concerns. Pine and Egg Island Lighthouses are manned but the light at Cape Caution is unmanned.

Two elements affect the sea conditions on a passage through Queen Charlotte Strait: weather and the state of the tide when reaching Cape Caution. Unfortunately you can't always adjust your departure to take advantage of the optimum time for both of these considerations. By leaving early in the morning from either Port McNeill or Port Hardy you can complete a good part of the voyage before the afternoon northwesterly winds pick up resulting in headwinds and seas that slow progress and make the boat's motion uncomfortable. On the other hand, by departing with an ebb tide and timing your arrival off Cape Caution at low water, the vessel will also get a lift from the a flood tide as you pass through South Passage and enter Fitz Hugh Sound.

Most cruisers usually like to get an early start regardless of tidal considerations, especially if they have a low-powered vessel. If weather conditions dictate a stop-over then you can look for the most convenient refuge that can be reached depending on the direction of the wind and seas. Several anchorages are available it may be prudent to make the passage in two or more steps. For details on anchorages south of Miles Inlet see page 102, for those north of Miles Inlet see page 106.

Miles Inlet is a wonderful anchorage on the north side of the Strait and is a convenient refuge regardless of your direction of travel. The McEwen Rock light is a prominent landmark for avoiding coastal dangers and as a marker for the approach to the Inlet one mile to the east.

APPROACHING SCARLETT POINT LIGHTHOUSE FROM WNW, about 3 miles

Chart 3744

Goldstream Hbr.

HECATE Is.

Pruth Anch.

CALVERT Is.

QUEEN

CHARLOTTE

SOUND

Truman Pt.

Safety Cove

South Pt.

C. Calvert

Grief Bay

Clerk Pt. Fl.

Penrose Is.

SOUTH PASSAGE

FITZ HUGH SOUND

Green Is.

Addenbroke Is.

Dawson's Landing

Good Hope

Wadhams

RIVERS INLET

Fl.

100

Duncanby Landing

Fl.(3) 12s

Goose Bay

Milbrook Cove

SMITH SOUND

Table Is.

Takush

Jones Cove (Emerg'y ↯)

C. Caution

Miles Inlet ↯

Allison Harbour ↯

Gp. Fl (3) 12s

Storm Is.

Fl.

Blundan Hbr.

Helipad Bridge Houses Light on a lattice mast tower

EGG ISLAND LIGHT

Egg Is. Fl. 5s Fog Sig., 60s

Not to be used for navigation

Egg Is.   Table Is.   Cape Caution Light

APPROACHING CAPE CAUTION FROM 6m SSW
(White beaches along the coast indicates the cape is getting closer.)

Pine Is.
Gp. Fl.(2) 10s
2 Fog Sig, 60s

C. St. James

Bull Harbour

Nahwitti Bar

Hope Is.

Fl.

Nigei Is.

Walker Gr.

Scarlet

Fl. 5s

Fl.

Gods Pocket ↯

Fl.

QUEEN

CHARLOTTE

STRAIT

Fl.W. 10s
C. Scott

VANCOUVER ISLAND

GOLETAS CHANNEL

ROUTES PAST CAPE CAUTION

QUEEN CHARLOTTE STRAIT

Hardy Bay

Port Hardy ↯

Gp. Fl.(2) 12s

Round Is. Fl.

Airport

Port McNeill

0   10   20m
Approx. Scale   n. m.

40'

30'

20'

10'

51°00'N

50'

40'

30'   20'   10'   128°00'W   50'   40'   127°30'W   20'

MILES INLET and ANCHORAGES NORTH of CAPE CAUTION

The amphitheater-like entrance to **Miles Inlet** lies between McEwen Point on the north and Bramham Point on the south. Many small islets and detached rocks are clustered along the northern shore, and after about .5 mile the opening narrows to only 22m (75 feet). Its entrance is a narrow rock-walled corridor that branches to the northwest and southeast to form a T at its inner end.

Depths in the entrance vary between 3 and 4 fathoms. Good anchorage in 2 to 3 fathoms, mud, can be taken in both channels. The northwestern end is a lagoon sealed off by shallows that dry 4 m (13 feet) at low water. The bottom shoals quickly in the southeast arm past a rocky mid-channel islet, beyond which is an interesting area to explore by dinghy. Westerly winds blow through the entrance, but are more of a nuisance for causing sloppy seas outside the entrance than for their effect within the anchorage.

After passing Cape Caution the nearest anchorage is small and can be difficult to identify the first time it is entered. **Jones Cove** lies on the northeast side of Macnicol Point. When entering steer clear of a reef that extends 180 m (600 ft.) southwest of Turner Islands, and round the east point of Jones Cove entrance by at least 90 m (300 feet). The cove is small but offers some shelter in an emergency. However, when heavy seas are breaking in the area the entrance is difficult to identify and anchorage should be taken elsewhere if you are unsure of the proper approach.

Takush Harbour is about 7 miles east of Table Island. It provides excellent protection from all winds and is worth visiting for its beauty as well as for a refuge from stormy weather. The most popular spot is in Anchor Bight, the west arm of the Harbour entered between Gnarled Islets and Anchor Islets. Bull Cove, on the east side of the entrance south of Bull Point, appears to be very small but it offers snug, secure protection for 2 or 3 vessels in 4 to 5 fathoms, mud.

Smith Sound can be entered from the south through Alexandra Passage between Egg Island and Macnicol Point (about 5 miles north of Cape Caution) or through Radar Passage north of Egg. The Sound can be entered from the north through Irving Passage south of False Egg Island. There are several dangers in both entrances and a large scale chart should be used in determining safe courses. The main dangers are drying rocks that are usually visible or are indicated by breakers.

Milbrook Cove is on the north shore of Smith Sound close to the east of Shield Island. A buoy marks Milbrook Rocks midway in the entrance which should be passed on the west. Once in the cove stay in mid-channel and pass between the two islands in the north end of the cove to anchor behind them in 4 to 5 fathoms, sand. This is a snug and pleasant anchorage.

Duncanby Landing is on the south side of Rivers Inlet. Approach by passing SSE of Bull Island until clear of the southern extremity of Cow Island. This is a welcome stop-over at a friendly marina with fuel, water, showers, marine supplies, a restaurant and improved docking facilities. Anchorage may be taken on the west side of the island .8 mile west of the facilities. Information may be obtained by calling (250) 949-3583.

Penrose Island is located between the entrance to Rivers Inlet and Darby Channel adjoining Fitz Hugh Sound. Anchorages on the island are described on page 108.

Slingsby Channel leads east on the north side of Bramham Island, and Schooner Channel is northward on the east side; both lead to the **Nakwakto Rapids** and entry into complex sounds and inlets beyond. These Rapids have the highest tidal currents in British Columbia (16 kts. at springs).

SLINGSBY CHANNEL

Nakwato Rapids
v. strong currents

51° 05'N

To Cape
Caution

BRAMHAM IS.

Cougar
Inlet

04'

Morphy Rk.

McEwan Pt.

Miles Inlet

McEwan Rk.

Skull Cove

Schooner Channel

Allison Hbr.

03'

Queen

ruins

City Pt.

02'

Charlotte

Major It.

Murray
Labyrinth

Strait

Eliza Is.

Emily
Group

ANCHS. ON N SIDE OF

From Port Hardy

QUEEN CHARLOTTE STRAIT

127°40'W

127°30'W

0   1   2   3 n.m.

Approx. Scale   n. m.

Lagoon – access by
dinghy only

Not to be used for navigation

Shallows
dries 13 feet
overfalls

Chart 3550, 3605

3

McEwan Pt.

4

N

W'ly. winds affect
entrance

From McEwen Rk

QUEEN
CHARLOTTE
STRAIT

DETAIL

Bramham Pt.

MILES INLET

1000'   0   ½   1 m.

Approx. Scale   n. m. & ft.

PENROSE ISLAND MARINE PARK and DAWSONS LANDING

At the southern end of Fitz Hugh Sound is Calvert Island on the west and numerous islands, islets, rocks and reefs on the east, the largest being Penrose Island. It provides several anchorages, the most useful one for cruisers being **Fury Cove** on the west coast. This is an ideal departure point to use when southbound for it is easy to exit and conveniently close Queen Charlotte sound. It is best to make your first entry to the cove during settled weather, for the intricate entry can be quite intimidating when seas are breaking on the many offlying rocks and reefs lining the western edge of the archipelago. The identification of Rouse Reef is of prime importance, for .75 mile to the southeast of it the opening through Schooner Retreat to Exposed Anchorage becomes evident. The many treed islets merging one with the other seem to be confusing, but the entrance is clear and once within Exposed Anchorage a turn to the only narrow opening to the northwest leads into the sanctuary of Fury Cove. Anchorage for many vessels can be taken in the bay in 3 to 5 fathoms, mud. In addition to being a protected anchorage the view to the west provides a sneak preview of sea conditions in Fitz Hugh Sound.

There are a multitude of dangerous rocks and shoals in Klaquaek Channel which separates Penrose Island from Walbran and Ripon Islands to the east. It is essential that the most recent edition of Chart 3934 is used. If the chart you are using has been published prior to August 12, 1998 you should make a note of two rocks reported in the immediate area by the Prince Rupert Notice to Mariners for that date at the following locations: 51°29.49'N and 127°42.1'W and at 51°29.51'N, 127°41.9'W.

Anchorage may be taken in **Frypan Bay** tucked into the center of the inner part of a cove in the south part of the bay. Another spot is in the center of the wider cove to the east, allowing for the shoals that restrict the useable space. The southern coves of **Big Frypan Bay** provide secure anchorage in 4 - 5 fathoms, mud.

East of Klaquaek Channel is a very popular anchorage in **Sunshine Bay**. Follow a mid-channel route in the narrow entrance, but favor the port side just before the channel turns eastward. Anchor in the center of the bay in 5 fathoms, mud. The next channel to the north leads to an unnamed basin with an islet in the middle. Pass to the east of the islet giving sufficient clearance to avoid a rock off its southeastern tip and another near the northeast end where a shoal extends in a northeasterly direction. Anchor northeast of the islet in 4 fathoms, sand. It is important to move slowly within these restricted areas in order to identify the location of rocks and shoals.

Moorage can be found on the floats in **Finn Bay** where divers congregate to explore the clear waters of the bay. A rock with a least depth of 2 m (6.5 ft.) is on the north side of the bay approximately .2 mile within the entrance. In southeasterly weather Finn Bay provides very good protection.

Dawsons Landing is about 12 miles up Rivers Inlet near the north end of Walbran Island. The store has a good selection of groceries and is a liquor outlet. Fuel, water and moorage are available. In days gone by this was once a very busy spot during the fishing season but reduction of the fishing fleet due to a lack of salmon has resulted in much less activity during the summer months.

PENROSE ISLAND

Chart 3934

O   ½   1

Approx. Scale n.m.

Not to be used for navigation

DARBY CHANNEL

Lone Is.

Bosquet Pt.

Finn Bay

Finn Lake

Frypan Bay

Fury Cove

Rouse Reef

Exposed Anchorage

Big Frypan Bay

KLAQUAEK CHANNEL

Rouse Point

Fury Is.

Penrose Island Marine Park

Sunshine Bay

Schooner Retreat

FITZ HUGH SOUND

Marine Park Boundary

Ironside Is.

Frigate Bay

Joachim Is.

Safe Entrance

N

Dimsey Pt.

Barry Rock

RIVERS INLET

SAFETY COVE, FIFER BAY and GREEN ISLAND ANCHORAGE

Calvert Island shelters the entrance of Fitz Hugh Sound off Queen Charlotte Sound. The triangular profile of highest mountains of the Cape Range (602 m/1,975 ft.) can be seen from a considerable distance. Cape Calvert is the SE extremity of Calvert Island, but it is not an obvious landmark. Clark Point, slightly northeast has a light and is more noticeable. The shore, with the bulk of Entry Cone above the point, is steep and hides any indication of the indentation of the cove, which lies about 6 miles to the north. Calvert Island is a welcome sight after passing Cape Caution and there are several anchorages where you can recuperate after a long day's run. Details for Penrose Island anchorages are on the previous page.

THE HEAD OF SAFETY COVE

Safety Cove penetrates almost a mile into Calvert Island and is about .3 miles wide. Two islets lie off the northern point, but are not particularly noticeable on an approach from the south. The cove's wide entrance makes it easy to identify. It is deep throughout, but shoals quickly at the head where an extensive mud and sand bank dries for almost 300 m (1,000 feet) from shore. Anchorage can be taken anywhere in the middle of the cove in 10 to 12 fathoms, mud. There is usually a breeze in the cove which can become gusty if a gale is blowing on the ocean side, but the anchorage is secure. This anchorage is popular with large craft and fishing vessels. The coast adjacent to the entrance points are productive areas to troll for salmon.

APPROACHING SAFETY COVE FROM SSE, nearing the entrance

About four miles to the north the forested islands of Blair and Addenbroke jut into Fitz Hugh Sound. There are two beautiful anchorages in the vicinity and a night spent at either one is very pleasant. **Fifer Bay** is a large irregularly shaped indentation in the middle of the western shore of Blair Island. It provides excellent protection from all winds for a limited number of vessels. When entering, care is needed to avoid the reef extending off the north end of the entrance islet and the rock slightly to the northeast. The passage to south end of the bay appears narrow but anchorage within is beautiful and secure.

A mile north of Fifer Bay is the more spacious well protected anchorage at **Green Island**. Entry can be made from the south by proceeding north of Fifer Bay through a narrow channel separating Blair Island from an unnamed island east of Sweeper Island. Fishing is usually productive in this passage. Many vessels can anchor with good protection in the outer and inner bays in 4 to 6 fathoms, good holding mud. Interesting trips can be taken in the dinghy exploring the varied coastline of the island's shores. The mound of clam shell fragments mark a midden.

FIFER BAY & GREEN IS. ANCH.

Approx. Scale n.m.

0   1200'   ½   1   1½ n.m.

Green Island Anchorage

foul

foul

SOUVENIR PASSAGE

SALVAGE ISLAND

FAIRMILE PASSAGE

51°38'

CORVETTE ISLANDS
shoal

PATROL PASSAGE

ADDENBROKE ISLAND
F.G.25m

51°36'

BLACK ISLAND

FIFER BAY

127°30'

N

Not to be used for navigation

Chart 3727, 3744, 3934

CALVERT ISLAND

Safety Mtn

South Passage

Bay Pt.   Clerk Pt. behind   Entry Cone   South Pt.   Safety Pt.

APPROACHING SAFETY COVE FROM N. distant about 1 mile.

51°32'N

North Pt.

Safety Pt.

Good fishing

127°56'W

Forested hillside

House with a galvanized roof visible behind trees.

Stony Beach

Shoal

Low col and hill behind

Rough road in a cutting into its bank

12½   10   15   17   soft

FITZ HUGH SOUND

Good Fishing

Forested hillside

South Pt.

N

SAFETY COVE
CALVERT ISLAND

Approx. Scale n.m. & feet

1000'   ¼   ½ m.

Not to be used for navigation

CALVERT ISLAND

Safety Mtn 2550'

Cape Calvert   Grief Bay   Clerk Pt. (Light)   Entry Cone 185'

Low out towards open ocean

Fitz Hugh Sound

To Safety Cove

APPROACHING CALVERT ISLAND FROM S. distance about 4 miles.

PRUTH BAY and GOLDSTREAM HARBOUR

These anchorages are within Hakai Recreation Area and are a short day's travel from anchorages just described. Each has its own attraction and is well worth visiting. Kwakshua Channel lies between Calvert Island and Hecate Island to the north. The entrance off Fitz Hugh Sound is about 7 miles north of Safety Cove. The channel is about 5 miles long with remarkably parallel, steep-to sides. At the eastern end it divides into several fingers, while the main Kwakshua Channel turns sharply northward in a right-angled turn.

Keith Anchorage lies on the south side, opposite Whittaker Point at the turn of the channel. Telus (the province-wide telephone company) microwave towers stand atop the low summit, and a small house and dock lie at the head of the bay. Anchorage can be taken here although winds may blow down the channel through the low passes.

Pruth Bay lies at the western end of Kwakshua Channel where it divides into three fingers. Anchorage in about 6 to 7 fathoms is best towards the head of the center finger, off the long pier and walkway of the Hakai Beach Resort. The unobtrusive buildings of the resort are tucked behind a screen of trees. A trail leads from the beach across the neck of land to a lovely sandy beach on the Pacific side of the island. A fantastic mask is carved into a cedar tree just off the trail.

Anchorage can also be taken .5 mile north of Whittaker Point. The south part of the cove is deep and shoals rapidly at the eastern side. Two small islands (separated by a drying rock) mark the northern part of the cove. Pass on either side of the rock to enter the northern section for anchorage. There is sufficient space for two or three boats, sand bottom.

Proceeding north in Kwakshua Channel, Meay Islets and the surrounding reef and shoals constrict the channel, which is otherwise clear. At the northern end you may choose to go to the west to use **Adams Harbour**, a snug spot though not recommended during strong westerlies, or turn northeast to pass through the narrow channel between Rattenbury Island and Hecate Island. In both cases, use the chart as a guide, generally favoring the Rattenbury Island side. Eagles nest alongside the channel on Rattenbury Island. Upon leaving Kwakshua Channel you enter Hakai Passage where the effect of the open sea is felt.

Goldstream Harbour, at the northern tip of Hecate Island, is on the south side of Hakai Passage as it joins Fitz Hugh Sound. An unnamed island lies off the tip to form the harbor, which is entered from the east. Midway into the harbor the channel is narrowed by Evening Rock (a drying reef) in mid-channel, and Hat Island which lies off the Hecate Island shore. Pass between to enter the basin where good anchorage can be taken in 7 to 12 fathoms, sand and mud.

The best nearby anchorage on the east shore of Fitz Hugh Sound is **Kwakume Inlet,** ESE of Goldstream Harbour. Give clearance to a rock awash about .1 mile west of the entrance. The narrow entrance is between a heavily treed islet on the north side of the north opening and two smaller islets topped with 4 or 5 trees to the south. The S opening is foul and should not be used. The actual entrance is easily lost in the background trees but when one is directly in front of it, it becomes obvious. Anchor in the south part of the bay in 3 - 4 fathoms, mud. Fishermen often raft together in the northern part where a rock awash at 1.6 m (5.5ft.) is half way between the southeast tip of the islet and the shore. **Koeye River Anchorage**, 5 miles to the north is strongly affected by west winds funneling down Hakai Passage and can be quite a rolly and uncomfortable spot.

Chart 3727, 3784

N°

HAKAI PASSAGE

To Namu

128°00'W

51°44'N

Fl.

Kelpie Pt.
reefs
Umme Pt.

No entrance

20

HECATE Is.

Hat Is.

Evening Rk. (dries)

Detail – Goldstream Hbr.

1000'   0   ¼   ½ m

Approx. Scale – feet & n.m.

NOTE:– This smaller anchorage
is shown in a larger scale;
twice as large as that below.

42'

Mainguy Rk.

Port Reef

Fl. 6s

Odlum Is

Donald
Is

Rattenbury Is.

Eaglenest

Boas It

Adams
Hbr.

Choked Passage

41'

Meay It

Drying reef

A good small
anchorage
Float Camp

CALVERT & HECATE IS.

ANCHORAGES

2000'   0   ½   1 m

Approx. Scale feet & n.m.

51°40'N

Whitaker Pt.   HECATE   ISLAND

Steep rock walls

KWAKSHUA   CHANNEL

From Fitz Hugh
Sound

Hakai Resort

Pruth Bay

39'

Path across
to ocean
side (Mask)

Keith
Anch.

CALVERT   ISLAND

House
& dock

⊙ Microwave Twr.

0|8'   0|7'   0|6'   128 05'   0|4'   0|3'   0|2'   0|1'

Telus Microwave
Tower

Calvert Is.

Houses at end of bay

House & dock

Keith Anch.

Pruth Bay Anch.

APPROACHING PRUTH BAY ANCHORAGE FROM KWAKSHUA CHANNEL

NAMU

Namu is in Whirlwind Bay on the east shore of Fitz Hugh Sound. For many years, when fishing was a major economic resource in B.C. waters, this small community was very active. Now, the ruins are a stark reminder of a vibrant natural resource that was mismanaged and abused.

The rotting remains of cannery buildings and various workshops are visible when entering the bay through either Morehouse or Cloverleaf Passes on either side of Kiwash Island. Several owners have had proposals to rejuvenate the facilities but their plans have not materialized.

When approaching the facilities the vessel passes south of a small red buoy marking Loo Rock, about 90 m (300 feet) NNW of an open cove where a small float is located. At the present time limited moorage is provided and fuel is sometimes available at a floating dock around the corner. Many buildings in reasonable condition are scattered about and a caretaker lives in one of the houses on the hill. A trail beyond the houses provides a pleasant, but sometimes muddy walk.

Whirlwind Bay is not a good anchorage, for it suffers from willi-waws and is too deep. Neither Rock Inlet nor Harlequin Basin nearby offer anchorage. Anchorage can be taken in **Fougner Bay** in Burke Channel, just 3 miles north. There are many islets and rocks but the chart can be used to guide an entry to find protected anchorage.

Burke Channel leads northeasterly to the coastal town of Bella Coola, about 50 miles distant. If the weather is good this can be a very attractive trip, as the channel lies between high peaks which increase in height towards the head of the channel. **Eucott Bay**, three miles northeast of Fougner Point, provides good anchorage in 2.4 to 3.7m (8 to 12 ft.). Nearby is Eucott Hot Springs, and a float on the east shore marks the location of a fresh water pipe.

In Dean Channel **Sir Alexander MacKenzie Park** is northeast of Elcho Point. A monument commemorates MacKenzie's historic trip overland as the first European to reach the North Pacific Ocean in July, 1793. Nearby is the rock in which he made a lasting inscription, "Alex MacKenzie from Canada by land 22nd July 1793." This epic journey was completed twelve years before the expedition led by Lewis and Clark reached the mouth of the Columbia River in November, 1805.

The Inside Passage proceeds north through Fitz Hugh Sound into Fisher Channel, past Fog Rocks, across to Pointer Island and into Lama Passage. An excellent all-weather anchorage at **Codville Lagoon** can be entered off the east coast of Fitz Hugh Sound opposite the entrance to Lama Passage. Enter from Fisher Channel taking care to avoid reefs to starboard in the inner part of Lagoon Bay (a circular bight leading to the narrow entrance channel). When transiting the entrance channel, favor the south side to avoid the mid-channel rock, covered 1 fathom, located in the narrowest part. Onshore, a 30-minute hike leads to Sagar Lake where warm water swimming and a spectacular red sand beach can be enjoyed.

An interesting side trip is to proceed north in Fisher Channel then follow Cousins Inlet branching to the west ending at **Ocean Falls**. This pulp-producing company town was active until 1980 when the supply of cheap logs ran out, the operation terminated and Ocean Falls became a ghost town. A pretty retirement community has grown in the wide valley seen before the dam comes into view. Unfortunately a massive aquaculture farm (raising smolt to feed farmed salmon) has taken over much of the bay and has degraded this once attractive area though the dam constructed for power production still creates an impressive backdrop. Moorage is available on a long dock on the north side of the inlet. Take a walk through the town's remains or a mile to the west where a bar and grocery store overlook the inlet. The high annual rainfall in the area is legendary.

55'

Chart 3784, 3785

BURKE CHANNEL

FISHER CHANNEL

Fougner Bay

Dries

Dries

dries

7

10

9

8

6

5

2

2½

3

3

2

N

Edmund Pt.

54'

Not to be used for navigation

NAMU

FITZ HUGH SOUND

0   ½   1m

Approx. Scale n.m.

Harlequin Basin

△475

53'

To Lama Passage

Que Que Rks.

Rock Inlet.

△500

Cliff Is.   Dries

Dries

50'

Loo Rk.
Buoy R.

Cloverleaf Passage

51° 52'N

Sunday Is.

Kiwash Is.

Whirlwind Bay

Log Rk.

Fl.

Namu Harbour

FITZ HUGH
SOUND

Namu

See detail

Clam Is.

Morehouse Passage

Abandnd.
Cannery

Houses

Incinerator
(garbage disp.)

Boardwalk

Radio

Machine Shop

Office

To Safety Cove

Store

B.C. Packers

Fuel
(at times)

Lapwing Is.

Imp. Oil float

Empty Buildings Except
For Caretaker's House →

54'   51'

53'

127° 52'W

51'

Detail - Namu

0   500'   1000'

Approx. Scale - feet

BELLA BELLA and SHEARWATER

Lama Passage leads westward between Hunter Island and Denny Island for about 7 miles, then turns northward. There are some coves on the south shore in Cooper Inlet, just before the junction with Hunter Channel. There are many rocks in their entrances, but a small vessel can find a passage into **Lizzie Cove** or **Jane Cove** for a snug anchorage.

The narrowing channel of Lama Passage leads north past the ferry terminal at McLaughlin Bay to the small town of **New Bella Bella**. The fuel dock (open from 8 am to 5 pm sharp) is prominent on the waterfront. Care is needed when tying up, for metal projections on the docks can damage and mark a hull particularly when wash from passing vessels causes your boat to move. Limited, rolly moorage is available at the adjacent government dock. At the head of the pier is a liquor store, grocery/general store, hotel, bank and post office. A modern hospital is a couple of blocks to the south. Many fishing vessels moor at the public docks at the north end of town where the entrance is marked by a light. Rafting is necessary because it is usually crowded.

There is little activity at the old town of Bella Bella across Lama Passage. However, around the point and past Spirit Island there is the large bay of Kliktsoatli Harbor where the **Shearwater Marina** and **Fishermans Inn** are located. To enter, take a mid-channel course through Clayton Pass between Shearwater Island and Denny Island.

Moorage is available at the elongated dock, and beyond that a dilapidated floating wharf is used by local craft. Registration and payment for moorage is done at the cash register in the restaurant which overlooks the bay. A grocery store, laundromat and shower facilities are behind the restaurant. A marine supply store adjoins the slipway and workshops where boat repairs are done. A fuel dock is prominent on the little peninsula to the southeast behind which is a ferry dock. A scheduled Air BC service operates from the resort, as does a water taxi service to and from Bella Bella. A small public wharf is found in the little cove beyond the shipyard float, but most transient vessels moor at the resort or anchor in the bay.

Kakushdish Harbour is SE of Cypress Island and secure, quiet anchorage can be taken in 5 fathoms, mud. A shallow bar in the channel has a least depth of about 1.5 fathoms and beyond is a large bay bordered by shoals and swamps, home to millions of mosquitoes.

Lama Passage continues northward, passing between Campbell and Saunders Islands, the western of three channels, into Seaforth Channel. A buoy off the south point of Saunders Islands marks a shoal. The channel is about 300 m (1,000 feet) wide at its narrowest point, and the meeting of the tides seems to collect logs and debris here. The ferries and cruise ships in the Inside Passage use this pass, and at such times it can become crowded. Dryad Point Lighthouse on the northern point is an important reporting station. Once in Seaforth Channel the route turns northwest to pass Dall and Regatta Rocks before heading westward toward Ivory Island, Reid Passage, and Milbanke Sound.

Gunboat Passage continues east from Dryad Point and is a narrow and delightfully scenic route leading into Fisher Channel. This is the shortest route to Ocean Falls from Shearwater or Seaforth Channel. The route is well marked and careful attention to ranges and markers brings a vessel through in comfort.

REID PASSAGE and OLIVER COVE

As Captain Vancouver's survey teams once found, this little passage offers a route to dodge the seas and weather in Milbanke Sound and to take a protected route into the lower part of Mathieson Channel. The route proceeds northward to cross via Oscar Passage into Finlayson Channel, or north to Kynoch Inlet for a side-trip visit to Fiordland Recreational Area.

Seaforth Channel becomes wider and more open to the sea as you approach Ivory Island. A major reporting lighthouse is at the southwestern end of Ivory Island, on Robb Point. In strong northwesterlies choppy seas develop which come into Seaforth Channel. The outside route through Milbanke Sound into Finlayson Channel may be uncomfortable at such times. East of Ivory Island, in the rock-strewn area between it and Harmston and Watch Islands there is a passage (marked by a light and red buoy) leading up to Reid Passage.

There are many large and small drying rocks in Blair Inlet and Powell Anchorage, but most are visible, especially near low water. From the red buoy a course set directly to the entrance of Reid Passage passes comfortably clear of these scattered rocks.

Carne Rock, with a light on it, lies in the middle of the passage. A shoal lies about 300 m (1,000 feet) SSW of Carne Rock, so favor the east side to pass these dangers. The least depth in this passage is about 4 fathoms.

Oliver Cove is a Marine Park on the eastern side near the northern end of Reid Inlet. A reef projects some distance from the southern point and there rocks fringing the northern point where the Marine Park sign is set. A dangerous rock, covered about .5 fathom lies in the middle of the opening of the bay. Entry to the bay is clear in the northern third of the entrance and anchorage may be taken in 5 - 6 fathoms, good holding mud. Two small, treed islands block the northern section but good anchorage can be taken in the south side. The remains of two old log cabins can be seen in the trees behind, as well as the posts and beams of what was a barn. They lie on the ground as they were assembled, and second-growth trees grow up through them. The head of the cove shoals to grass-covered mud flats.

The north end of Reid Passage can be exited by passing near the southern tip of Leighton Island before setting a course towards the southern end of Martha Island in Perceval Narrows. This route should clear the intimidating and extensive field of Lizzie Rocks at the southern tip of Lake Island. A course can then be set up Perceval Narrows into the broad opening of Mathieson Channel. When southbound, the approach to the north end of Reid Passage must be carefully plotted, for the islands and islets are confusing in their similarity.

Even in fog a slow, careful passage could be made through this section unless conditions make it absolutely inadvisable to travel. Do not attempt Lady Trutch Passage which is blocked with rocks. Moss Passage and Oscar Passage are discussed in the next page.

In calm weather the shortest route from Seaforth Channel to Finlayson Channel is via Milbanke Sound. Courses should be laid to clear the dangers off the coast, passing to the east of Vancouver Rock, before standing up into Finlayson Channel. However, between Ivory Island and Klemtu only 7 miles are saved, so that whatever the weather one might prefer the more interesting route via Reid Passage and Mathieson Channel.

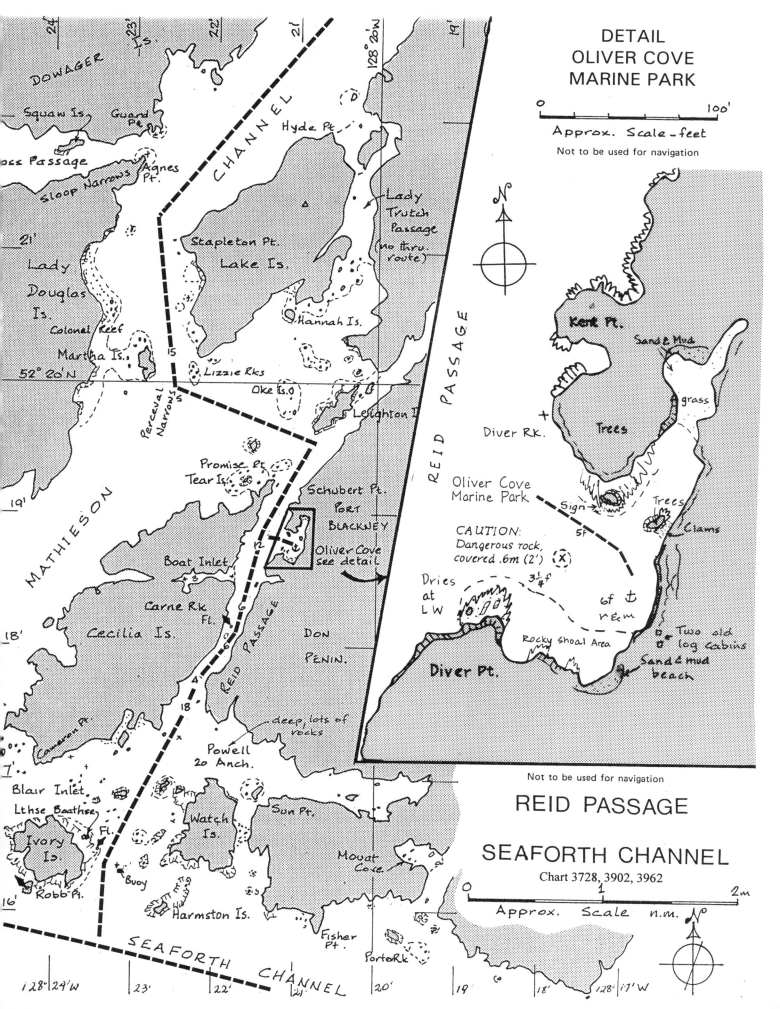

DETAIL
OLIVER COVE
MARINE PARK

0   100'

Approx. Scale – feet

Not to be used for navigation

DOWAGER

Squaw Is.   Guard Pt.

oss Passage

Sloop Narrows

Agnes Pt.

CHANNEL

Hyde Pt.

Lady Trutch Passage (no thru route)

21'

Lady Douglas Is.

Stapleton Pt. Lake Is.

Colonel Reef

Martha Is.

52° 20' N   15

Hannah Is.

Lizzie Rks

Oke Is.

Leighton I.

Perceval Narrows

Promise Pt.
Tear Is.

Schubert Pt.
PORT BLACKNEY

Oliver Cove see detail

19'

MATHIESON

Boat Inlet

3

Carne Rk. Ft.

Cecilia Is.

DON PENIN.

18'

4

6

REID PASSAGE

18

deep, lots of rocks

Powell 20 Anch.

7

Blair Inlet

Lthse Boathse

Ft.

Ivory Is.

Robb Pt.

Buoy

Watch Is.

Sun Pt.

Mouat Cove

Harmston Is.

Fisher Pt.

PortoRk

16'

SEAFORTH CHANNEL

i28° 24' W   23'   22'   21'   20'   19'   18'   128° 17' W

REID PASSAGE

Kent Pt.

Sand & Mud

grass

Diver Rk. +

Trees

Oliver Cove
Marine Park

Sign

5f

Trees

Clams

CAUTION:
Dangerous rock,
covered .6m (2')   (X)

Dries
at
LW

3¼f

6f

r & m

Rocky shoal Area

Two old
log cabins

Sand & mud
beach

Diver Pt.

Not to be used for navigation

REID PASSAGE

SEAFORTH CHANNEL

Chart 3728, 3902, 3962

0   1   2m

Approx.   Scale   n.m.

OSCAR PASSAGE and NEARBY ANCHORAGES

There are several routes which cross from Mathieson Channel to Finlayson Channel. Jackson Passage, separating Susan and Roderick Islands, is about .25 mile wide throughout and narrows even more at the eastern end where it passes through Jackson Narrows. Here it is barely 180 m (600 feet) wide and the channel has many rocks. While this passage offers much of interest, it is challenging and should be attempted only at or near high water slack. The eastern end of Jackson Narrows is a small undeveloped Marine Park.

Oscar Passage is the southern route, separating Dowager and Susan Islands. It is wide, deep, and free from dangers. Even when Finlayson Channel and part of Mathieson are foggy, Oscar Passage may be clear. The steep shores, particularly on the north side make the trip similar to transiting a canal.

There are two handy anchorages about 1.5 miles south of the eastern entrance of Oscar Passage. A cove with two lobes indents Dowager Island, and **Arthur Island** lies in front of them. The approach to the anchorages may be made on either side of Arthur Island, the southern channel being the wider of the two. At low tide the reefs that extend from the points near the eastern entrance reduce the width to about 60 m (200 ft.); as this entrance is deep (15 fathoms) a mid-channel course is satisfactory. The west cove is larger than the east cove, but a little more exposed to southerly winds blowing through the opening between Arthur and Dowager Islands. The head of the cove is shoal and dries; thus it should not be approached too closely. Anchor in 7 to 10 fathoms, stone and mud bottom. This cove can accommodate several boats.

The east cove is separated from the other by a short, rocky point. It is considerably narrower and smaller and is sheltered by the bulk of Arthur Island lying before it. There are rocky outcrops along each side—leaving is room for only one or two boats. The bottom is rock and mud and varies from 6 to 8 fathoms.

Tom Bay in the southern end of Mathieson Channel, extending south from Symonds Point, provides anchorage in 8 to 10 fathoms; some kelp is found. An anchorage across Mathieson Channel N of De Freitas Islets is **Salmon Bay** which is entered between Carmichael Point and Ursus Point. The head of the bay is shoal, so anchor well off in 10 fathoms, soft mud.

The best anchorage in the vicinity is immediately before the eastern entrance to Jackson Narrows, in **Rescue Bay**. Rocky islands and shoals limit the width at the entrance but a mid-channel course is free of dangers. Drying rocks and shoals line the bay, particularly its western shore, but good anchorage is available for many vessels in mid-bay. Watch for a drying rock about .1 mile from the head. This attractive spot provides excellent protection and is strategically located for a stop-over to break the passage of Mathieson Channel or when waiting for the proper time to pass through Jackson Narrows.

Moss Passage at the southern end of Dowager Island (and Mathieson Channel) is a narrow passage leading to Finlayson Sound. At its eastern end it contracts to only 90 m (300 feet) at Sloop Narrows, where tidal currents are strong. Pass well south of the drying rock south of Guard Point, and continue to stay south of Squaw Island in the Narrows. Though Moss Passage widens at its western end there are many rocks, islands and kelp patches to be avoided, and extra care is needed for safe passage. During foggy weather this passage is inadvisable.

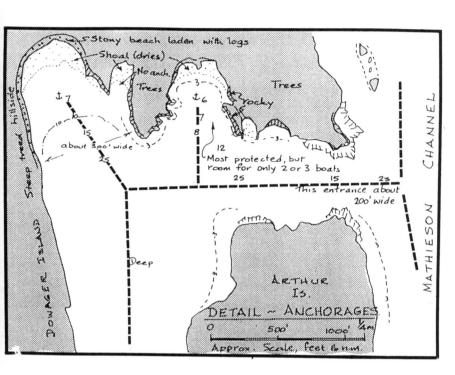

Snowy mountains behind

Point A   Arthur Is.

APPROACHING ARTHUR IS. ANCHORAGES FROM SE, distant abt. 1½ miles

Stony beach laden with logs
Shoal (dries)
No anch.
Trees   Trees
Rocky
⏚ 7
⏚ 6
10   3
15   7   8
about 300' wide   12
25   Most protected, but
                         room for only 2 or 3 boats
                         25   15   25

Deep

This entrance about 200' wide

Dowager Island
Steep hillside

hillside

MATHIESON CHANNEL

ARTHUR
Is.
DETAIL ~ ANCHORAGES

0   500'   1000'   ¼m
Approx. Scale, feet & n.m.

RODERICK ISLAND

128°17' W

MIALL ISLET
×

JACKSON NARROWS MARINE PARK

52°31' N
1'

SUSAN ISLAND

RESCUE BAY
⏚ × ×
4f

To Klemtu, &
Sarah or Jane
Passages

FINLAYSON CHANNEL

SUSAN Is.

Steep rocky slopes

OSCAR   PASSAGE

Brown rock wall

Bulley Bay

Legace Pt
③

DOWAGER   Is.

MATHIESON CHANNEL

Anchorages,
See detail
above

⏚
⏚

OSCAR PASSAGE &

ARTHUR IS. ANCH'S

Point A
in sketch

Arthur Is.

52°27.5'N

To Seaforth
Channel, via
Reid Passage

0   1   2   3 m

Approx. Scale n.m.

Not to be used for navigation

128°25'   24'   22'   20'   18'   128°16' W

KLEMTU

This pretty village lies behind aptly named Cone Island on the west side of Finlayson Channel. At the north end of Cone Island two important passages, Jane Passage and Sarah Passage, connect Finlayson with Tolmie Channel. In turn, Tolmie Channel runs north alongside Sarah Island to join Graham Reach and continue the Inside Passage. Note: a one–knot current in Tolmie Channel runs south during flood conditions, contrary to charted information. Finlayson and Tolmie Channels are also joined at the north end of Sarah Island by Hiekish Narrows, where the passage is clear except for Hewitt Rock. A shoal extending 300 m (1,000 ft.) from the rock is marked by a light at its southeastern end. Transit of Heikish Narrows within an hour or two of slack water is trouble-free even for low-powered vessels.

Klemtu is well placed as a stop along the Inside Passage. The village is in Trout Bay, on the west side of Klemtu Passage about one mile south of the northern end of Cone Island. There is easy access to fuel and water on the dock adjacent to the ferry terminal at the northern edge of the village. If the fuel dock manager is not around he can be called on CB Ch 14, call sign 44. Two stores selling groceries, fishing gear and general goods serve the community. Near the ferry dock is the Kitasoo Band Store and coffee shop. Open six days a week the store also offers banking services. On the south side of the bay is another store, open all week, 9 to 5 and 6:30 to 10 p.m.

There is a government dock and a seaplane landing float at the middle of the cove in the western shore. This dock is usually filled with local fishboats and rafting is necessary if you want temporary moorage. The dock in the southern part of the cove is used by local fishermen for repairing their nets; this area is shoal. While shopping, you can sometimes tie for a short period at the end of the fuel dock.

Anchorage within Trout Bay is not recommended because of the shoals and regular traffic. Anchorage can be found in the middle part of **Clothes Bay**. Anchor off the passage behind the drying rocks in about 5 fathoms. Wash from channel traffic discourages anchorage in Trout Bay.

Fog rolls up Finlayson Channel and into Klemtu Passage, most often in the summer and fall though sometimes in the spring. Klemtu Passage is narrow but deep. Both Jane and Sarah Passage have hazards that limit their width, but are otherwise deep and free of problems. On the north (inside) point of Sarah Passage is Boat Bluff crowned by an attractive and photogenic lighthouse. Further up Tolmie Channel where it passes Split Head at the top of Swindle Island is a well marked passage, just past a mid-channel shoal called Parry Patch. By slightly favoring either shore the patch is easily passed and weak tidal swirls cause no difficulty.

There are three anchorages in the area on the east side of Finlayson Channel. **Nowish Cove** is about 5.5 miles SE of Klemtu. Enter from north of Nowish Island and use plenty of scope as the water is deep (10 -15 fathoms) and an eddy current is evident. **Mary Cove** is about 5 miles north of Nowish Cove. Anchor in 10 fathoms at the head of the basin. The best is **Bottleneck Inlet,** 1.2 miles north of Howay Point. The 90m (300 ft.) wide entrance is difficult to identify until you are close to it and the channel has a least depth of 3 m (10 ft.). The elongated channel leads to a wider part followed by the basin at the head of the bay, where anchorage can be taken anywhere. This secluded and peaceful hideaway is the epitome of a perfect all-weather anchorage: calm, beautiful and large enough to hold many vessels. **Work Bay,** located on the west side of Finlayson Channel west of Adze Point, provides good anchorage in the northeastern end of the bay in 7 fathoms. **Cougar Bay,** 10 miles north, on the west side of Tolmie Channel, has a poor reputation for dragging but you could try the small cove on the east side of the bay in 10 fathoms.

APPROACHING KLEMTU FROM NNW i.e. down Tolmie Channel

KLEMTU — FINLAYSON CHANNEL

Not to be used for navigation
Chart 3711, 3734

SECTION 4 - Klemtu to Prince Rupert

Green Inlet is the site of a Marine Park on the east side of Graham Reach across from Princess Royal Island. Located 1.5 miles NNE of Quarry Point, the entrance is north of Netherby Point. Snug anchorage can be taken in **Horsefly Cove** on the north side of the inlet, .6 mile inside the entrance. A stern line to trees or snags on shore assists holding since secure anchorage using only one anchor can be difficult to obtain. A small section in the middle of the cove with depths of about 5 fathoms is surrounded by much deeper water, making the use of a stern line to the overhanging trees with the anchor set in about 8 – 9 fathoms, mud. Another spot where anchorage may be taken is reported to be off the green flats on the south side of the entrance channel.

This is a well-named cove for the size, voracious appetite and number of horseflies and deer flies in this spot are beyond description. Four miles within the entrance is Baffle Point where tidal rapids make exploration of the tidal lagoon possible by dinghy at high water slack. .

The most used anchorage in the area is at **Swanson Bay,** a wide bight on the east side of Graham Reach north of Green Inlet. A rather narrow shelf off the southeast side of the bay provides tolerable anchorage in 3 to 4 fathoms with limited swinging. Watch the state of the tide and check for sunken logs which line parts of the shore. The best spot is in the northern part of the bay slightly west of a blunt knob jutting into the bay. Avoid the large sand and grass shoal off the beach. An interesting walk can be taken around the ruins of a sawmill and pulp mill where a tall brick smokestack is almost hidden by the surrounding forest.

* * * * *

Vessels proceeding to the Queen Charlotte Islands often follow the route described until Grenville Channel branches off to the north in Wright Sound. By continuing west until passing through Otter Passage they then turn north in Principe Channel and proceed until reaching the north end of Banks Island. The winds accelerate here and often make entrance to Larsen Harbour exciting while you thread your way through heavy kelp patches until passing through the entrance. Although buoys in the windy harbor are often occupied by fishing vessels there is still plenty of room for anchoring. The shortest distance from the B.C. coast to the Queen Charlotte Islands is between Larsen Harbour and Lawn Point. This makes Larsen Harbour a favorite departure point. In addition, its location provides a favorable slant to northwesterly winds for sailing vessels making the passage.

Orca (Killer Whale)

Looking down Fraser Reach towards Butedale

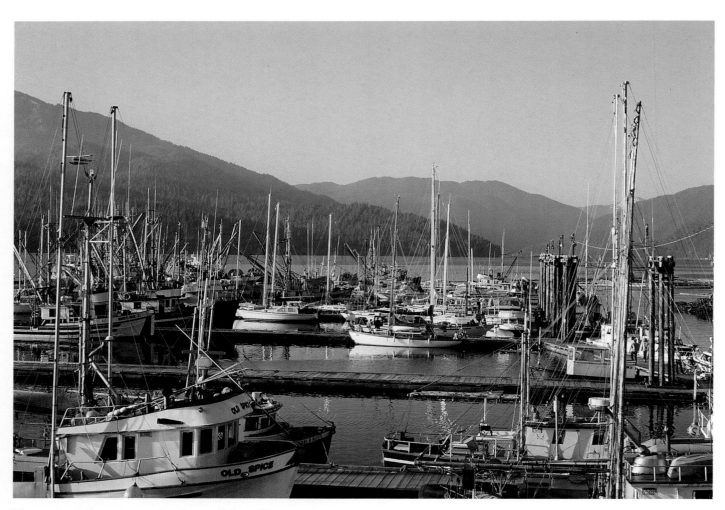

Pleasure craft are in a minority at Prince Rupert

FIORDLAND RECREATIONAL AREA

An alternative route to traveling from Mathieson Channel to Finlayson Channel via Oscar Passage, Jackson Passage, or Moss Passage, is one which proceeds northward in Mathieson Channel. After exiting at Mathieson Narrows the route continues west in Sheep Passage until reaching the upper end of Finlayson Channel where Hiekish Narrows leads to the junction of Tolmie Channel and Graham Reach in Princess Royal Channel.

By proceeding north in Mathieson Channel until reaching the junction with Kynock Inlet you can visit **Fiordland Recreational Area**. This huge park covers 225,000 acres, encompassing the land surrounding all of Kynock and Mussel Inlets, land bordering part of the northern end of Mathieson Channel and part of Pooley Island. It is well named for the steep, precipitous granite cliffs rising more than 1,000 m (3,200 feet) are as spectacular as any found in the world. The sheer mountain faces are laced with waterfalls, particularly following a shower, making this one of the most beautiful areas on the B.C. coast. McAlpin and Lizette Falls in Mussel Inlet are worth seeing.

The most spectacular part of this park is **Kynock Inlet,** an 8.5-mile long inlet which joins Mathieson Channel about 15 miles north of the junction of Jackson Passage. It is entered between Kynoch Point on the south, and Garvey Point on the north. About 1.5 miles north of Garvey Point is a conspicuous waterfall followed by Desbrisay Bay (Big Bay) which is too deep for anchoring. Clouds and rain often obscure the scenery but if you can outlast the weather it is indeed worth the wait. Though it can be breezy, the only anchorage is clear of the drying flat and shoals extending from the head of the inlet. Anchor in 6 to 8 fathoms, sand, after checking that the vessel is well clear of the extensive shoals.

The eastern end of the inlet terminates in Culpepper Lagoon which can only be entered at slack high water. This is a fascinating spot to explore by dinghy though some venturesome sailors enter at high water slack and anchor just inside the lagoon or further up in 10 to 15 fathoms off the large shoal which extends from the head of the bay.

Two other anchorages found in adjacent waters are:

Windy Bay is located in the southeastern curve of Sheep Passage. The entrance is to the west of the treed islet near the east entrance point. Foul, rocky ground separates the islet from the shore. The best all-weather anchorage is off the steep-to drying flat about .3 mile from the head of the bay in 10 12 fathoms. This bay is well named for when southeasterly winds blow in Mathieson Channel the Venturi effect accelerates the winds as they pass through the low part of the mountains south of the bay, resulting in gusty blasts which sweep the bay and create a considerable chop.

During settled weather anchorage can be taken southeast of the islet in 6 to 8 fathoms, mud. This location provides a ring-side seat for viewing the antics of a congregation of seals living in the vicinity. As the tide falls, a large flat rock provides a hauling-out and rest area where the largest bulls preempt the best spot before it is even visible. As the tide falls and more of the rock is above the waterline, the rest of the herd congregate until 30 or more pile on, arguing and growling until the tide rises, their rock gradually submerges and they slide into the water to fish for the next meal.

Bolin Bay is 3 miles north of Windy Bay and is almost due west of Mathieson Narrows. With good protection in all but easterly winds, this little niche is tucked below towering mountains. Shoals at the head of the bay shelve rapidly; anchor in 10 - 12 fathoms, mud.

FIORDLAND RECREATIONAL AREA

0   5   10

Approx. Scale n.m.

Not to be used for navigation

Chart 3962

KHUTZE INLET and BUTEDALE

The entrance to Khutze Inlet (on the east shore of Graham Reach) is almost 13 miles north of Hiekish Narrows. The mile-wide entrance to the inlet is between Griffin Point on the south and Asher Point on the north. Steep, sometimes precipitous, mountains surround the inlet except for Khutze River mud flats which are over a mile long and block the half-mile wide head of the inlet. When entering the inlet favor the north shore to pass Green Spit, which extends from the southern shore and leaves a clear passage (about 300 m/1,000 ft.) wide about 1.5 miles east of Asher Point. Anchorage east of the inner end of the spit may be taken in about 6 - 8 fathoms, good holding mud. Fishing is productive near the spit.

By proceeding 3.5 miles past the end of the spit and favoring the southern shore you pass Pardoe Point to arrive at an anchorage area near a spectacular waterfall. Anchor close to shore west of the waterfall in 6 - 8 fathoms, sticky mud. Very shallow shoals off the waterfall drop off quickly and must be given plenty of clearance to avoid grounding when the tide falls or tidal currents cause the vessel to swing. If you anchor at high tide the nearest land to the east is over a mile distant and it is easy to assume you have plenty of swinging space, but when the tide falls the heavy odor of rich clam mud tells you the soft shoals are <u>very</u> close at hand. The calls of waterfowl and the constant sound of the lovely waterfall make this an unforgettable spot.

Graham Reach continues about 5 miles to the north before joining Butedale Passage at Redcliff Point, marked by a light. Two miles west of the Point at the south end of Fraser Reach is a bight. **Butedale*** is at the head of the bight and north of the buildings is a spectacular waterfall. Here, torrents of water tumble down even in late summer when many of the other falls have almost dried up. The docks and buildings are in ruins and the entire area is a shambles. Although several people have proposed developing this prime location it continues to deteriorate with only a watchman to oversee the dilapidated remains. A path leads to a large lake where fishing is good, but the mosquitoes are ravenous. An Indian summer village was located here long before the arrival of Europeans when it became a busy fish cannery and then a popular stop for vessels traveling the inside Passage. Now, it is a reminder of the vagaries of time.

When winds are light or from the southeast, passable anchorage may be taken on the narrow shelf midway into the bay, though it is open to wash from ferries and cruise ships rushing up and down the channel and there is risk that the anchor could foul on logging debris. Some vessels tie between the rotting pilings at the south end of the bay. In the southeast corner is an unstable log dock where one or two boats may tie if permission is obtained from the caretaker.

In the spring the waterfalls along Graham and Fraser Reaches are among the most appealing attractions of travel along the Inside Passage. They appear in all shapes and sizes from single large falls to tiny threads and multiple cascades. Fraser Reach has the better of Graham Reach in the variety and beauty of its waterfalls.

*Butedale is on Princess Royal Island, one of the few areas inhabited by the rare Spirit or Kermode Bear but without regard for this endangered species the Provincial government has given permission to Interfor Corp. to log the island. International pressure is mounting to declare the Island a protected area.

APPROACHING BUTEDALE FROM 128 WNW, i.e. down Fraser Reach

KHUTZE INLET & BUTEDALE

Approx. Scale n.m.
0 1 2 3 4 5

Not to be used for navigation

Chart 3739

Work Is.
Butedale
Butedale Passage
Butedale Falls
Redcliff Pt.
53°10'

128°42'W

Princess Royal Island

GRAHAM REACH

Aaltanhash Inlet

Asher Pt.
Green Spit
Khutze Inlet
Baudre Pt. — Waterfall
53°05'
Canoona B.
Griffen Pt.

128°35'   128°30'   128°25'

FRASER REACH

Butedale Passage

N

53°10'N

GRAHAM REACH

Not to be used for navigation

BUTEDALE
Prominent Falls

Butedale Lake

Walk
Ruins

Woodstave penstock (leaking)

10
3
Ruins

Detail – Butedale

Approx. Scale n.m. & feet
1000'   0   ¼   ½ n.m.

Graham Reach   Butedale   Falls   Fraser Reach   Work Is.

APPROACHING BUTEDALE FROM ESE, i.e. up Graham Reach

COGHLAN ANCHORAGE and HARTLEY BAY

Coghlan Anchorage lies in the channel between Promise Island and the mainland at the southern entrance into Grenville Channel. Promise Island is dome-shaped with two peaks and stands out before the mountains in the background.

Enter the anchorage from the south, past Thom Point on Promise Island. Harbor Rock in the center of the passage is marked by a light. The anchorage lies beyond, on the shelf off a mud and stone beach, opposite Brodie Point. Holding is good on the shelf but exposed to the SE.

Opposite the anchorage are two buoys of white painted tires belonging to local fishermen who return to them nightly. The channel turns eastward around the top of Promise Island at Stewart Narrows. A short distance beyond is the Indian village of **Hartley Bay** where fuel, water and basic provisions are available. The fuel dock operates from 9 a.m. to 5 p.m., Monday to Friday but the friendly attendant often gives service outside of these hours. The first-aid post up the hill has a nurse in attendance. A heli-pad is located here and float plane service also serves the community. The friendly people of the village are very helpful and happy to share local information with cruisers. No liquor is sold in this 'dry' village.

Grenville Channel leads northwestward from Wright Sound to Arthur Passage where it opens into Chatham Sound, thence to Prince Rupert. The south entrance is at Sainty Point, where a light is located. A bay adjacent to the light has no anchorage, being deep close inshore. Grenville Channel appears dead ended, for it narrows and has a slight jog that gives this impression. This 45-mile long, almost straight, and narrow passage, with steep mountains on both sides is one of the most unique parts of the Inside Passage. The succession of steep points off the mountains receding into the distance tends to make the channel look even narrower; huge cruise ships dwarfed by the landscape give perspective to the scene.

Several inlets indent the east side of Grenville Channel and anchorage can be found in Lowe, Klewnuggit, Baker, and Kumealon Inlets. Waterfalls are not as numerous as along Fraser Reach.

Lowe Inlet, a Marine Park about 14.5 miles from Sainty Point, is the first anchorage available when traveling from the south. The entrance is between James Point and Hepburn Point. A light on a small island in Grenville Channel is located about .25 mile NW of James Point. A short distance after turning into the inlet there is a 6-fathom bank on the south side between Hepburn and Don Points on which a vessel may anchor. The channel then narrows to .25 mile and the inlet extends for about 1.75 miles towards the northeast.

A prettier anchorage is at the far end of Lowe Inlet in **Nettle Basin**. It is reached by passing through the narrows between the peninsula of Pike Point and Mark Bluff. Anchor behind Pike Point on the southern side of spectacular Verney Falls in about 12 - 15 fathoms. Some current is felt from the falls so extra scope should be allowed. Salmon jump the falls in season and a trail on the north side of the falls provides a nice hike to another waterfall.

Tides enter both ends of Grenville Channel, meeting at about Evening Point. In the narrow sections of the channel the current is evident to low powered vessels (especially when there is a large tidal differential between high and low tide) so they find it advantageous to start through on the last of the flood and benefit from ebbing currents when the tide changes. Most well powered vessels proceed through at all stages of the tide since the influence of the current is generally negligible.

GRENVILLE CHANNEL FROM SOUTHERN ENTRANCE

COGHLAN ANCH.
HARTLEY BAY
GRENVILLE CHANNEL

0   ½   1   1½
Approx. Scale. n.m.

129° 16'W

18' 17' 15' 14' 13'

Store
Church
Halsey Pt.
Hartley Bay
Rock Breakwater
Boardwalk Sutton Pt. Fuel

Matsey Bay
Nessie Pt.

Dawson Pt.

Stephens Pt.
Stewart Narrows
Mud & Stone beach
Otter Shoal
Govt. Buoys
Letita Pt.
Coghlan Anchorage
6¾
3¾
Buoys
Brodie Pt.

Chart 3711, 3742

N

Harbok RK.
Fl. G
PROMISE
Mt. Brodie △

23'

Mt. White △
ISLAND

Mt. Frye
Mt. Smiles △

DOUGLAS CHANNEL

Fl.
Sainty Pt.

Thom Pt.
53° 22'N

Grenville Channel Entrance
c. Farewell

WRIGHT   SOUND

Not to be used for navigation

Coghlan Anch. behind island

Sainty Pt Light

Grenville Channel

Promise Is.

APPROACHING GRENVILLE CHANNEL FROM ESE, distance about 5 miles.

KITIMAT and the KITLOPE

This cruising area with its many anchorages, a large town for provisioning, good fishing and beautiful scenery can be a side-trip on your return from Alaska, or a destination in itself. It can be approached either by continuing north of Hartley Bay in Douglas Channel or by way of Ursula Channel. Weather forecasts for Douglas Channel cover this area.

The Inside Passage proceeds north in Fraser Reach to turn west in McKay Reach before transiting Wright Sound and then entering Grenville Channel. At the east end of McKay Reach a 10-mile side-trip north in Ursula Channel leads to the entrance to **Bishop Bay** where the first of several hotsprings in the area are located. Docking facilities are being expanded and are administered by a local Indian band. A walkway leads to refreshing hotsprings, where two basins are arranged for a choice of covered or outside bathing. Good anchorage in the bay is difficult to find though it is possible in 8 to 12 fathoms, poor holding sand and mud.

By following Ursula Channel to Verney Passage you can proceed north through Devastation Channel and then Douglas Channel to **Kitimat**. **Kitsaway Anchorage** is a beautiful anchorage off Devastation Channel west of Kitsaway Island. It provides excellent protection for many vessels in 2 - 3 fathoms, mud and shells. Crabs and clams are outnumbered only by horseflies and deer flies.

Continuing northward, **Weewanie Hotsprings** is about 6 miles distant on the east shore of the channel. Avoid the drying rock 18m (60 ft.) off the south point. Two buoys provide moorage and a ladder provides assistance in reaching the undeveloped hotsprings. Where Devastation Channel joins Douglas Channel there can be a marked increase in wind velocity if southerly winds are blowing. An excellent refuge from rough conditions can be found by anchoring at the head of **Eagle Bay** (southwest of Coste Island) in 6 - 8 fathoms. Though wind gusts can sweep through the gap at the head of the bay, the holding is good and the water is fairly calm.

The town of **Kitimat** has an economy centered on the huge Alcan Aluminum smelter. Moorage is available in three places. The small dock marked "Public" on the chart is usually filled with local fishboats, but you can raft up. A stop here is "a must" to visit the gallery of renowned Haisla carver and artist, Sammy Robinson, whose studio is near the head of the ramp. A short distance to the north is **MK Bay Marina**, a full-service marina with all the amenities. For slip assignment call (250) 632-6401. On the opposite side of the bay is friendly and rustic **Moon Bay Marina** which also has fuel, water and moorage. For information call (240) 632-4655. You can reach Kitimat by taxi, hitch-hiking or by bus; its a walk of about .5 miles to the bus stop.

Gardner Canal should be traveled during settled, sunny weather to view the spectacular colors in the rocky precipices, along with waterfalls and glimpses of glaciers. Unfortunately the views are marred in places by clear cuts. You must stop at Europa Hotsprings to enjoy their unique, natural setting. During stormy weather this trip should be avoided for gusty winds are magnified in the convoluted passages and the scenic mountains are hidden by clouds and fog. Since the Alcan Company town of Kemano has been terminated and the docks decommissioned, the anchorage outside the harbor remains the only choice for moorage in the area. By continuing to the end of Gardner Canal where the **Kitlope River** delta fans out for a considerable distance you reach the edge of a huge ecological reserve which is the largest temperate coastal watershed in the world. Check the depth sounder regularly, for shoals extend well off the mouth of the river and the cloudy water gives no indication of depth. Anchorage may be taken in **Chief Mathews Bay** where the Haisla Indians have constructed a longhouse.

KITIMAT and the KITLOPE

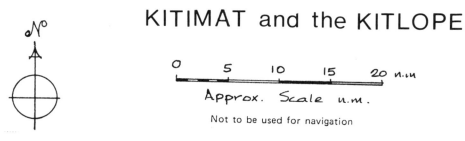

0   5   10   15   20 n.m.

Approx. Scale n.m.

Not to be used for navigation

Chart 3724, 3737, 3742,
3743, 3902

129° 00'   128° 00'

53°58'

Kitimat
Moon Bay → F MK Bay Marina
Marina   ▪Kitamaat

Jesse   Clio Bay
Falls   KILDALA ARM Landing
          ⚓-I   Alcan Caretakers
                    Eagle Bay

                    Weewanie Hotsprings
Maitland Is.

HAWKESBURY
ISLAND

Kitsaway
Anchorage

GRENVILLE CHANNEL
                              Bishop Bay
                              Hotsprings   Europa
                                                Hotsprings   Kemano Bay
Hartley   GARDNER CANAL
Bay F
                                                        Chief
Promise Is.   GRIBBELL IS.   Mathews
PITT IS.   Bay
                    VERNEY PASSAGE   Longhouse
                    URSULA CHANNEL
DOUGLAS CHANNEL
DEVASTATION CHANNEL

GIL
ISLAND
                    FRASER REACH   Kitlope
                                                         River

CAMPANIA IS.   Butedale
                                        Khutze Inlet
PRINCESS
ROYAL   Fish Ladder   GRAHAM REACH
ISLAND

KLEWNUGGIT INLET

This is a very beautiful anchorage, isolated and secure, but a long way in from Grenville Channel. Klewnuggit Inlet Marine Park includes East inlet, Brodie Lake, Freda Lake (lightly indicated on the sketch) and the surrounding land. It is well worth the effort to visit this area, for the scenery is magnificent.

When turning in to the wide entrance of the inlet give a safe clearance to Morning Reef, marked by a light. A partially drying, submerged reef runs between Evening Point and the light. Do not turn in until the inlet is well abeam and a route into the center of the inlet can be taken.

APPROACHING KLEWNUGGIT INLET FROM SE, up Grenville Ch.

A deep anchorage lies between Harriot Island and the long peninsula which projects southward into the Inlet. However, for small boats, better anchorage is around this peninsula in the northwestern inner bay of **East Inlet**. This spacious anchorage is seldom visited by more than one or two boats at a time. In this protected bay, surrounded by forested slopes and rocky peaks you are truly isolated from the outer world. Crabbing is excellent. The head of the bay is shoal.

Exposed Inlet, the southern portion of Klewnuggit is exposed to winds coming through gaps in the mountains, but during settled weather or southerly winds anchorage may be taken. Drying flats at the head of the bay lie off a large swamp.

ENTRANCE INTO KLEWNUGGIT INLET

Silas Pt.   Bare Pt.   Rogers Pt.   Morning Reef

APPROACH TO KLEWNUGGIT INLET FROM NW. distant abt. 4 miles.

KLEWNUGGIT INLET

GRENVILLE CHAN.

Dome Peak to N.

NW Inner Bay

Not to be used for navigation

129°45'W

0   ½   1m

Approx. Scale n.m.

Best anch. beautiful location!

9

rock

clear-cut logged patch (1984)

10

Silas Pt.

20

7

20

Dries

rocks

Dries

20

Harriot Is.

West Is.   SHIP ANCH.

EAST INLET

Bare Pt.

Drieso

Deep

Rogers Pt.

25

KLEWNUGGIT INLET

15

50

GRENVILLE

Morning Reef

Morning Pt.

Nabannah Bay

Inner Pt.
Do not cut too close to point

Brodie Lake

CHANNEL

Evening Pt

Exposed Inlet

53°40'N

Dome Peak at head of inlet

Exposed Inlet is shallow and extends SE abt 2 miles but is in a low gap open to winds.

Inner Pt.

LOOKING UP EAST INLET TOWARDS NW INNER BAY ENTRANCE

BAKER INLET and KUMEALON INLET

Baker Inlet, 10 miles further north on the eastern shore of Grenville Channel, provides anchorage at the eastern end. The entrance through Watts Narrows (60 m/ 200 feet wide) is deep but has strong currents; use Prince Rupert slack water times when entering. When traveling north the entrance is easy to miss in spite of the light on the south side of the entrance. A white house at Po-aae River on the west side of Grenville Channel indicates the location of the Narrows.

Three miles north of Baker Inlet, on the northeastern side of Grenville Channel is Kumealon Inlet. The 450 m (1,500-foot) wide entrance is between Lerwicke and McMurray Points. Give a safe clearance to foul ground located .2 mile offshore south of McMurray Point. There is a logging camp in the small bay beyond the entrance, with a small float in front¬depth unknown.

The main anchorage lies further up at the head of the inlet. Stay about 60 m (200 feet) off the north shore to pass the rocky patch extending into mid-channel from the southern shore. Beyond the rocky area the eastern end of the inlet forms a basin, where anchorage in 10 - 12 fathoms can be taken. At the north side of the basin a narrow, rock encumbered channel with tidal falls leads from Kumealon Lagoon. It cannot be entered except by dinghy at slack water.

A smaller but more convenient anchorage lies at the entrance, west of Lerwick Point. There is room for only two or three boats here.

ENTRANCE TO KUMEALON IS. ANCHORAGE

Chart 3773

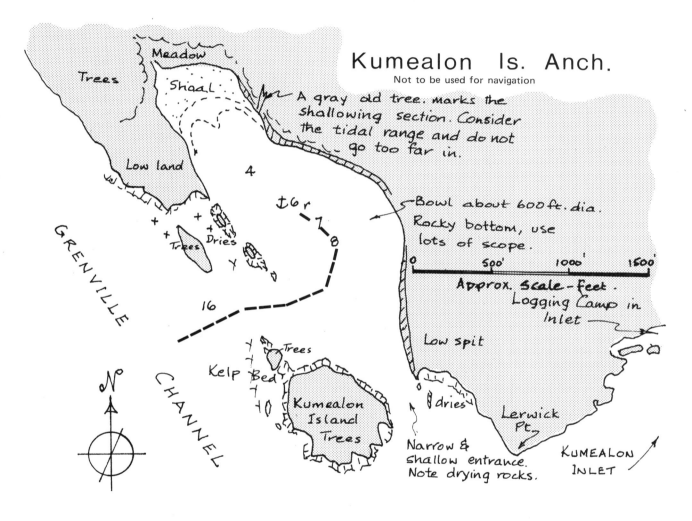

Kumealon Is. Anch.
Not to be used for navigation

Trees

Meadow

Shoal

Low land

A gray old tree. marks the shallowing section. Consider the tidal range and do not go too far in.

4

$\pm 6r$

7

8

Bowl about 600 ft. dia. Rocky bottom, use lots of scope.

|0 500' 1000' 1500'|

Approx. Scale-Feet.

Logging Camp in Inlet

16

Low spit

GRENVILLE CHANNEL

Trees

+ Dries

N

Trees

Kelp Bed

10

Kumealon Island Trees

dries

Lerwick Pt.

Narrow & shallow entrance. Note drying rocks.

KUMEALON INLET

Steep rock face

Anch. entr.

Kumealon Inlet

APPROACH TO KUMEALON INLET ANCHORAGE FROM W.

McMICKING ANCHORAGES

From the northern end of Grenville Channel the Inside Passage continues through Arthur Passage and Malacca Passage to Chatham Sound and the approaches to Prince Rupert. Anchorages in this area are the closest ones south of Prince Rupert and can be used as a resting place or to await reasonable weather and sea conditions for approaching the city.

McMicking, Elliott and Lewis Islands are on the western side of Arthur Passage. Chismore and Kelp Passages are narrower channels that separate the three islands on their western sides from the shore of Porcher Island. Kelp Passage is constricted with rock and shoal and should not be attempted.

Lawson Harbor lies in a bight on Lewis Island and is marked by a beach on the southern shore where some ruins remain. Avoid the rock off the north end of Break Island. By anchoring in the middle of the basin you should clear the rocks in the SE corner. The holding is good though there is exposure to the north and the effect of passing cruise ships is felt. For a more spacious anchorage continue through Bloxam Pass (currents of about 1 knot are normal) to enter the basin south of Cocktail Point.

Chismore Passage forms a basin south of Elliott Islands which provides good anchorage on the Lewis Island side. Approach this basin using a mid-channel course through Bloxam Passage, between Elliott and Lewis Islands. When northbound in Arthur Passage pass well clear of Herbert Reefs, which are marked by a concrete post and light.

Porcher Island Cannery, south of Ada Islands on the northeastern tip, and Hunt Inlet on the north side of Porcher Island can also be used as a refuge. Both have narrow entrances, with rocky ledges near the approaches.

The crossing of the southeastern part of Chatham Sound to Prince Rupert is well marked with lights and buoys on all rocks, shoals and islands. From Herbert Reefs the flashing green lit buoy off Cecil Patch can be passed on its east side; then the light on Genn Islands passed on its west. This clears the sand and shoal areas of the Skeena River entrances. The course from Genn Islands must clear the Horsey and Agnew Bank buoys south of Ridley Island. The coal terminal and grain elevator of the deep sea port (marked by strobe lights) are visible even in daylight, a sure sign that Prince Rupert is near.

APPROACHING PRINCE RUPERT FROM SE, i.e. from near Genn Is. Light

McMICKING IS. ANCH.

ARTHUR PASSAGE

0   1   2 n.m.

Approx. Scale n.m.

Not to be used for navigation

Chart 3717, 3927, 3909

Light Structure   Lewis Is.   Chismore Range   Porcher Is.   Elliot Is.

Herbert Reefs   Lawson Hbr.   Bloxam Pass

APPROACHING McMICKING ISLANDS ANCHORAGE FROM N

To Prince Rupert

Lamb Pt.   Bamfield Is.

20

Fl.G Cecil Patch

Hanmer Island   Fl.R

Elizabeth Rock

McMicking Is.

8

8

Chismore Passage

Chalmers Anch.

No entry

Elliot Is.

Bloxam Pass

Lawson Hbr.

3

Kennedy Island

12

Chismore Range

PORCHER ISLAND

8

10

A

Herbert Reefs

5

Lewis Is.

No entry

Kelp Passage

Henderson Pt.

To Grenville Channel

Porcher Is.   McMicking Is.

Lewis Is.   Elliot Is.

Cecil Patch Light

Genn Is.   Little Genn Is.   Hanmer Is.

To Prince Rupert

Light

Herbert Reefs   ARTHUR PASSAGE

APPROACHING McMICKING ISLANDS ANCHORAGE FROM SE

PORT EDWARD in PORPOISE CHANNEL

Until recently the facilities in Port Edward were available only to private vessels and fishboats but this facility now has moorage space available and welcomes transient cruising vessels. Port Edward is a convenient spot where cruisers can moor to get away from Prince Rupert which sometimes becomes overcrowded during July and August. This quiet little village is a convenient spot to stop, particularly if winds in Chatham Sound create beam seas which can make travel uncomfortable for the approach to Prince Rupert Harbour from the south. Similarly, when vessels are returning from Alaskan waters this provides a suitable spot to stop, since it reduces the following day's southbound travel exposed to beam seas. An early start the next morning can be done in relative comfort before westerly winds pick up in Brown Passage.

This harbor may be approached from the south or from the northwest. At low tide Flora Bank becomes evident as it dries, and with any wind, breakers mark Agnew Bank and other shoal waters. From the south you will find the turn into the Porpoise Channel fairway marked by Agnew Bank light and bell buoy "D24." The Porpoise Harbour Entrance range and port and starboard hand buoys lead to the entrance to the Channel. From the northwest follow the deeper (15 fathoms) waters of the channel, where waters are less disturbed, to avoid the shoal areas and drying reefs. Caution is advised when transiting Porpoise Channel for tidal streams at the entrance can reach 2 knots and there is a strong northward set to tidal currents at the northeast end of the channel during a falling tide. A mid-channel course takes you past commercial structures lining the shores until the moorage facilities come into view.

The **Harbour Authority** located at Port Edward has control of moorage facilities here and in Prince Rupert (Fairview and Rushbrook). Moorage is on a first-come, first-served basis; vessels tie to the docks and then register at the harbor office. Showers, restrooms and a laundromat are available and docks have water and power (110V, some with 220V). Plans are in the works to establish a fuel facility but at present the nearest source of fuel is in Prince Rupert at the Fairview dock. Moore's Boatworks can provide mechanical and electrical services and the boatyard can repair wood, fiberglass and aluminum vessels. The travelift has a 15-ton capacity. There is a post office, laundromat, general store and bank in the town and bus service connects the community to Prince Rupert. The eating establishments offer take-out food but for restaurant dining you must go to Prince Rupert.

The **North Pacific Historic Fishing Village**, about 5 miles south of the basin, is a National Historic Site. It provides a fascinating view of the once-thriving fishing industry that made this an active economic community. Features of the Village include tours, live performances, exhibits, craft shops, restaurants and bed and breakfast accommodation.

When in Prince Rupert the **Museum of Northern BC** is well worth visiting. Features include a Heritage Walking Tour, a visit to the Kwinitsa Railway Station Museum, performances at the longhouse, and an opportunity to watch craftsmen in the First Nations Carving Shed.

Chinook Salmon
(Oncorhynchus tshawytscha)

RM

Details

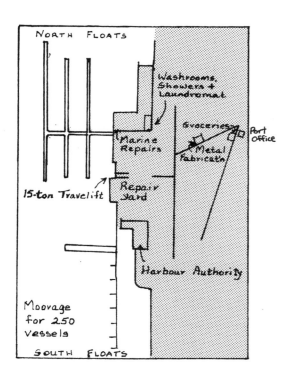

Port Edward

North Floats

Washrooms, Showers + Laundromat

Groceries

Port Office

Marine Repairs

Metal Fabricath

15-ton Travelift

Repair Yard

Harbour Authority

Moorage for 250 vessels

SOUTH FLOATS

Fairview

Floating Log Breakwater

Coast Guard Harbour Office

Co-op

Fuel Dock

PORT EDWARD
Porpoise Harbour

Approx. Scale n.m.

Not to be used for navigation

Chart 3955, 3958

PORPOISE

Booms

Ridley Terminals

Port Edward

Ridley Island

TSIMPSEAN PENINSULA

5f

Chimney

Bn

HARBOUR

1f

Porpoise Chan

2km

Lelu Is.

5f

2f

1f

1f

Range 73°

(Dries)

Dries.

1f

D24

Agnew Bank

Flora Bank (Dries)

Shoal

1f

5f

Kitson Is.

PRINCE RUPERT

This attractive city with a population of about 13,000 is the largest city in northern B.C. Almost 45% of the population are First Nations people and this is reflected in the rich artistic craftsmanship shown in wood and argillite carving, basketry, and jewellery making.

Prince Rupert is a **Port of Entry**, where you must report when arriving from Alaska. The harbor is a magnificent natural basin, protected from seaward by Digby Island. Prince Rupert lies on the flat part of Kaien Island, overlooked by the high, steep bulk of Mount Hays. The approach from Ketchikan passes inside the screen of Dundas and Melville Islands along Chatham Sound to Venn Passage or carries on to Petrel Rock (Bouy #D.39, Fl G), then turns south of bell buoy #D33 before entering the harbor. From Dixon Entrance pick up the lighthouses and buoys of Brown Passage, 16 miles WNW of Petrel Rock. See the last sketch in the book.

The harbor entrance between Kaien and Digby Islands is well marked at the various ledges and shoals, and is wide enough to accommodate the heavy traffic of a busy deep sea port. Much driftwood collects here with the tidal flow and a careful lookout is needed.

At the harbor entrance deep sea terminals are passed followed by the Fishermen's Co-op and **Fairview Public Floats** behind a breakwater. These are often filled with fishing vessels; a detailed sketch of them is on the previous page. The B.C. and Alaska Ferry Terminals are next. The harbor front turns northwesterly after the Railway Barge Terminal and the downtown part of Prince Rupert is visible. The Atlin Docks are designed to accommodate small cruise ships and mega-yachts. To arrange moorage at all docks (except at the Yacht Club) call (250) 628-9220.

Beyond the cruise ship docks are the **Prince Rupert Yacht Club** floats, a good place to moor when space is available. Reservations are recommended and can be made by calling (250) 624-4317 or VHF Ch 73. Confirm your arrival if you expect to check in after 5 p.m. on the day of your reservation for after that time space is rented on a first-come, first-served basis. When facilities are filled up moorage outside of the breakwater on the "T" may be offered but it is recommended for use only by vessels 40m (60 ft.) or larger because it is affected by chop and wash from passing vessels. Wireless internet (ADSL) is available.

Transients may find moorage at **Rushbrook Public Floats** located near the top of the harbor. A floating log breakwater protects the floats and the entrance is at the northern end. It may be necessary to raft up during the summer months. After tying up, report to the harbormaster. Water is available on the floats and garbage disposal is at the head of the pier.

Rushbrook is about a mile out of the main city center. While taxis are available, walking is commonplace. On the way in you will pass Smiles Seafood, a highly recommended eating place. The waterfront road joins the Prince Rupert downtown core near the Courthouse and the Visitor's Bureau and Museum. Shopping centers, craft shops and the Post Office are along 1st, 2nd, and 3rd Avenues. A laundromat is on McBride, just up from the Courthouse. For a nominal charge showers can be had at the Pioneer Rooms on 3rd Avenue in an old, but clean boarding house. The Esso fuel dock has a shower and laundromat.

Vessels arriving from Alaska please note: South of Prince Rupert all calls to marinas must be made only on VHF Ch 66A as this has been designated as the marina channel for the rest of the province. They should not be called on VHF Ch 16.

TSIMPSEAN PENINSULA

20'

Seaplane Base

VENN PASSAGE

3k

RUPERT HARBOR

Rushbrook Public Floats
See detail
Fuel docks
P.R. Yacht Club
Smiles
Cruise ship dock
Safeway

Floating Log Bkwtr.

Museum
Court House
Shownt
Laundromat

Transient

Trees
Bald Eagle's Nests

Reserved for Sailing Assn
(Enquire at dock)

Reserved for Comm. fishing boats

DIGBY ISLAND

Prince Rupert Airport

PRINCE

Rail Barge Term.

B.C. & Alaska Ferry dock

Fairview Floats

P.R. Fisherman's Co-op

P.R. Shipyard
Shipping docks

PRINCE

P.O. Box Rupert

Shopping Center

Hospital

Official use boarding & loading area

Garbage disposal

Head Harbormaster
Parking

½m to downtown

Rushbrook Public Floats

KAIEN ISLAND

Microwave Tower

Steep slopes

C.N. Railroad

Yellowhead Hwy.

N

54° 15'N

15'

Fl.G

Fl.G

D.47

Spire Ledge

CHATHAM SOUND

Fl.R
Barrett Rk.

Industrial Area

Fl.G
Patrel Rk

Kestrel Rk.

Approach from Dixon Entrance

Georgia Rk

Fl.G
D.43

25'

130° 20'W

Grain Elevator
RIDLEY ISLAND
Coal Terminal

PRINCE RUPERT

Port of Entry

Approach from Grenville Channel via Arthur Passage

0   1   2
Approx. Scale n.m.

Not to be used for navigation

Charts 3955, 3958

Prince Rupert   Microwave Tower   Ridley Is. Coal Terminal

Industrial emissions

Digby Is.   Petrel Rk Buoy   Buoy D.43

APPROACHING PRINCE RUPERT FROM W, i.e. from Dixon Entrance routes

Section 5 - Prince Rupert to Wrangell

Two points of interest that should be mentioned in this section are Crab Bay, a good anchorage (but limited as to use depending on direction of travel), and a highlight of the Southeast Alaskan coast, the Anan Bay Bear Observatory.

Crab Bay, on the east coast of Annette Island opposite Mary Island, is just to the north of Kwain Bay. When entering the bay caution must be exercised to identify and avoid reefs on each side of the entrance.

The bay provides excellent protection for 4 or 5 vessels over 3 - 4 fathoms, mud and sand. Shore access is available over the gravel beach. The anchorage can <u>only</u> be used by southbound vessels departing Alaskan waters since Customs in Ketchikan do not recognize it as a temporary stop-over for northbound vessels. Foggy Bay is the <u>only</u> spot authorized for anchorage by Ketchikan Customs before check-in.

Not to be used for navigation

Anan Bay Bear Observatory is between Ketchikan and Wrangell, about 10 miles north of the turn-off to Zimovia Strait on Bradfield Canal. Temporary anchorage toward the east end of the shelf is possible. Note: the shoal projects some distance into the bay and then drops straight down. Better anchorage for the night is in Frosty Bay, about 10 miles south, with calm, deep water.

A half-mile boardwalk leading to the observatory is at the mouth of the lagoon. Make noise by talking or rattling a can with pebbles to alert bears in the vicinity of the trail as to your presence. Mink, marten and river otters are sometimes seen along the creek next to the trail.

Black and brown bears can be safely observed from a blind overlooking a waterfall where they fish for pink salmon or "humpies" attempting to jump the waterfall. Anan Creek has one of the largest salmon runs in Southeast Alaska. A Forest Service Ranger is available during the summer to answer questions.

Vixen Harbor

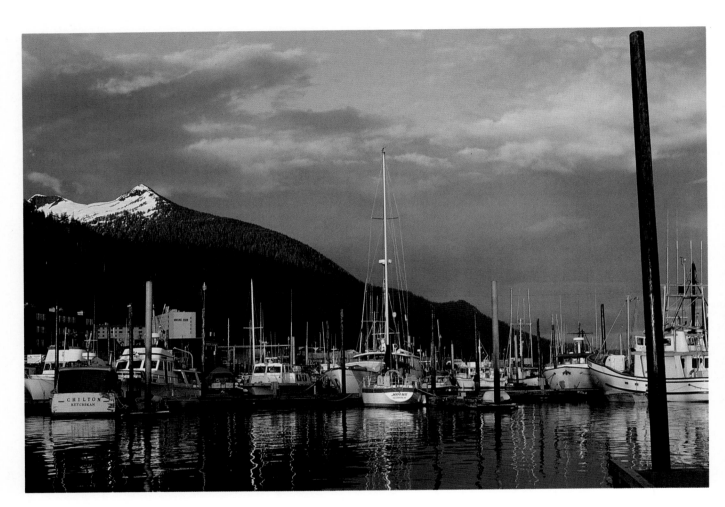

Bar Point Basin at Ketchikan

133°   132°   131°

Wrangell

F P
(160)

Eastern Passage

Zarembo
Is.

Not to be used for navigation

Wrangell Is.

STIKINE STRAIT

Etolin Is.

ZIMOVIA STRAIT

(144)   Anan Bay

Burroughs Bay

Frosty Bay

56°   56°

CLARENCE

ERNEST SOUND

Vixen Hbr.

Behm Narrows

Chictamin R.

Cleveland Peninsula

(158)

Prince
of
Wales
Is.

Meyers Ck.

(156)

P (154) F

Thorne
Bay

Helm
Bay

Naha
Bay

Revil'lagigeda
Is.

BEHM CANAL

Walker Cove

Rudyerd Bay

Carroll
Inlet

Thorne
Arm

Smeaton Bay

Kasan
Bay

Skowl
Arm

Knudson
Cove Hbr.

Tongass
Narrows

Ketchikan
F (152)

Granna
Is.

Hyda Burg

F (150)

Nichols Passage

Annette
Is.

Crab
Bay

(144)

REVILLAGIGEDO CHANNEL

Boca de
Quadra

Moira
Sound

Metlakatla

55°

Cordova
Bay

Kendrick
Bay

SEALED PASSAGE

Duke
Is.

(148)

Pearce
Canal

55°

(228)

Barrier Is.

Pearse Is.

PORTLAND INLET

C. Muzon

C. Chacon

U.S.
CAN.

Main Passage

Zayas Is.

(230)

Port Simpson

(230)

DIXON   ENTRANCE

Caamano P.
Dundas Is.

Brown Passage

Venn
Passage

(146)

F (142)

133°   132°   131° Prince Rupert

VENN PASSAGE (METLAKATLA PASSAGE)

Venn Passage is a narrow passage that is a convenient short-cut for vessels traveling to and from Alaska. The upstream direction for buoyage is laid out considering a vessel's passage from seaward when approaching Prince Rupert. The eastern end of the passage is marked by the McIntosh Rock daybeacon which is within Prince Rupert Harbour limits. Numerous drying reefs and sand banks are adjacent to the passage making careful navigation essential. Buoys, daybeacons and sector lights provide clear references as to the safe route through the passage. Use of the latest edition of Chart 3955 is mandatory.

To take advantage of the current (3-knot maximum) vessels depart Prince Rupert just before high water and by so doing obtain a slight lift through Venn Passage past the village of Metlakatla. It is well to remember that near high water the shoal areas are submerged by the high tides experienced (up to 6m/20ft.) so caution is advised throughout the passage. Powered vessels drawing less than 1.8m (6 ft.) can transit the passage at any state of the tide.

Historically, this has been one of the longest continuously inhabited areas of North America. Just across the channel from the village is Pike Island with five archaeological sites, three of which are village sites that were last inhabited some 1800 years ago. Petroglyphs can be seen at low tide and within the towering forest are depressions in the ground pinpointing the location of longhouses that have deteriorated and disappeared through the passage of time. Tours originating from the Museum of Northern BC in Prince Rupert provide the only access to Pike Island.

The Tsimpsean village of **Metlakatla** with a population of about 130 is a remnant from a more recent era that has a fascinating history. In 1857 William Duncan, an Anglican missionary arrived in Fort Simpson and began to convert native Indians to Christianity. By 1862 he realized that in order to create lasting results it would be necessary to remove his converts from the heathen influence of the surroundings as well as the degrading effects of some of the white people in Fort Simpson. Along with 350 converts he established the new church-oriented community of Metlakatla. Here there was a quiet channel filled with salmon and shellfish, good beaches for canoes and rich soil for gardens. Thirty-five houses were erected by the fall of 1862, each white-washed and with four glass windows. Hundreds more natives moved to the village and eventually the population numbered 1,200.

For 25 years they worked to make this a Utopia, building two-storey houses, a school, sawmill, cannery, a cooperative store and an octagonal church that could hold up to 700 people. They acquired a trading schooner, a brass band, fire brigade and community affairs were run by a village council. Both adults and children attended classes in reading writing, arithmetic and Bible study. Though some attended services with nose rings and painted faces, they trusted the gentle missionary and cooperated to build a peaceful, happy community. Considerable funds raised by the London Missionary Society helped to finance symbols of 19th century English society.

But in 1887 a disagreement with inflexible Anglican church hierarchy combined with authoritarian Canadian government actions led to an untenable situation. William Duncan approached President Cleveland of the U.S. for help, and Annette Island in Alaska was given as a reserve and the village of New Metlakatla was born. The exodus consisted of four hundred Metlakathlans who became the forbearers of the present inhabitants of the thriving community located on Annette Island. William Duncan developed and continued to build the foundation for another successful community and eventually retired in New Metlakatla until his death in 1918.

FOGGY BAY

The distance between the Ports of Entry of Prince Rupert and Ketchikan is about 90 miles; between them lies Dixon Entrance. This is more than a normal day's travel for the average yacht though use of Venn Passage eliminates quite a few miles and one must use Charts 3955 and 3957. Foggy Bay and Brundige Inlet on Dundas Island are anchorages that will help to break the distance to be covered into convenient stages. One method would be to use Brundige Inlet for the voyage north, and Foggy Bay for the trip south. However, the crossing of Dixon Entrance is a major step and a skipper might prefer to cross when he can. If Foggy Bay is to be used on the northbound trip, you **must call U.S. Customs in Ketchikan** at (907) 225-2254) from Prince Rupert for permission to stop in Foggy Bay before entering Ketchikan the following day.

The initial portion of the crossing is in Chatham Sound, in the lee of Dundas Island. It is after passing Green Island Lighthouse and the light on Holiday Island at the northwestern tip of Dundas Island that the yacht faces the 10 miles of the actual crossing of Dixon Entrance. Tree Point Lighthouse in Alaska is a welcome sight indicating the crossing is completed, but the swell still crashes on the lee shore as you travel into Revillagigedo Channel. Seven miles from Tree Point is Foggy Point and the entrance into Foggy Bay. The swell marks the reefs and rocks that surround the bay, and can present an intimidating sight when the seas are high.

It is preferable to enter anchorages Foggy Bay anchorages during the lower part of the tide when the various rocks, reefs, and shoals are clearly visible. When turning into the Inner Cove of **Foggy Bay,** clear the reefs that extend about .5 mile north of Foggy Point, then steer to pass south of the submerged reefs that extend about .75 mile south and southeast of DeLong Islands. Ahead, on the east side of the bay an obvious opening leads into Very Inlet. The approach to an excellent anchorage lies south of this opening, behind a large, wooded island. As you close the shore the entrance becomes clearer, but never obvious because the land behind appears to enclose it. Stay clear of the reefs in the entrance, until the channel leading behind the island is visible. Though narrow, a mid-channel route leads easily into the wider basin where secure anchorage can be taken in 5 to 6 fathoms, mud. The southern openings into the basin at the south end of the large island are shallow, drying at low water. They give a view into the outer bay where swell and breaking seas mark the reef.

Somewhat exposed anchorage can be taken in the outer cove of Foggy Bay about 1.5 miles south of the approach to the inner cove. Here, a pipeline from a spring provides good water. Anchorage can be taken in Very Inlet, but it can only be entered at high water slack because of the rapids at the narrows, hence it is not useful for a transient vessel.

Additional anchorages in the area include **Kah Shakes Cove,** about 5 miles north of Foggy Bay and **Crab Bay** on Annette Island, but they cannot be used by northbound vessels departing from Canadian waters since Customs clearance in Ketchikan must first be completed. Similar regulations apply to **Ray Anchorage** and **Morse Cove** on Duke Island. The latter anchorage has a narrow entrance with a drying rock near mid-channel and thus should be entered at low water, but since there are many rocks in this area it is not a recommended choice. In Canadian waters anchorage can be taken in **Brundige Inlet** on Dundas Island. Refer to the last sketch of the guide for their location.

Chart 17434

De Long Islands

Foggy Point

APPROACHING FOGGY BAY FROM NW, distant about 3 miles

54° 58'N

FOGGY BAY
Revillagigedo Channel

Not to be used for navigation

0   500'   1000'   ¼   ½

Approx. Scale - n.m. (& feet)

De Long Islands

Trees

Entrance to
Very Inlet

7

Trees

3

On the approach this
opening is the one clearly
Visible, but the better
entrance is shown below.

Kelp

13

This reef almost covered
at HW. Favor the N side.

13   6

30

Trees

Foul

Width at narrows about
60', with a controlling
depth of 2½ fathoms.
Long reef exposed
at LW.

F O G G Y

Seas break on these
outer reefs. Give them
a clear berth as shown.

N

Trees
(abt. 40' high)

4

6

B A Y

⚓m 54° 5_

See Chart 17434 for position
and other details of the bay.

Dries at LW

5

2

130° 58'W

130° 57'W

130° 56'W

De Long Islands

Reef   Foggy Bay
(Outer Cove)   Foggy Point

APPROACHING FOGGY BAY FROM SE, distant about 3 miles

METLAKATLA

This Tsimshian village on a Federal Native Reserve is located on Annette Island about 50 miles from the Brundige Inlet anchorage on Dundas Island and approximately 16 miles south of Ketchikan. It not only provides moorage for transient vessels but it is the last fuel stop in Alaska available to southbound vessels.

Nichols Passage branches off from Clarence Strait and separates Gravina Island from Annette Island. The entrance to the Passage is between Hid Reef on the southeastern end of the Passage and Point McCartey to the northwest. This is the edge of an extensive field of rocks clustered at the southern tip of Gravina Island and is marked by light shown from a skeleton tower with a red and white diamond-shaped daymark. Another rock, marked by a buoy, which uncovers .6 m (2 ft.) is about .3 mile ESE from Point McCartey.

The microwave tower in the cove south of Cedar Point is prominent and a lovely white sand beach is seen at the northern end of the cove. Close approach is unwise for numerous rocks line Cedar Point and the coast to the north. Rock patches on both sides of Port Chester leading to the village of Metlakatla are marked by buoys. About 1.5 miles south of the village is Yellow Hill, composed of several bare, rounded knolls. Flood currents in the Passage set north as much as 2.8 knots on the flood and is strongest in the vicinity of Walden Rocks, at the northeastern end of Nichols Passage where it meets Tongass Narrows.

Metlakatla has a number of commercial wharves and is also a State ferry terminal. There is regular seaplane service to Ketchikan. Two small craft basins (controlling depth 3 m/10 ft.) with a capacity for over 50 vessels are located in the town about .5 mile from the town center. Transient moorage with power is provided, but water is not available on the docks. The harbormaster monitors VHF Chs. 12, 16 and 18 or can be reached by telephone at (907) 886-4646. The fueling station is on the same ramp as the northerly airplane dock. To arrange for propane or fuel call Annette Island Gas at (907) 886-7851 or give them a call on VHF Ch 72. Tidal currents affect the line-ups waiting to take on fuel as there is no fuel float and the vessel must be tied to pilings. One of the crew must then climb up the ladder to the top of the pier in order to hand down the fuel hose.

*An Indian reserve about 5 miles from Prince Rupert, B.C. has the same name and should not be confused with its Alaskan namesake. The ancestors of natives in the Alaskan reserve moved from Canada in 1887 as a result of a power struggle within the Anglican Church hierarchy combined with Canadian federal government authoritarian actions.

Soon after their arrival in New Metlakatla the industrious group built a total of 91 structures including an octagonal school house, boarding homes for boys and girls, a sawmill, store and newspaper office. A cannery was established that regularly produced up to 8,000 cases of salmon annually. Even before the turn of the century the village became a bustling tourist destination as steamers brought visitors from distant lands eager to have their photograph taken with a Metlakathlan and bring home souvenirs of silver jewellery, wood carving and baskets of woven bark. Present-day New Metlakatla is a fitting tribute to the efforts of the missionary, William Duncan and the 400 loyal people who followed him.

Bostwick Pt.
Bostwick Inlet
Tongass Narrows
N
Gravina Is.
NICHOLS PASSAGE
Kelp Rocks
Warburton Is.
PORT CHESTER
Metlakatla
Annette Is.
55°08'
Cedar Pt.
Pt. McCartey
Micro Tower
Clarence Strait
Aero Bn.
Hid Reef
131° 40'

0   1   2   3
Approx. Scale n.m.

Not to be used for navigation

Chart 17435

RM

DETAIL

Breakwater

Breakwater

B C D

A

Transient Moorage

Garbage

Harbormaster

Metlakatla Harbor

0   500
Approx. Scale - feet

Transient Moorage

B

Port Chester

Breakwater

Telephone

Garbage

Launch Ramp

City Float

200   0   200
SCALE IN FEET

KETCHIKAN

The southernmost **Port of Entry** in Alaska, Ketchikan is a growing and active city. Its facilities sprawl along the east bank of Tongass Narrows. The approach and entry to Ketchikan is straightforward—one merely continues up Revillagigedo Channel into Tongass Narrows.

There are several mooring basins in the vicinity, all under the control of the harbormaster who monitors VHF Ch. 16 or can be reached at (907) 228-5632. Approaching from the south, the first facility is **Thomas Basin.** The entrance lies between a rock breakwater and a floating log boom protector. Transient moorage areas are shown on the sketch, but they are usually filled, so you normally takes a vacant berth while checking in. The advantage of Thomas Basin is that it is close to the downtown area of Ketchikan. There is a good market close by on Stedman Street. Customs Officers require the skipper to report to the office in the Federal Building, past the cruise ship docks; they do not come to the boat as in some Ports of Entry. A two-ton hoist is available.

A telephone booth at the creek near the float walkway allows you to contact the Harbormaster whose office is at Bar Harbor Basin. Since most berths in the area are rented, the harbormaster will inform the skipper which berths are temporarily empty.

The next moorage is at the **City Floats.** They are at the downtown waterfront, and even if space is available the wash from harbor activity creates an uncomfortable moorage. Better moorage is available in **Bar Harbor,** about one mile northwest, where floating and rock breakwaters protect the floats. Washrooms, shower and laundry facilities are in the Highliner facility at the south end of Bar Harbor South. Though this basin lies about a mile from the downtown area, all facilities such as supermarkets, restaurants, bars, etc. can be found along the way and are closer to Bar Harbor than to other moorages.

The fuel docks are south of Thomas Basin, just northwest of the Coast Guard base which is passed when entering the harbor. The Alaska State Ferry dock, as well as the local ferry to the airport (located across Tongass Narrows) are northwest of the Bar Harbor Basin. Other facilities where transients may find moorage include Ketchikan Hole-in-the-Wall Harbor in George Inlet, about 7 miles from the city center and Knudsen Cove Harbor, just around the corner to the north in Behm Canal, about 14 miles from the center of town.

Ketchikan is a major stop for cruise ships and during the summer they seem to overwhelm the city with hordes of tourists making the streets so congested and rushed that it looses some of its charm. The downtown area has the usual tourist attractions, gift shops, coffee shops and marine stores. Creek Street, once a red light district, is now a tourist area with many small specialty stores. Several walks can be taken to explore the city and its immediate environs. Brochures describing these walks can be obtained at the Ketchikan Visitors' Bureau on Front Street. The Totem Heritage Center is of special interest for restored totems and a display of other native crafts. About 3 miles south of Ketchikan is a large collection of totem poles at the Saxman Totem Park. Another collection, with a replica of a community house is 10 miles north at Totem Bight State Historic Park.

Misty Fiords National Monument lies a short distance to the east. The scenery is spectacular and if time permits it is well worth visiting. On a clear day, an aerial view is breath-taking. However, Ketchikan and Misty Fiords lie in the 'wet' belt, and have up to 410 cm (162 inches) of rain per year. Cloudy days are the norm for more than two-thirds of the year so if you experience a sunny day with blue skies you are indeed fortunate!

KETCHIKAN

0   500'   1000'

Approx. Scale - details (feet)

Port of Entry

Chart 17428, 17430

Parking

Tongass

Harbor Master

Grid

T - Transient berths

Concrete Breakwater

Detail –
Bar Harbor North

16
15
14
13
12
11
10

9
8
7
6
5
4
3
2

Highliner: Showers + Laundromat

Breakwater

Bar Harbor South

Bar Harbor Basin
See detail.

KETCHIKAN.

City Float

Airport

Fy

Safeway

City Center

A

Thomas Basin
See detail

Fuel

F

Coast Guard

TONGASS

NARROWS

PENNOCK
Is.

Detail – Thomas Basin

City Center

Creek St

US Customs

Federal Bldg

Breakwater

Spruce Mill

1

T

2

3

4

T

5

Log
Boom

Grid

Breakwater

0   ½   1

Approx. Scale n.m.

THORNE BAY

Thorne Bay is a convenient stop-over and is a fueling station strategically located approximately 50 miles north of Ketchikan and 60 miles southwest of Wrangell. It is situated about half way up the eastern coast of Prince of Wales Island, southwest of the junction of Ernest Sound and Clarence Strait.

A large island almost blocks the mouth of the entrance to the bay which is 2.5 miles west of Tolstoi Point. When approaching from the east look for the sharpest indention in the horizon to pin-point the entrance. The featureless, tree-covered rolling hills on the coast make the entrance difficult to identify until the 6m (20 ft.) light on the island south of Thorne Head comes into view.

Entrance to the bay should be made only at slack water to avoid the eddies and rips occurring in the narrow channel when the current is running. A shoal area close to the north shore of the channel, north of the large island, extends over half way into the channel. This part of the channel has thick kelp which is towed under when the current runs strong. Follow a mid-channel course until reaching the western part of the channel where the bay begins to open. At the western end of the channel, off the southern tip of the northern shore a shoal extends in a southerly direction about two-thirds the distance across the channel. To avoid this shoal favor the southern side until well into the bay. NOAA Charts 17420 and 17423 must be used when approaching the bay.

The "city" of Thorne Bay has a population of about 650 and is a community whose economy is centered around logging, sportsfishing and tourism. Vessels up to 15m (50 ft.) can find moorage in the slips, with space for larger vessels along the breakwater float. Water, power and pump-out services are available on the docks; a laundromat, post office, liquor and grocery stores are a short walk away in the town center. The Tackle Shack has a short dock where fishing gear and gasoline are sold. A convenience store, diesel and gasoline are available at The Port which is open Monday to Saturday from 6 am to 6 pm and from 9 am to 4 pm on Sunday. Propane is available Prince of Wales Gas, telephone (907) 828-3969. Basic medical services with visiting physicians are available on Mondays from 8 am to 12 am and 1 pm to 3 pm. For more information on the area call (907) 828-3380 or visit their website at www.thornebayalaska.net

Thorne Bay is connected to the rest of Prince of Wales Island by an extensive system of roads originally built by logging companies which have operated on the island for many years. At one time Thorne Bay was the largest logging camp in the U.S. and it was from those temporary beginnings that the community evolved. Float-planes, barges and ferry service link the town to Ketchikan.

Lyman Anchorage is another handy stop-over on the southwestern shore of Clarence Strait about 28 miles south of Thorne Bay and 6.5 miles northwest of Streets Island. Its outer part is an open bight about 1 mile wide at its entrance with and inner harbor extending another .6 mile to the southwest. Entrance can only be made at high water, for it has a controlling depth of .5 fathom. Excellent protection can be enjoyed here with good holding in 4 to 5 fathoms, mud.

Other anchorages in the area include **Ratz Harbor**, about 10 miles north of the entrance to Thorne Bay on Prince of Wales Island and across from it at **McHenry Anchorage** on Etolin

THORNE BAY

PRINCE OF WALES IS.

Approx. Scale n.m.

Chart 17420, 17423

Not to be used for navigation

Gasoline

Launching Ramp

Seaplane Float

Seaplane Float

Pump-out

Breakwater

Hbr. Details

Approx. Scale feet & n.m.

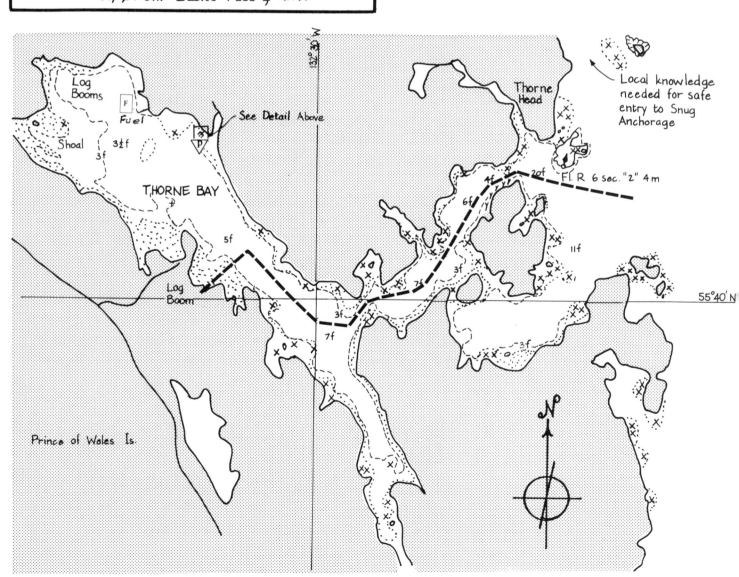

Log Booms

F
Fuel

Shoal

3½f

3f

THORNE BAY

See Detail Above

Thorne Head

Local knowledge needed for safe entry to Snug Anchorage

Fl. R 6 sec. "2" 4m

20f

4f

6f

11f

3f

5f

Log Boom

3f

7f

3f

55°40'N

Prince of Wales Is.

N°

MEYERS CHUCK

Proceeding north from Ketchikan, the exit from Tongass Narrows is marked by the Guard Island Lighthouse. Here there is a choice of several directions to follow: northeast up the Behm Canal to traverse the Misty Fiords; west across Clarence Strait to Kasaan Bay and Kasaan, or north towards Wrangell. When going north the course lies along the west coast of Cleveland Peninsula. Ernest Sound opens from Clarence Strait at Lemesurier Point; about 1.5 miles southeast of the point is Meyers Chuck.

This is a small, convenient harbor to use to split the distance from Ketchikan to Wrangell. Unfortunately, generators on shore run constantly and their fumes degrade the attractive setting. If fuel is required it must be taken on in Thorne Bay, described on the previous page. Meyers Chuck is formed by the protection given by Meyers Island and a screen of smaller islands against the side of Lemesurier Point. As you approach the harbor from Clarence Strait the microwave tower (visible above the trees) pinpoints the location of the settlement. Meyers Island lies north of the tower. The entrance to the harbor lies between the northern end of Meyers Island where a light is displayed, and a pole marking the reefs of the small islands north of the light.

Misery Island (the large island lying .5 mile northwest of Meyers Chuck) has rocks awash at its southern end which are indicated by a green marker. When entering, approach the entrance from due west, south of the green marker to avoid the reefs that lie about 120 m (400 feet) off the northwestern corner of Meyers Island. Do not approach Meyers Island closer than .3 mile until the entrance is clear. At the entrance the depths reduce sharply to about 3 fathoms but the opening is clear midway between the buoy and the light. After turning into the small harbor, you will find the State-operated public float in the northeast corner. A seaplane float extends northwesterly, near the gangway. A reef that dries at low water lies further east of the seaplane float. The main floats are open to transient moorage. A harbormaster is not located here but if you require information call the DOT at (907) 465-1781.

This settlement is devoted primarily to fishing. There is a small store with limited supplies and a Post Office from which mail is picked up weekly. The post office is open on Tuesday from 11 am to 2 pm and on Wednesday for one hour after the mail plane arrives. The closest fuel docks are across Clarence Strait in Thorne Bay. The southwestern corner of the harbor has pilings and is used by fishermen for their nets.

Anchorage in 7 – 8 fathoms, mud and broken shells over rock, can be taken in the harbor if moorage is not available. Anchorage can also be taken in the narrow arm beyond the small islands forming the eastern side of the harbor. It is necessary to go out the entrance and travel around the northern island to enter the anchorage area. The water in the harbor ices up during the winter.

Lemesurier Pt.   Misery Is.   Microwave Tower

APPROACHING MEYERS CHUCK FROM SSE, distant about 3 miles

APPROACHING MEYERS CHUCK FROM WNW, distant about 2 miles.

Misery Is.

Clarence Ship Is.
Strait

MISERY IS.

Dries

Gr. Marker Bn.
Dries

Chart 17423, 17385

Lemesurier Point

N

#3 Marker

1½

3

5

5

T3

5

Red Fl 4sec
#4

15

Post Office

Dries

7 Meyers Chuck Lodge

Mud + Shell

Reef

Float Plane Dock

Heliport

8

Public
Floats

School

6

Telephone

Foul

MEYER'S IS.

Grid

3

MEYERS CHUCK

Not to be used for navigation

Microwave Tower

132° 15' W

RNEST SOUND

McHenry Ledge
R #2. Fl. 2 sec.

See also Vixen Hbr
in these charts

UNION BAY
(Magnetic disturbance)

Reef

Lemesurier
Point

Cleveland Peninsula

Misery Is.

55° 45' N

Meyers Chuck
See detail

Cleveland Penin.

500'   0   ¼

Approx. Scale   n.m.

MEYERS CHUCK
Clarence Strait

VIXEN HARBOR

If you travel to Wrangell by the scenic route which uses Ernest Sound and Zimovia Strait then Vixen Harbor is a very pretty anchorage to use either after Meyers Chuck or as an alternative to it. The entrance is narrow and not obvious until it is carefully lined up, but it is a well sheltered anchorage backed by a beautiful mountain.

At Lemesurier Point (the southern point at the entrance to Ernest Sound) several dangers lie offshore. Lemly Rocks are about .25 mile off the point while McHenry Ledge is about .75 mile east. Strong magnetic disturbances occur between Lemesurier and Union Points—as much as 30 degrees was noticed at the time of writing. Since compass courses cannot be relied on, good visibility is needed to be certain of the vessel's course and location. This is especially true in this area as the current sets towards Union Point.

It is necessary to proceed about .25 to .5 mile off the coast until the entrance into Vixen Harbor can be ascertained. The shallow southern entrance is more obvious at first. However, even though it is more evident, do not attempt the southern entrance for shoals reduce it far more than the main entrance. Line up the northern entrance from offshore and steer carefully through using a mid-channel course. The pilot indicates a width of 30 m (100 yards) but this may be the distance between high water shorelines. At low tide, reefs extending out from both sides reduce the actual channel width to about 18m (60 feet), but the depth is at least 1.5 fathoms.

Once past the islands the harbor opens up nicely. Anchorage can be taken in about 4.5 fathoms, mud. The view of the mountains to the southeast is spectacular and the anchorage is peaceful.

On leaving, clear the entrance and set a visual course until well clear of the magnetic effects of the area before relying on the compass. Other anchorages in the area include the cove behind **Magnetic Point** and a smaller cove behind the nearby islands where houses have been erected.

Zimovia Strait is a pretty, much used route to Wrangell. The Narrows are clearly marked and are interesting to traverse. Whaletail Cove looks inviting as an anchorage, but is unusable since the entrance is shoal.

Other anchorages in the area include **Ratz Harbor**, about 10 miles north of the entrance to **Thorne Bay** on Prince of Wales Island and across from it on Etolin island is **McHenry Anchorage**.

APPROACH TO VIXEN HBR. FROM SW, i.e. across Union Bay

Chart 17385, 17422

Shallow S. entrance is more evident on approach. Main N. entrance Union Pt. (note ledges)

APPROACHING VIXEN HBR. FROM NNE (ZIMOVIA STR.), distant 1 mile.

Ledges extend off Union Pt. Give it a wide berth.

IMPORTANT – Clearly identify the N. entrance, then Line up the narrow opening and steer a mid-channel course.

Reefs exposed at Low Water

Shoal

10

In Channel Minᵐ width 60'. Control depth 9' at Low Water

3

1½

Do Not Use

Heavily Wooded

Trees

2

Bare

Trees

Shoal

2½

10

Trees

6

Shoal

Shallow

4½ ⌘m

2

A beautiful mountain on this side.

4½

Detail unknown

Shoal

ERNEST SOUND

Union Pt.

Strong magnetic disturbances will affect your compass in this area.

Vixen Harbor

Magnetic Pt.

UNION BAY

Cleveland Peninsula

Not to be used for navigation

55° 45' N

Reef

Lemesurier Pt.

See detail chart in this guide.

Meyers Chuck

VIXEN HARBOR

Ernest Sound

0   (500')   ¼

Approx. Scale n.m. (feet)

132° 15' W   132° 10' W

WRANGELL

Wrangell lies near the north end of Wrangell Island. It may be approached from Clarence and Stikine Straits, up Zimovia Strait, or up Eastern Passage and around the northern tip of the island. The combination of the magnificent backdrop of the Stikine Mountains and the town's frontier appearance draws many cruise ships to the area.

After passing the cruise ship terminal the main harbor extends along the shore, but the small craft harbor is in a bight behind Point Skekesti, where a wooden breakwater extends partly across the entrance to provide shelter in the southern cove. This cove is divided into an outer and inner harbor. In the outer harbor the floats on the western side are used by commercial vessels. Fuel docks are also on this side. The long floats on the eastern side have transient moorage which is almost always filled—you can expect to raft up. The harbormaster's office is at the head of the walkway with a shrimp cannery lying behind it. He controls moorage in the harbor and monitors VHF Ch. 16 or can be reached at (907) 874-3736.

The inner harbor is approached through a connecting channel having about 2 fathoms, marked by day beacons. Here the floats cater to small craft and power boats with very reasonable moorage fees. But limited turning room makes the area awkward for large sailing vessels.

The harbormaster at Wrangell also controls **Shoemaker Boat Harbor**, about 3.5 miles SSE on Zimovia Strait near the Wrangell Institute. The breakwater protecting the harbor is visible when approaching Wrangell. This facility can accommodate over 250 vessels and although it is a cleaner area than elsewhere, its 5.5-mile distance from the city center is a disadvantage for transients. Power is available on the floats but not water.

Wrangell was originally located at the mouth of the Stikine River because it controlled the route into the interior. Its history is varied, for Russian, British and American flags have flown over the town and it was an important trading point for the Tlingit Indians. On Shakes Island are several totem poles and Chief Shakes Community House, which can be approached by following a wooden walkway near the harbormaster's office. The old false front business houses along Front Street and other buildings in the streets behind give evidence of the age of the town. The Visitors' Bureau (near the cruise ship terminal at the northern end of the town) can provide information on the location of petroglyphs and many other points of interest.

THE STIKINE PEAKS BEHIND WRANGELL FROM WORONKOFSKI IS.

Cruise Ship Dock ↑

To Town of Wrangell
Ferry, Stores, etc.
⅛ mile.

WRANGELL Is.

Chart 17382, 17384, 17385

Case Ave.

Alaska Lumber
& Pulp

Shakes St.

Light Fl.R 4s

Wooden
Breakwater

Seaplane
Dock

Shrimp
Cannery

Harbormaster

Walkway

56° 28' N

Inner
Harbor

Pt. Shekesti
(Shustak Pt)

Pump-out

Grid

Shakes
Is.

Chief Shakes
House

Reliance Float

Totem pole

G#7

3

Outer Harbor

Fuel F
docks

Transient

G#5

R#8

2

R#6

2

Sub.
Piling

Piling

R#4

N

STRAIT

132° 23' W

WRANGELL

Not to be used for navigation

0   100'   300'   500'   ⅛m

Approx. Scale n.m. and feet

SECTION 6 - Wrangell to Juneau

Additional views found in this section:

One of The Twins   Pt. Hughes (distant, across the sound)   Sunset Is.   Pt. Windham   N. Point of Hobart Bay

VIEW NW UP STEPHENS PASSAGE ON LEAVING HOBART BAY, OUT 1½ MILES.

Unnamed Cove   Shoals off this point   Williams Cove

TRACY ARM ANCHORAGE

In Tracy Arm

Devil's Thumb, a spectacular peak near Petersburg

134°

133°

132°

58°

⑯176

Taku

Port Snettisham

Tracy Arm

STEPHENS

SEYMOUR CANAL

PASSAGE

Not to be used for navigation

⑭174

ADMIRALTY

Holkham Bay

Endicott Arm

Ford's Terror

ISLAND

Pt. Hugh

Windham Bay

Gambier Bay

Hobart Bay

⑫172

Pybus Bay

FREDERICK SOUND

Port Houghton

Farragut Bay

C. Bendel

Thomas Bay

57°

Pt. Gardner

KEKU STRAIT

Portage Bay

⑩170

57°

⑧168

KUPREANOF IS.

CHATHAM

Petersburg

F

Wrangell Narrows

⑯166

Duncan Canal

Dry Strait

Stikine R.

⑭164

Kui'u Is.

⑯216

Woewodski Is.

Mitkof Is.

STRAIT

Tebenkof Bay

SUMNER STRAIT

SNOW PASSAGE

Zarembo Is.

STIKINE STR.

F

Wrangell

⑯160

Woronkofski Is.

NIMOVIA STR.

Wrangell Is.

R. Baker

⑳220

Prince of Wales Is.

Etolin Is.

⑳222

C. Decision

Kosciusko Is.

56°

134°

133°

132°

WRANGELL NARROWS

This waterway, the shortest route between Wrangell and Petersburg,. is a well known and exciting part of the trip which also provides the southern entrance at Point Alexander on Mitkof Island (off Sumner Strait) is about 20 miles west of Wrangell. The Narrows consist of 21 miles of waterway with more than 66 navigation markers, leading to Petersburg in the north, where it opens on to Frederick Sound. At night, with its myriad of flashing red and green lights it is easy to understand its nickname of "Christmas Tree Lane."

It is not possible with the small charts and brief comments of this guide to describe the many details of the Narrows, nor is it intended. This guide merely describes significant and interesting aspects of the passage.

The ship channel narrows in places to 90 m (300 feet) wide, and though the major section the controlling depth is 6 m (19 feet). Any larger vessels that might be encountered are most likely to be the Alaska State Ferries, which use the narrows at high tide.

For small boat use when navigating the channel it is recommended that NOAA Chart #17375 (which divides the Narrows into two sections printed side by side) be cut along the vertical division; then match and tape the two sections together in a long continuous chart of the waterway. By folding this into four it gives a handy and useful chart size reference at the helm for the actual transit. It will assist navigation if a check mark is placed as each odd (or even) beacon is passed. This will not only determine position but will also allow a skipper to make a quick decision as to whether he can move off the channel (and to which side) if a large vessel is met in the Narrows. With the aid of the chart the passage can be taken easily by all small craft. High-speed powered vessels should slow down to reduce the turbulence of the wake they create.

For most slow-speed small craft going either way, the <u>passage should be commenced on the last part of the flood</u>. The currents enter Wrangell Narrows from both ends to meet at about Green Point (9 miles from Petersburg and 12 miles from the southern entrance). Thus, a prudent skipper will arrange his entry to carry a favorable current all the way through.

In foggy weather it is strongly recommended that the passage be delayed until it is clear, even if the vessel is equipped with radar. If fog is encountered when in the passage it is wise to haul well off the channel at the first opportunity to anchor and wait for clearing. Though yachts can do this at several places the best site is at **Halfmoon Anchorage** (about 8.5 miles from the southern entrance), where depths are 2 to 3 fathoms, mud. Other areas off the channel may have hard or rocky bottoms and kelp,

Dry Strait appears to be an apparent alternative route north from Wrangell, but it should not be attempted without local knowledge. Considerable shoaling and muddy water with strong currents can put a stranger in difficulties. Keku Strait, further west of the Narrows cannot be used, as navigation markers have been removed. The only alternative to the Narrows is to proceed through Sumner Strait, around Cape Decision and up Chatham Strait.

⑫ N. Entrance – strong currents can be felt in channel.

DETAIL – W. PETERSBURG FLOAT.

Approach

100' Float.

1f

56° 50'N

#63

W. Petersburg

FREDERICK SOUND

Fl R #62

PETERSBURG
See detail next page

Chart 17375

Scow Bay.

100' Float

2

Papkes Landing

To Petersburg

⑪ From marker 49 north to Petersburg the channel widens & passing is not a problem. However, strong winds blowing down channel can create steep waves.

⑩ From marker 44 to 48 stay in the channel; shoals border it closely.

Fl G #49

⑨ Green Pt. Currents meet here & change

Fl R #50

North Flat

South Flat

⑧ From marker 8 to 42 the dredged channel is 300' wide. Keep to the channel except for emergency anchoring.

40'

Papkes Landing
See detail above ⑦

④ Beecher Pass connects with the Duncan Canal; Anch. can be taken W. of Keene Is., but cross currents here should be watched.

Boulder Flats

⑥ Dredged anch. for large vessels

Blind Slough

Halfmoon Anchorage
⑤ Emergency use.

North Ledge

Not to be used for navigation

shoal

small boats

2

3

1

3

6

3

10

Large vessels

3

DETAIL – TEMP. ANCHORAGE
Open to SE winds.

Keene Is.

8

Beecher Pass

WOEWODSKI IS.

Strong currents Watch for drift

Hicks Point

Battery Is.

③ The narrow channel E of the Battery Is. can be used by small vessels. It is marked by buoys.

Fl R #2

For NAVIGATION USE US CHART No. 17375

Fl. G. #1, Pt. Lockwood Rk

② Anchorage, see detail above.

December Pt
No anchorage

Midway Rk

WRANGELL

NARROWS

① S. Entrance. On the flood, rips occur off Point Alexander.

Pt. Alexander
Fl. 4s

56° 30'N

133°

SUMNER STRAIT

rips

132° 54'W

0   1   2   3   4 m

Approx. Scale n.m.

PETERSBURG

The charming town of Petersburg lies at the northern end of Wrangell Narrows, on the tip of Mitkof Island. This busy town is more concerned with fishing and lumbering than with tourists. This refreshing attitude is reflected in the prosperity of the people, the expanded boat harbors, and in the number of large seiners and fishboats. The Norwegian heritage of many of the inhabitants is celebrated each May 17 (Norwegian Independence Day) during the annual "Little Norway Festival." Other signs of this pride are seen in the rosemaling on building fronts and the replica Viking vessel in the harbor.

There are three major boat harbors in Petersburg, but the main transient accommodation is the northernmost, between the Whitney-Fidalgo Seafoods pier and the Petersburg Fisheries Cannery docks. The harbormaster's office is at the head of the dock or he may be reached by calling VHF Ch. 16 or CB Ch. 9. A reasonable mooring charge is assessed, and depending on the location, electrical power may be available. A water tap is on the transient dock. The people of Petersburg are very friendly and helpful.

In the same building as the harbormaster's office are restrooms and a large coin-operated stainless steel shower. Although it often has a queue when the fishing boats come in, it's worth the wait! Adjacent to the showers is the Visitor Center where maps and guides can be obtained. A grid is just below the walkway. Garbage and waste oil disposal facilities are nearby.

Main Street is half a block from the dock. There are two major grocery and hardware stores, The Trading Union and Hammer & Wikan. Also within walking distance are a hospital, post office and an intriguing little museum.

If the budget is tight, there is open mooring at the West Petersburg Public Float, across Wrangell Narrows in the community of Kupreanof. However, there is no public transportation back and forth to Petersburg.

The weather is dominated by rain; with an annual average of 2.7 m (106 inches). Heavy weather gear and boots are right in style for everyday wear in Petersburg. In fact when rain is pounding on the deck you will likely hear the local radio announcer cheerfully reporting, "Today we'll have a few sprinkles!"

Exiting the Narrows from Petersburg brings you to Frederick Sound where icebergs from the glacier can often be seen. The spectacular mountain view behind Petersburg is highlighted by a granite rock pinnacle, the Devil's Thumb. Just 25 miles southeast is Le Conte Glacier, the southernmost tidewater glacier. It is well worth visiting, but shoaling at the entrance to the bay makes entry difficult without local information.

A cruising destination for boaters from Petersburg is Tebenkof Bay, about 50 miles distant. This popular bay with its numerous anchorages is described on page 202.

4

Private dock

3

Transient

T

T

2

North Harbor

Cannery

Grid

2

2½

2½

2½

2

Transient this side

Boat Launching

Boardwalk

Prolewy Pt.

Middle Harbor

Store + Restaurant

Sasby Is.

sients

0   100   300   500'

Approx. Scale - detail (feet)

West Petersburg.

Public Float

Dredged channel

Fuel Float

Standard Oil

F

Ferry

P'bg South Harbor

Mitkof Island

N. end of Wrangell Narrows

NOTE:- North Harbor only has transient berths. Check with Hbrm'ster, if a large vessel, for temp. berths in other harbors.

Telephones

Main Harbor Master's Office

Washrooms

Shower - coin operated

Tourist Information

Frederick Sound

#63
Fl. 4s.
Bell

R#62
Fl. R 4s.

Strong tidal currents

Dredged Channel

56°49'N

Petersburg

Petersburg Fisheries.

Stores

P'bg North Harbor (Transient berths)
See detail above

Supermarket

P'bg Middle Harbor

132°57'W

Chart 17375

PETERSBURG

Not to be used for navigation

0   ¼   ½

Approx. Scale n.m.

PORTAGE BAY

This protected and very pleasant anchorage lies on the south side of Frederick Sound, indenting Kupreanof Island. It is very different from the bays that lie on the other side of the Sound, with their glaciers coming down to sea level. Portage Bay provides a good stop for vessels proceeding along Frederick Sound to or from Petersburg.

Low points at each side of the entrance are marked by the two small Portage Islets roughly .75 of a mile west of the entrance. On the east side the mountains of the Missionary Range rise between the bay and Petersburg, with some snow usually remaining throughout the year.

Stay about a mile offshore, and when the entrance is clear begin the approach. Both East and West Points project into the opening with shoals that reduce the useful passage to about 150m (500 feet). The tidal flow into and out of the fairly long bay can attain considerable velocity at times. However, except at the maximum tides vessels can enter and usually use a natural range to guide the vessel into the channel.

East Point has a light on a tower with a green daymark. The tip of the grassy verge should be aligned on Hook Point (with a gap in the trees and a hut now hidden in undergrowth), and on a low peak behind—as shown in the sketch. Follow this bearing till at the entrance, first round West Point, then East Point, staying about mid-channel. West Point has a red daybeacon on it. Once in the bay past East Point, a large shoal bay lies to the west and a booming ground to the east. You can anchor in about 5 fathoms in the area of the booming ground, but a better anchorage is found further in.

A prominent logging camp lies on the east side about a mile and half into the inlet. Anchor in the middle of the bay, slightly beyond the camp, in about 4 to 6 fathoms, mud. Do not go too close to the shore. The main part of the bay is large enough to accommodate many boats.

Further into the bay Stop Island marks the beginning of shoaling, and this area is called Goose Bay. Harrington Rock is about .25 mile north of Stop Island.

KAKE

The village of Kake is about 12 miles west of Point Gardner at the entrance to Frederick Sound, and about 15 miles west of Portage Bay. Kake has public floats, stores, lodges, and a grid. Its tall totem pole is visible from well offshore. A fuel dock and propane source is about a mile south of town.

The best protection during stormy weather is two miles south of the town at **Portage Cove Harbor.** The harbor office is open 8 to 5 and the harbormaster monitors VHF Ch. 16 and can be reached at (907) 785-3804 or CB Ch. 15. The village is at the entrance to Keku Strait, but the Coast Guard has removed all navigational markers to discourage its use.

Portage Cove Hbr.

PORTAGE BAY FROM N, distant about 5 miles

Boulder Pt.
See entr. detail below.
West Pt.
Bn.
Portage Is.

PORTAGE BAY

FREDERICK SOUND

Portage Is(⚬⚬)

Boulder Pt.

West Pt.

57°00'N

Currents at entrance.
East Pt.

Booming ground.
If clear, anch. nearer
entrance is possible.

Hook Pt.
Cabin amid
new trees.

Logging Camp

5 5½ 5

Stop
Is.

133°20'W

Goose
Cove

0   1   2

Approx. Scale   n.m.

N

Not to be used for navigation

Chart 17367

151°Mag. (1985)
Low Peak
Hook Point (hut in trees)

Boulder Pt.

Grass verge of
East Point.

West Pt.

ENTRANCE   BEARING   TO   PORTAGE   BAY

Hall Peak   Missionary Range

(Entrance Pass behind) Portage Is.

APPROACHING   PORTAGE   BAY   FROM   W, distant about 2 miles.

THOMAS BAY

Ten miles north of the buoys at the Petersburg entrance to Wrangell Narrows, and across Frederick Sound is the entrance to Thomas Bay. This is the first opportunity to see a glacier fairly closely. The entrance to Thomas Bay lies between Point Vandeput in the northwest and Wood Point in the southeast. Although the two points are about 2.25 miles apart, shoaling and reefs at the mouth of the bay are extensive, thus reducing the opening to a narrow buoyed entrance. Depending on the state of the tide, considerable turbulence and swirls may be encountered at the entrance, but by watching the course and drift with care there is no difficulty in entering.

Puffin

The water here is noticeably milky with glacial silt. The shape of the bay may be likened to a lazy T, resting on its side. The east side of the cross arm of the T is a range of peaks, whose flanks descend in steep sides to the water. Several landslides mark the tree-clad slopes, and numerous waterfalls can be seen.

The northern arm ends at Baird Glacier. Though not a tidewater glacier at this time, it is not very far back from the water's edge, and apart from the lack of ice discharged into the bay it provides very scenic views. Do not approach the end of the inlet closer than half a mile, for considerable shoaling occurs due to the discharge of silt down the glacial river.

Near the end of the northern arm, a narrow steep-walled inlet leads off to the east. This is **Scenery Cove**, a small version of Fords Terror. Almost overhanging walls hem the sides, which shoal quickly at the head. In very settled weather it is possible to anchor on a 9-fathom shelf extending off the northern entrance point of the cove. Anchor off a prominent scar on the face. You can then take a dinghy to the flats below the face of the glacier and walk up to explore it. However, a better and safer anchorage is available in the south arm of Thomas Bay. **Ruth Island** lies roughly north/south and on its southeastern side are two coves. Both can be used as anchorages, though the southern one is preferable.

Anchorage is also possible close to the shore south of a prominent cascade behind Spray Island. But like Scenery Cove, this anchorage has very limited shelf area close to a steep mountainside.

The southern arm of Thomas Bay has the terminal river of Patterson Glacier, which has receded so far back that its only visible remains are the moraines.

THOMAS BAY
FREDERICK SOUND

Chart 17367

Approx. Scale n.m.

VIEW OF BAIRD GLACIER FROM SSW

Ruth Is. S.E. Cove

Not to be used for navigation

HOBART BAY

Cape Fanshawe marks the point where Stephens Passage opens northward off Frederick Sound. These are wide stretches of sea, where weather conditions can create rough water. There is an anchorage near the Cape in Cleveland Passage behind Whitney Island. It is in 6 to 8 fathoms at the southeastern end, tucked east of East Spit (a rocky shoal awash at low water which projects out from the mainland). While the pilot recommends entry from the north around Whitney Island, small vessels can enter from the south by keeping a mid-channel course and allowing for a clear berth of East Spit. However, this anchorage is relatively open; swell affects it and gusty southeast winds often blow down the nearby mountains.

The course northward passes Five Fingers Islets, on which is a lighthouse often mentioned in local weather reports. This is useful for reckoning the weather in Stephens Passage. Port Houghton is the first large bay on the mainland, but it is too deep for anchoring.

Hobart Bay opens into the mainland about 5 miles further, and at first appears to be a shallow indentation. It is marked by small islands, The Twins, two miles west and by the larger Sunset Island, about 5 miles north.

Entrance Island lies in the center of the entrance to Hobart Bay. Behind it a long, high arm projects outwards, almost closing the opening into the inner part of Hobart Bay. A stand pipe and several houses mark a large logging operation, with snow-clad peaks in the background.

The anchorage and moorage lie in a small L-shaped inlet on the southern side of **Entrance Island**. As you approach the island from either direction a large fault becomes visible. On the rocky south shore there is a small niche with a house behind the stony beach. This is seen before the true opening is visible. Turn into the small inlet, where the State maintains a 30 m (100 foot) float in the western niche. It is unconnected to the shore, except for two underwater cables that affect the ability of all but very small vessels to use the south side of the float. The house previously seen on the approach is on the neck of land behind the float. This is a quiet and restful spot, used primarily as a weather lay-over by vessels traveling these waters.

It is possible to enter the remainder of Hobart Bay through the narrow, rock-strewn entrance, and to find other anchorage immediately northwest of the entry. But the currents and multitude of rocks discourage such exploration, especially when the quiet moorage at Entrance Island is available.

There are two other anchorages in this area. The best one is **Cannery Cove** in Pybus Bay located on the west side of, and across Stephens Passage. When anchoring in **Windham Bay** you should anchor in a niche near the entrance or proceed far into the bay and anchor at the head.

APPROACHING HOBART BAY FROM SSE, distant about 5 miles

Chart 17363

Snow peaks

Standpipe

Entrance Island

Large Logging Camp

ENTRANCE IS. IN HOBART BAY FROM NNE, distant about 1 mile

STEPHENS PASSAGE

The Twins

Entrance Is.

see detail

BAY

Standpipe

Logging Camp

HOBART

Pt. Hobart.

ENTRANCE IS.

HOBART BAY

0   1   2   3

Approx. Scale n.m.

ENTRANCE Is.

Grass

Old Float

5

6

Grass

CAUTION: Note that underwater cables reach from shore to float.

3½   100' × 12' Float

Private

7

Eagle nest

Trees

Shed

House

8

Garden

Trees

Heavily Wooded

0   500'

Approx. Scale — feet

Not to be used for navigation

HOLKAM BAY

Holkam Bay has a 5-mile wide opening between Point Coke in the north and Point Astley in the south. Harbor Island along with several smaller islands stretch across the bay toward Wood Spit and its extension of tidal flats and islands. Tracy Arm and Endicott Arm are two long fiords that extend roughly north and southeast respectively from the bay. High, snow-clad mountains and glaciers form the backdrop for these arms.

This is a spectacular and very scenic area, with long fiords and calving tidewater glaciers. Though there are few secure anchorages, a visit to this area is truly worthwhile. Tourists are brought high-speed craft from as far away as Juneau.

Tracy Arm

Enter Tracy Arm by going around the north point of Harbor Island to pick up the unlit range on Harbor Island that leads through the shoal areas at the mouth. A day beacon is located on the opposite shore. Currents can be up to 4 knots, and swirls and tidal effects will be encountered in the entrance. For entering the Arm use the detailed information on Chart 17360.

Tracy Arm extends north for about 9 miles before turning east in a sinuous passage between steep, Yosemite-like cliffs for 13 miles to its head. Here the North and South Sawyer Glaciers discharge into the sea. Icebergs are encountered throughout the passage, becoming more numerous as you come closer to the glaciers; the South Sawyer Glacier is the more active of the two. Approach to the glaciers depends on ice conditions which can vary from year to year. The water in Tracy Arm is very deep and the only anchorage possible is near the entrance taking care to avoid the rocky shoal at the east point of the entrance. Though this anchorage is of reasonable depth and protection, it is open to the southeast; in bad weather it would be better to retreat to Taku or elsewhere.

Endicott Arm

This Arm can be entered from the north by passing behind Harbor Island, or from a point 1 mile north of Point Astley you can steer for prominent Sumdum Glacier in order to reach the entrance. Wood Spit Light marks the southern part of this half-mile wide entrance which is more easily entered than Tracy Arm. Swirls will be encountered here. It is about 27 miles along the Arm to Dawes Glacier which discharges ice directly into the sea.

About 5 miles into Endicott Arm is an anchorage at **Sanford Cove** on the south side, abreast of Sumdum Island. It is an indifferent anchorage, deep and on a narrow shelf. The anchorage in Tracy Arm is preferred as a base, even with the few additional miles involved.

Fords Terror is a spectacular, narrow, steep-walled inlet about 5 miles long. It is on the north side of Endicott Arm and about 13 miles from Sumdum Island. About 1.25 miles into this inlet it narrows and shallows considerably. Since currents run up to 15 knots, accompanied with overfalls, entry is possible only at high water slack. This occurs about 20 minutes after high tide in Juneau. The best spot to anchor is in the west arm, off a waterfall in the northwest corner.

Chart 17300, 17313

TRACY ARM

Steep rocky walls

Peaks

N. Sawyer Gl.

Calving glaciers.
Access depends
on ice in Arm.

S. Sawyer Gl.

57° 50' N

Williams
Cove

See detail

6 ⚓
8 6
   7
7 8 4
5 0
    20
    30
    40

Pt. Coke

Swirls

Entrance Range
See Chart 17360

▲ Mt. Sumdum
6660'

Sumdum Gl.

TRACY & ENDICOTT ARMS

HOLKAM BAY

Harbor Is.

HOLKAM

BAY

Swirls

Fl. 2.5s

Wood Spit

Sumdum Is.

Bushy Is.

0   5   10 n.m.

Approx. Scale n.m.

Not to be used for navigation

Bares

FORD'S
TERROR

57° 40' N

Pt. Astley

Anch. on narrow
shelf.
Sanford Cove

⚓

Shoal

Enter and leave only
at high water slack.

Pt. Lookout

⚓ A possible anch. in very
settled weather. Not closely
examined.

Pt. League

WINDHAM BAY

Abandoned
Village

ENDICOTT ARM

Glacier

Sunset Is.

To Dawes
Glacier

STEPHENS PASSAGE

Sumdum
Gl.

? Icebergs   To Tracy Arm   Harbor Is.   To Endicott Arm   Wood Spit

APPROACHING ENTRANCE TO HOLKHAM BAY FROM

TAKU

This harbor is within 20 miles of Juneau. One would not normally make so short a run near one of the major ports of a trip, but it has one inestimable benefit in providing a safe harbor if strong winds are blowing down Taku Inlet.

Taku Inlet is 15 miles long and opens into the east side of Stephens Passage just beyond Taku Harbor. It has a spectacular backdrop of glaciers and peaks. Taku Glacier is advancing and producing sediments which make the upper part of the Inlet shoal. Stephens Passage is well known for the strength and bone-chilling temperatures of the winds that funnel down from the icefields above. While passage in summer is never as bad as in winter (when icing is an additional problem) it can be a rough and uncomfortable trip. In such cases it is wise to retreat to the security of Taku Harbor and wait for calmer weather before proceeding.

Taku Mountain (640 m/2,100 feet) is a prominent, conical landmark rising to the north of the entrance to the bay. There is a light is on Grave Point at the southern tip of Taku Mountain. Stockade Point, off a low, forested peninsula marks the southern boundary of the entrance. The entrance itself is wide and deep and has no difficulties.

The ruins of a large cannery wharf are near the northeastern corner of the protected harbor. About 200 m (600 feet) south are the T-shaped public floats having a 60 m (200-foot) face and a 30 m (100-foot) cross arm, which are connected to the boardwalk on shore by a float (walkway). The main floats have at least 2 fathoms or more alongside. No facilities are available, but Juneau is close by. Watch for old pilings when maneuvering in the dock area.

The harbor is shoal both at its northern head and in the southern section. Anchorage is possible in the southeastern part in 7 to 9 fathoms, soft bottom. Some minor current effects may be noticed. Winds can swirl off the mountains around the harbor, but the harbor itself is secure.

Limestone Inlet, the narrow opening less than 2 miles south of Taku Harbor, is an ecological research area and has no anchorage.

Slocum Inlet, about 5 miles north of Taku Harbor, is shoal and does not provide an anchorage. On the south shore is Butler Peak an even more conical peak than Taku Mountain, but half its size. All of these shores are steep and heavily wooded. The power line route is evident along the coast.

Grand Isle, in the middle of Stephens Passage, is prominent from the south and has steep slopes. Though it can be passed on either side the usual route passes it on the east.

Apart from the discomfort of the winds down Taku Inlet, the trip can be enjoyed for its scenery and to savor the approach to Juneau. From Juneau excursion flights can be taken over the glaciers and icefields. Taku Glacier Lodge, where overnight accommodation and guided tours can be arranged, is situated at the head of the inlet. Information on these facilities can be obtained at the Visitor Information Center or by inquiring at the Merchants Wharf in Juneau.

Detail – Taku Floats

Private Log Float

Rock

3   1½

200' Floats

Rocks bare
at Low tide

Boardwalk

TAKU HARBOR

STEPHENS PASSAGE

Chart 17314

0   ½   1 n.m.

Approx. Scale n.m.

Not to be used for navigation

STEPHENS

PASSAGE

N

Taku Mtn.
△ 2140

Prominent conical peak

Grave Pt
Fl 2·5s

ruins

Taku
See detail above.
58° 04 N

3

10

10

⚓

3

Stockade Pt.

Arthur Peak
3670 △

134° 00'W

Glass
Penins.   Grand Is.   Taku Hbr.   Pt. Coke
         Gastineau Ch.   Pt. League
             Stephens Passage   To Holkham Bay

APPROACH UP STEPHENS PASSAGE TO HOLKHAM BAY FROM SE

SECTION 7 - Juneau to Glacier Bay to Sitka

Additional views found in this section:

R&W Steel Tower

Microwave Twr.

Douglas & West Juneau

Green Bn.

To Aurora & Harris Harbors

Cruise ship area

JUNEAU HARBOR

Douglas Boat Basin

DOUGLAS HARBOR

In the ice pack before Muir Glacier

Blue Mouse Cove

Not to be used for navigation

Skagway (184)

Chilkoot Inlet

Chilkat Inlet

Haines (184)

Sullivan Is.

59°

Muir Inlet

Pt. Sherman

Adams Inlet
Muir Pt. (196)

Blue Mouse Cove (194)

Berners Bay
Pt. St. Mary

GLACIER

Sandy Cove

BAY

Boat Hbr

Bear Track Cove

James B.

Lincoln Is.

(192)

Bartlett Cove

Shelter Is.

C. Spencer

Gustavus

(190)

Pt. Retreat

Auke Bay
Airport

Taku
Inlet

(182)

Pt. Dundas

ICY PASSAGE

Pleasant
Is.

Juneau

Lemesurier Is.

Douglas Is. (180)

ICY

STRAIT

Inian Pass

(186)

CROSS

(189)

SOUND

Pt. Couverden

Hawk Inlet

Elfin Cove

The Sisters

(198)

(188)

C. Bingham

Hoonah
Port Frederick

CHICHAGOF

ADMIRALTY

YAKOBI

Lisianski Inlet

Is.

Pelican

Freshwater
Bay

58°

(200)

C. Cross

(210)

ISLAND

CHATHAM

Tenakee Inlet

Tako (176)

(202)

STRAIT

Khaz Bay

ISLAND

SEYMOUR CANAL

LYNN CANAL

STEPHENS PASSAGE

Mansfield Penin

136° 135° 134°

59°

58°

Joins page 209

JUNEAU

This is the state Capital and the largest city of the Southeast. The city lies along the west bank of Gastineau Channel beneath the steep flanks of Mount Juneau, and it extends northwesterly to Mendenhall Valley and Auke Bay. The town of Douglas is across the channel. The main port area is a cruise ship anchorage, while facilities for yachts are beyond the bridge joining the communities of Douglas and Juneau. The bridge has a clearance of 15 m (51 ft.).

Some transient moorage is available at the Juneau **City Floats** near the ferry terminal, but the main transient moorage facilities are at **Harris** and **Aurora Harbors** immediately beyond the bridge. The harbormaster's office is on the southeast corner of Aurora Basin and he controls all transient moorage. Report to him on arrival, either by calling on VHF Channel 16 (working Ch. 73) or checking into his office. If all transient slips are filled, you may have to take a vacant slip until directed elsewhere and be prepared to move if your are staying for an extended period of time. Harbor Washboard (with a dry-cleaner and laundry at the back) is the nearest shower and laundry facility, about 1.5 blocks south of Harris Harbor on the road leading to the bridge. A bank is nearby.

It is about .5 mile from Aurora to downtown Juneau; half that from Harris. The walk downtown along the street one block inland from the freeway goes past a supermarket, stores, restaurants, the post office, the Alaska State Museum and Centennial Hall. Both of the latter places are well worth a visit to learn about this part of Alaska.

The town of Douglas lies beyond Juneau in the Gastineau Channel. Operated by the City of Juneau, the **Douglas Boat Harbor** is located about 3 miles from the center of Juneau. Transient moorage is available on the first (of three) floats seen when entering the basin. Power and water are available on the float and there is no time limit on length of stay. Grocery stores and a restaurant are close by but fuel, repairs and any other services can only be obtained in Juneau.

Juneau is a tourist-oriented city. There seems to be a cruise ship or two docked almost all the time. There are many tourist shops in the downtown area. Perhaps because of this regular tourist parade and the winter's legislative period (marked by an influx of elected officials, staffs, and lobbyists) this city loses its friendliness when compared with other communities of the Southeast.

A visit to Mendenhall Glacier can be accomplished by city bus or rented car. Maps of hiking trails are found at the Center. The new community areas of Mendenhall Valley are served by a large shopping center which rivals the selection of goods found in Juneau. The airport is also located here.

JUNEAU HARBOR

Chart 17315

JUNEAU

Not to be used for navigation

0   500'   1000'   ¼ m

Approx. Scale enlarged section.

Freeway to
Mendelhall Glacier
& Auke Bay

AURORA HARBOR

Shoal

Egan Drive

GASTINEAU CHANNEL

Breakwater

2T

T-app.3

Bn

Pump-out

F

Gas Dock

"Breakwater" Motel

High School

Swimming Pool

Walking route
to city center,
P.a. stores
½ mile

T
Harbormaster's Office

Note:-
J – John or Head
T – Telephone
O – Oil disch. tank

Mt. Juneau
(Micro. Twr.)

134° 25' W

Gold Cr.

Aurora Harbor

SEE DETAIL ABOVE

Harris Harbor

JUNEAU

58° 18' N

R. Qk Fl

Launch Ramp

HARRIS HARBOR

Transient

Gov't Docks

To downtown Juneau
Showers & Laundry

Seaplane Float

Bridge 50' cl

WEST JUNEAU

Cruise ship anchorage

GASTINEAU CHANNEL

Douglas Is.

Bridge to Douglas
Clearance 50'

R. Qk. Fl.

0   ¼   ½

Approx. Scale n.m.

To Douglas

AUKE BAY

This handy starting point for the next stage of the cruise is off Stephens Passage, facing Favorite and Saginaw Channels. Coghlan Island is on the southwestern side of Auke Bay, about 1 mile northwest of Spuhn Island. Point Louisa and Indian Point are on the north shore of the bay, about 1.2 miles northwest and .6 miles north, respectively, of the northern extremity of Coghlan Island. Fairhaven is on the shore of the bay between these two points. After passing .2 miles south and east of Coghlan Island, enter the bay on a northeasterly course as indicated on the sketch.

Since this is the only deep-draft facility in the area it is the site of the Alaska State Ferry Terminal, the National Marine Fisheries Service and the National Parks Service Pier. The pleasure craft facilities that cater to both transient vessels and local boats are located in the northeastern part of the bay.

Auke Bay Public Float is about 300m (330 yards) north of the National Marine Fisheries Service Float. There are over 50 transient berths which can accommodate vessels up to 18 m (60 feet) in length on a first-come, first-served basis with the maximum allowable stay being 72 hours. The Juneau harbormaster controls the public floats and the 14m (45-foot) grid which is just to the north of the floats. The harbormaster monitors VHF Ch. 16 (working channel 73) and can be reached by phone at (907) 789-0819. Water and power are available on some floats. The two private marinas are filled with local vessels and do not have space for transients. Fuel, marine supplies and minor repairs are available at both marinas. A travelift is available at Dehart's Marina. Anchorage in 8 -11 fathoms can be taken as indicated and shore access is convenient.

A store with groceries, liquor and sundry items and a restaurant are one block up the hill and there is a telephone and a weather forecast device at the top of the gangway. Restrooms, waste oil receptacles, pump-out facilities and garbage collection facilities are available as shown on the sketch.

Juneau may be reached by a 33-mile trip around Douglas Island and up Gastineau Channel which is marked by lights, buoys, and daybeacons. An alternate route crossing Mendenhall Bar should be taken only by vessels having a fairly shallow draft and after a thorough and careful investigation of current tide and bar conditions. A generous allowance must be made for the fact that the actual height of high tide can differ markedly from the predicted high tide, with actual height usually less than the predicted height. A free diagram of the channel across Mendenhall Bar is available from the Aids to Navigation Branch of Coast Guard District office in Juneau or by writing to: Commander, 17th Coast Guard District, Federal Bldg., Box 25517, Juneau, AK 99802-5517. The channel is marked, but at low water the markers rest on the bars so current knowledge of the channel is essential before using this route.

AUKE BAY

Detail – Auke Harbor

Veterans Memorial Highway

Groceries Liquor

Rest Rooms

Andrews Marina

F Fuel →

Private Marinas

Launch Ramp

Dehart's Marina

Harbormaster

F Fuel

Pump-out

Washrooms Telephone Garbage

AUKE BAY

Transients Public Floats

Approx. Scale – n.m. & ft.

0   500'   1000'   ¼ m

Approx. Scale   n.m.

0   1   2 n.m.

Not to be used for navigation

Chart 17315

See Detail

Auke Lake

Ferry

10f

Shore Acres

Pt. Louisa

Mooring Buoys

10f

10f

⊥ 8-11f

×
×

G⊙ ×
3f

AUKE BAY

10f

Coghlan Is.

Aero Bn.

Mendenhall Peninsula

Spuhn Is.

N

Not to be used for navigation

LYNN CANAL

This long and beautiful inlet and its arms reach about 85 miles NNW from the junction of Chatham and Icy Straits. It is deep and varies in width from 3 to 6 miles. Lined on both sides by glaciers and peaks, this can be a very scenic trip.

Haines

On the west side of Chilkoot Inlet in Portage Bay, this town has a spectacular backdrop composed of the Cathedral Peaks. The small boat harbor is protected by a rock breakwater and entry should be made via the southern entrance. The harbormaster controls moorage and monitors VHF Chs. 12 and 16 or can be called at (907) 766-2448. A 4,000 lb. hoist is available on the dock.

Groceries, showers, a laundromat and restaurants are available in town and fuel and water may be obtained in the harbor. The ferry terminal at Lutak Inlet is a few miles out of town. The Haines Highway gives year-round access to the Alaska Highway.

The Chilkat Dancers give evening performances at Fort William H. Seward. Indian arts and crafts are readily available in the shops.

Skagway

Skagway lies near the end of Taiya Inlet off Chilkoot Inlet. The harbormaster monitors VHF Ch 16 or can be called at (907) 983-2626. The small boat harbor is protected by a breakwater and lies adjacent to the ferry terminal and the railway. Fuel and pump-out facilities are available as shown.

The population of 2,000 is greatly reduced from the 30,000 in the days of Soapy Smith. Skagway celebrates its gold rush history by maintaining the atmosphere with unchanged store fronts and locals in period costumes. A highway gives access in summer to the Alaska Highway.

Ship Loading area

TOWN OF SKAGWAY

RV Park

Not to be used for navigation

Tanks

Boat Launching

Parking
Harbourmaster
Walkway & ramp

135° 19' W

59° 27' N

Ferry Terminal

Pumpout

E

D

C

2
Seaplane
B

A

White Pass
& Yukon Rly.

N

Fl. 4s

F

Fuel
Float

Breakwater

Grid

Grid

Walkway
& ramp

4

10

approx.

10

TAIYA INLET

Cruise ship terminal

SKAGWAY

Chart 17317

0   100'   300'   500'   ⅛ m

Approx. Scale feet & n.m.

Not to be used for navigation

Breakwaters

Launching ramp

135° 26' W

Telephone,
Walkway & ramp

A

Grid

TOWN
OF
HAINES

Harbourmaster

CHILKOOT INLET

59° 14' N

N

B
2

C

D

E

2½

F

Dock

Breakwater float

Seaplanes

2½

Fl. R. 2·5s

HAINES

Approach channel

0   100'   300'   500'   ⅛ m

Approx. Scale feet & n.m.

ANCHORAGES AT THE SOUTH END OF LYNN CANAL

The junction of Lynn Canal, Chatham, and Icy Straits is a crossroads for yachts bound to or from Glacier Bay or Juneau. There are two very good anchorages in this area.

Funter Bay

Mansfield Peninsula projects NNW off Admiralty Island with Lynn Canal on its west side. Funter Bay is on the west side, about 10 miles south of Point Retreat (the tip of Mansfield Peninsula). It is a fairly large bay with several islands near the entrance.

On a northern approach Naked Island (with a light on it) and the pair of smaller islands called the "Kittens" should be passed on their west side. The northern point of the entrance to Funter Bay is Clear Point (with a light on it). There is a wide opening to the group of islands off the southern point of the entrance, Rat Island, Station Island and two smaller islets.

A State-operated 30m (100 ft.) float can be found at the ruins of the cannery wharf in the northern part of the bay, between Coot and Crab Coves. Caution is needed in this area due to the ruins of the wharf and a rocky ledge nearby. Open moorage is available and there are no facilities or services and vessels must retain all waste materials. Trails provide a welcome chance to stretch your legs on nearby public lands.

Swanson Harbor

Across Lynn Canal from Funter Bay is Swanson Harbor, formed by a group of islands lying off the land. Less than a mile off the southern tip of Couverden Island is Rocky Island, a prominent, rounded, grass-topped rock with a light. Set a course to enter the channel between Point Couverden and Rocky Island. Leaving Rocky Island astern, proceed northwesterly, follow along the southwest shore of Couverden Island, then take a mid-channel course between it and Entrance and Ansley Islands successively. Around the northwestern tip of Couverden Island is a bight with drying flats and a small island to the west. Here a 45 m (150-foot) State operated float is located, unconnected to the shore. Boats can moor on both sides.

At high tide the scenic mountains behind Juneau and Auke Bay can be seen from the float. When it is calm the float has many annoying deer flies but with a breeze they are not in evidence.

Alternate anchorage can be taken off the stony beach on **Ansley Island** at the side of the harbor on the shelf close to shore. Large vessels could anchor in the bight at the head. The gap between Ansley and Entrance Islands has rocks and reefs that discourage use. From Rocky Island courses may be set down Chatham or Icy Straits.

Mt. Robert Barron

Chart 17316

Clear Point behind — Naked Is. — Station Is.

APPROACHING FUNTER BAY FROM NNE, distant about 2 miles

From Juneau,
Aulke Bay, Haines
& Skagway

MANSFIELD
PENINSULA.

Funter   100' Float

LYNN

Naked Is. Fl. 6s.

58°15'N   58°15'N

The Kittens

Clear Pt.
Fl. G. 2.5 s.

150'
float

CANAL

Rat Is.

Station Is.   FUNTER BAY

Couverden
Rock

Float

Ansley Is.

See Detail

Couverden
Is.

Entrance Is.

Fl. R

Pt. Couverden

ICY
STRAIT

o Glacier Bay,
Hoonah, Elfin Cove,

135°05'W

Rocky Is.
Fl. 4s.

135°00'W

Not to be used for navigation

N

To Tenakee
& Angoon
Via Chatham
Strait.

134°55'W

ANCHS. AT THE S. END OF
LYNN CANAL

0   1   2   3

Approx. Scale n.m.

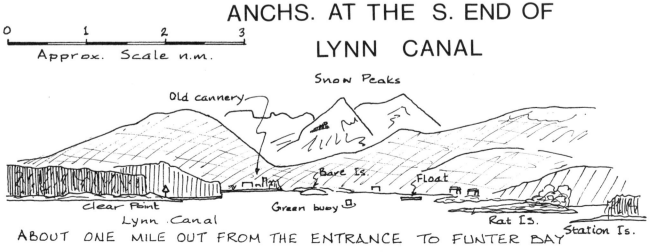

Snow Peaks

Old cannery

Bare Is.   Float

Clear Point
Lynn Canal

Green buoy

Rat Is.
Station Is.

ABOUT ONE MILE OUT FROM THE ENTRANCE TO FUNTER BAY

HOONAH

This is the largest Tlingit community in Southeast Alaska. The original Tlingit name of "huna" means "Place where the north wind doesn't blow" and warm ocean currents usually keep minimum temperatures just below freezing.

Enter Port Frederick after passing the light at Inner Point Sophia. The former fish plant docks just beyond the point is a facility for cruise ships waiting to enter Glacier Bay and the cannery is now a museum where machinery and equipment once used are on display. The fuel dock, marked by a large "Ace" sign, is outside the harbor. Since the fuel pier is on pilings and does not have a camel at the base it is necessary to use horizontal fenders when tying to the pilings. You must climb the ladder to pay for fuel so dock near it and use a pair of old gloves for grasping the dirty rungs. The fuel dock is open Mon. to Sat., 9 a.m. to 5:30 p.m. and can be contacted on Ch. 11 by calling "Hoonah Trading," or phone (907) 945-3211.

The transient float, operated by the town, is at the north end of the basin. Water and power are available on the docks and shower and laundry facilities are next to the harbormaster's office. The docks are very busy during summer months and reservations are recommended; contact the harbormaster at (907) 945-3670 or Fax (907) 945-3445. A walk along the gravel shore road brings you to the store, café, hardware and gift shops. The State ferry makes regular stops at Hoonah and daily air service links the community to Juneau.

Chart 17302

NEARING THE TURN TO SWANSON HARBOR FLOAT.

Not to be used for navigation

LYNN CANAL

No Use Ledge

Dries at LW

Pilings

Reef dries at LW

Pilings

58°13'N

Dries at LW

150' float

12   4

15

20   18   Shallow, stony beaches at L.W.

stony beach

Ansley Is.

Couverden Is.

ICY

SWANSON HARBOR

ICY STRAIT

STRAIT

135°07'N

1000   0   ¼   ½

Approx. Scale n.m. (and feet)

Chart 17316

No entry

Entrance Is.

Curve course to pass reef off Entr. Is.

Sketch above

Steep cliff   Snow peak

Ansley Is.

Light, Fl. R. 6s

Entrance Is. ———— Sharpe Ledge ——— Couverden Is.

ENTERING SWANSON HARBOR, LEAVING ROCKY IS. ASTERN ½ MILE

GLACIER BAY

This magnificent area with its high, permanently snow-clad peaks and over 20 large and many smaller glaciers are included in the 4,400 square miles of Glacier Bay National Monument. Tidewater glaciers in the Bay are Grand Pacific, Johns Hopkins, Lamplugh, Margerie, McBride, Reid and Riggs. The National Park Service controls entry to the Park.

The entrance to Glacier Bay is north off Icy Strait, and lies between Point Gustavus on the east and Point Carolus on the west. The bay is large, of varying width and extends in two major arms. It is about 45 miles north to the head of Muir Inlet and 54 miles northwest to the head of Tarr or John Hopkins Inlets. The western portion of the Park includes the peaks of the Fairweather range culminating in the wedge-shaped peak of Mount Fairweather (4,650 m/15,300 feet). The National Park Service regulations aim at minimizing the disturbance of humpback whales, an endangered species that feed in Glacier Bay. A maximum of 25 private vessels may enter the Park for up to 7 days from June 1 to September 30. There are reports of some vessels being limited to a 3-day visit. Meanwhile two cruise ships, 3 tour boats and 6 charter vessels are allowed in the Bay at any one time. **Vessels may not enter the Park, even to proceed to Bartlett Cove, without a permit or permission given by telephone or VHF in lieu of a permit.** Thus, if early or just arriving in the area other anchorages must be found while waiting.

Requests for applications for permits and information about the park should be addressed to: The Superintendent, Glacier Bay National Park, P. O. Box 140,Gustavus, Alaska 99826-0140. You may get permission to enter by phoning 907-697-2627 or by VHF Ch 12 or16 to KWM20 Bartlett Cove when within VHF range. Additional information can be accessed at www.nps.gov/glba/ and the e-mail address is GLBA_Administration@nps.gov.

Since applications are not accepted earlier than 60 days before the entry date requested vessels traveling from distant ports are adversely affected. Permits are not needed for visits concluding before June 1 or beginning after September 30. The most heavily booked period is July 4 to 15, the time when local vessels as well as boats coming from the south are in the area.

The application requires the following: vessel's name and number, skipper's name, address, phone number, the number of people on board, a description of the boat, the proposed date of entry (first, second, and third choices), and the duration of one's visit. Once in the Park an extension of up to 7 days may be requested provided that unused permits are available. Even with a permit, confirmation is required just before entry by calling the Park Office by telephone on VHF within 48 hours of the scheduled entry (no later than 10 a.m. on the day of entry. Note that this fixes your date of entry; if you are either too early or too late you are back to square one and have lost any benefit of early application. If this happens, it is worthwhile to contact the Park Office on a daily basis to see if a cancellation has occurred that makes a space available to you. Entry occurs when you cross the line between Point Gustavus and Point Carolus.

THE APPROACH TO GLACIER BAY FROM ESE, distant about 20 miles

Chart 17318

Grand Pacific Gl.
John Muir Gl. Riggs Gl.
Cushing Gl.
6/1 7/15 No Motorized Vessels
McBride Gl.
Margerie Gl.
Carroll Gl.
Rendu Gl.
Burroughs Gl.
Casement Gl.
59° 00'
Tarr Inlet
Plateau Gl.
Goose Cove
Russel Is.
Rendu Inlet
Wachusett Inlet
Queen Inlet
Muir Inlet
John Hopkins Inlet
G L A C I E R
Composite Is
Morse Gl.
Adams Inlet
NMV
Tidal Inlet
Adams Gl. 50'
Dirt Gl.
La Pérouse Gl.
Reid Gl.
Gilbert Penin.
Scidmore Gl.
Blue Mouse Cove
Hugh Miller Inlet
Tlingit Pt.
Sebree I.
John Hopkins Gl.
1 - Topeka Gl.
2 - Toyatte Gl.
3 - Kadachan Gl.
4 - Tyeen Gl.
5 - Charley Gl.
6 - John Gl.
7 - Clark Gl.
8 - Gilman Gl.
9 - Hoonah Gl.
10 - Kashoto Gl.
Hugh Miller Gl.
B A Y
Lone Is.
Geikie Rks
North Sandy Cove
Drake Is.
40'
Geikie Inlet
△ Mt. Bertha 10,000'
Mt. Crillon 12,728'
Geikie Gl.
Willoughby Is.
Beartrack Cove
B R A D Y
I C E F I E L D
Beardslee Is.
△ Mt. La Pérouse 10,728'
Strawberry Is.
Perouse Gl.
N
Young Is.
30'
Lester Is.
Berg Bay
Bartlett Cove
Not to be used for navigation
Park Hdqrs.
GLACIER BAY

NATIONAL PARK

0   5   10

Approx. Scale n.m.

Icy Point
Pt. Gustavus
Ancon Rk
Pt. Carolus →
Dundas Bay
58° 20'
PACIFIC
Taylor Bay
OCEAN
I C Y   S T R A I T
137° 00'
Cape Spencer
50'   40'
30'
20'
10'
136° 00'

GLACIER BAY Cont'd.

Other regulations apply to your vessel in the park, and a pamphlet outlining them is sent with any communication from the Park Service. Briefly, you are required to stay more than .25 mile from a whale and to travel mid-channel courses at less than 10 knots in designated areas (presently from the entrance to Strawberry Islands and/or Bartlett Cove).

ENTRANCE TO GLACIER BAY FROM S, distant about 2 miles

BARTLETT COVE

Located on the east side of the bay and 4 miles from the entrance, this cove is the main Park Service Ranger Office and Entry Station. A large lodge is located here and the Park Service maintains a pier, small craft floats and a fuel float. Vessels over 9 m (30 feet) must anchor out and may use the floats on a first-come, first-serve basis for not more than 8 hours in every 48 hours. Anchorage may be taken in the quadrant north to northeast of the pier in about 7 fathoms. Tour boats dock at the pier so allow for their passage. A seaplane landing area marked by seasonal buoys, is northeast of the pier where anchoring is prohibited. Dinghies and skiffs can be moored at the rear of the floats. Water is available at the floats but is so highly treated as to be almost unsuitable for drinking. Although supplies are unavailable, there is a garbage disposal station where trash must be sorted into recyclable containers made of <u>any</u> material, compostables (food waste), trash (waxed/plastic-coated paper, snack wrappers, tissues and disposable diapers). Batteries and biohazard wastes such as syringes and bandages must be clearly marked.

The Park Rangers provide information as to anchorages, ice conditions, regulations, etc. Not all areas are open to traffic. For example, Marble Islands are closed to foot traffic because of the sea birds. Other areas sometimes have restrictions related to bears.

Strong rips and tidal currents occur in the Narrows approaching Strawberry Island. Either channel past Willoughby Island may be taken, but the current is evident on both sides. Above Willoughby less current is evident.

Under certain conditions in summer, outflow winds of great velocity pour out the inlets that lead from the mountain and glacier massifs on the west. They whip up steep waves for varying distances downwind across Glacier Bay. Such winds scream out of Berg Bay, Geikie Inlet, Hugh Miller Inlet and Reid Inlet. These winds can make entering these inlets very difficult, and the anchorages in or near them dangerous. Keep this in mind when using these inlets. Fog and mist are frequent in the colder parts of the Bay in late summer. The Park Service broadcasts weather forecasts on VHF Ch. 16/09 at 8:45 a.m. and 5:45 p.m.

Chart 17318

One method to explore Glacier Bay is to move out of Bartlett Cove as soon as practicable to an advance base anchorage. Depending on the weather this will allow for exploration and return from the ice-filled arms where passage may be slow and sometimes difficult and stressful. **Blue Mouse Cove** is a good base for visiting Tarr and John Hopkins Inlets, with **Reid Inlet** a further advance base to use in good weather.

Other anchorages in the Bay, with their own attractions include the following: Berg Bay (care is needed because of the many rocks in the entrance; anchor on the north side of the west arm), North and South Sandy Cove, Tidal Inlet, Russell Island, Goose Cove Adams Inlet, North and South Fingers Bay, Beardslee, Entrance, Johnson Cove, Willoughby Island (north end), Shag Cove (in Geikie Inlet), and Sebree Cove (between Tlinglit Point and the southern part of Sebree Island).

Peak –	Mt. Perouse	Mt. Crillon	Mt. Bertha	Mt. Fairweather
Height –	10,728'	12,728'	10,000'	15,300'
Distance –	43 miles	49 miles	45 miles	67 miles

VIEW OF GLACIER BAY NATIONAL PARK PEAKS FROM BARTLETT COVE

BLUE MOUSE COVE

This is an excellent anchorage to use as a base for exploring the northwestern arms of Glacier Bay. It is a well protected cove at the end of Gilbert Peninsula about 29 miles from Bartlett Cove. Anchorage can be taken on two 8-fathom patches on the south and southwestern sides of the cove. A smaller but shallower anchorage is in a niche on the north side.

The west side of the cove looks out over Hugh Miller Inlet to a truly beautiful mountain scene. Winds can blow down the peaks and inlets behind the cove, but it provides better protection than any other nearby anchorage.

Ice is not a concern in Blue Mouse Cove though an occasional berg may ground on the shoals near the entrance. Access to the glaciers in John Hopkins and Tarr Inlets depends on the time of year and on the amount of glacial calving which has occurred. If John Hopkins Glacier has been active small vessels rarely get further than Lamplugh Glacier. Grand Pacific and Margerie Glaciers in Tarr Inlet have tended to be easier to approach. However, year to year conditions differ so greatly that you must take things as they come.

REID INLET

This advanced base has its own tidewater glacier, and anchoring here gives a very special feeling. However this should be considered as an anchorage to be used only during settled, fair weather. (Note the remark on outflow winds made earlier.) There is a shallow bar across the entrance. Suitable anchorage may be taken on the west side tucked in behind the drying area and the island. Park regulations prohibit the operation of generators in the inlet between the hours of 10 p.m. and 6 a.m.

Gullied Peak

one Is.

Blue Mouse Cove

Gilbert Peninsula

APPROACHING BLUE MOUSE COVE FROM WNW, distant about 2 miles.

Chart 17318

Occasional icebergs

GLACIER BAY

Low land, shrubs & trees

50

136°30'W

58° 48'N

20

10

Beautiful mountains beyond Miller and Charpentier Inlets

11

Small trees and shrubs (abt. 250')

7

6

13

N

Low Point

10

9

Stony beach

BLUE MOUSE COVE

GLACIER BAY

abt. 600'

1000'   0   ¼   ½ n.m.

Approx. Scale. n.m. (and feet)

Not to be used for navigation

Mt. Fairweather
15,300'

Hugh Miller Inlet

Blue Mouse Cove

Glacier Bay
To Tarr & John Hopkins Inlets

To Rendu Glacier

APPROACHING BLUE MOUSE COVE FROM ESE, distant about 3 miles

An alternative anchorage on the other side may be available but as the movement of ice varies from year to year current ice conditions determine the preferred anchorage spots.

When the bergy bits in the inlet are not numerous, the vessel can be taken to within 2.5 mile of the glacier. It is not difficult to land on the shores of the inlet near the anchorage and hike over an easy trail to the face of the glacier. Rumbling, creaking sounds give evidence of the movement of the glacier, advising caution near the glacier's face, as immense slabs of ice may break away (calve) with little or no warning. Since the tidal range is very high in these latitudes the dinghy should be secured above the high water line to avoid a cold, bone-chilling retrieval when the tide comes in.

NORTH SANDY COVE

This anchorage provides a base for exploring Muir Inlet, and lies about 20 miles from Bartlett Cove. The cove can be approached from the northwest via either channel past Puffin Island. The best anchorages are along the southern shores. No-see-ums are prevalent here, and they can be annoying if one is anchored close to the shore. Another anchorage, though exposed to the south, is at Sebree Cove, between Tlingit Point and the southern end of Sebree Island. Give safe clearance to Tlingit Point to avoid the rock south of the islet off the point.

The inner recesses of Adams inlet, Wachusett Inlet and Muir Inlet can only be visited by motorized vessels before June 1 and after July 15. During this period seals are birthing their offspring which they leave on ice floes while they search for food. It is essential that the young seals not be disturbed for they slip into the water and become lost, resulting in their death. Consequently only canoe and kayaks are allowed in these areas during this critical period when the young are so vulnerable. Canoes and kayaks can be rented at the Glacier Bay Lodge, just to the north of the Park Headquarters in Bartlett Cove.

It is about 20 miles from North Sandy Cove to the restricted area of Muir Inlet where Muir Glacier which has receded so much that it is no longer a tidewater glacier. Adams Inlet, about 8 miles along, has strong tidal currents at the entrance which is strewn with rocks. Seven miles further brings you to Sealers Island, a small island close to the east shore of Muir Inlet. East of the island is shoal and narrow Goose Cove, where anchorage may be taken. A Park Ranger is stationed here.

Though there are fewer glaciers along Muir Inlet it is an exceptionally interesting and revealing journey. The rapid retreat of Muir Glacier over the last few decades has exposed the whole spectrum of development of glaciated land. Near North Sandy Cove the steep mountainsides are covered with timber and other vegetation. But as you travel further into the inlet the terrain becomes steeper and more barren. Proceeding on from Riggs and McBride Glaciers (which can be easily reached), the land is raw and stark. Glacial streams and moraines mark the sides. Since Muir Glacier has receded so much in recent years that it is no longer a tidewater glacier, bergy bits are not as prevalent as they once were.

An additional attraction of this area is that the cruise ships do not come up this narrow, inlet. This area is favored by campers and kayakers who often camp on the flat area near McBride Glacier.

APPROACHING NORTH SANDY COVE FROM NW, distant about 3 miles.

North Sandy Cove

Puffin Is.

Sturgess Is.

Chart 17318

NORTH SANDY COVE

GLACIER BAY

Not to be used for navigation

1000' 0 ¼ ½ n.m.

Approx. Scale n.m. (and feet)

N

136° 00' W

Steep hillside.

Steep cliff

50

Shoal
Large boulders
Steep

10

Puffin Is.
Low trees & shrubs

30

NORTH SANDY COVE

reefs uncover at L.W.

Stream

Bears seen occasionally.

Sand & stone beach

58° 43' N

⌄6

⌄7

7⌄

7   16

6

⌄7

Sand & stone beach

Trees and shrubs

Meadow

Covered only at very H.W. No Passage

SOUTH SANDY COVE

Mt. Wright behind.

Muir Point

Muir Inlet   To North Sandy Cove   Sturgess Is.   S. Sandy Cove

APPROACHING NORTH SANDY COVE FROM SE, distant about 3 miles.

ELFIN COVE

The small village of Elfin Cove lies in a beautiful setting on the south side of Cross Sound and is well worth visiting if Glacier Bay is on your itinerary. Both North and South Inian Pass connect Icy Strait to Cross Sound. The route through North Inian Pass is longer but with less current than South Inian Pass. A good anchorage, **Inian Cove**, is on the north side of the Inian Islands. Anchor in the wide end of the cove, where a mooring buoy and dolphins are in place. A prominent light, North Inian Pass Light, is on the northwest point of the next small island to the west.

South Inian Pass is the shorter and more attractive route to Elfin Cove. It should be traversed near slack, for the current can be strong (approaching 9 knots on the ebb), and when a westerly wind opposes the ebb severe tidal rips and steep waves and swirls occur at the western end of the pass. At times this may make the passage extremely difficult.

Point Lavinia, marked by a light, is the southerly point of the western entrance to South Inian Pass. Elfin Cove is in a small inlet in the north shore of the Inian Peninsula south of Point Lavinia. A large island, with a couple of smaller ones nearby, lies at the entrance to the cove. Passage is possible on either side of the large island. The harbormaster controls moorage in both the inner and outer harbors; he monitors VHF CH. 16 or can be called at (907) 239-2203. The eastern entrance leads directly into the outer harbor of Elfin Cove where most transient vessels lie (open moorage). Rafting may be necessary as the float is only 60m (200 ft.) long, with vessels mooring on either side. A seaplane landing is at the tip and a long wharf connects the float to the shore. Apart from water at the gangway and limited use of power, no facilities are available. During northerly winds uncomfortable swells run into the outer harbor making the inner harbor inviting.

Another dock is to the west, behind the large island, where fuel may be obtained. Fish buyers transact business at this dock. Beyond this float a route via a narrow dredged channel (the Gut) leads into the inner harbor. Most of the local fishing vessels berth here. The channel should be entered at or near high water as it is only 12m (40 ft.) wide and has a controlling depth of 2.4m (8 ft.). Markers indicate the route.

The village of **Elfin Cove** clusters around the edge of the harbors. The Post Office, general store, laundry and most of the houses are close to the boardwalk which is built up along the steep, rocky edges of the cove. Some vacation homes are also around the boardwalk. The permanent summer population is less than 50, which is augmented by fishing boats based here, and other transient visitors. However, in winter life in the cove reverts to an isolated, inward-looking existence where there is little contact with the outside world for the few hardy souls remaining.

When you sit at the end of the dock and look across to Brady Glacier beneath the tall peaks of Glacier Bay, the lure that takes people north and draws some to stay seems all too clear.

APPROACHING ELFIN COVE FROM N distant about 2 miles

ELFIN COVE

CROSS SOUND

Chart 17302, 17303

Approx. Scale n.m.

Cross Sound

Fl. 4s.

Approx. 3 fathom Line

10

Seaplanes
Outer Hbr.

3 6

3

Nº

Washroom
+ Telephone

3

Fuel
Dock

Bn
G#1

1½

Bn
G#3

FL.R.4s.

2

2

Bn.R#4

ELFIN COVE

1½

Grocery
& Hdware

Sidewalk

Grid

Channel dredged
to 8' × 40'wide (1976)
Enter at HW only.

Bn
G#5

4

Inner Hbr.

3

3

Detail - Elfin Cove Harbor

0   500   1000   1500

Approx. Scale (feet)

Not to be used for navigation

N. INIAN PASS

From Icy Strait

Fl. 4s

Inian Cove

INIAN   ISLANDS

136° 20'W

INIAN
ISLANDS

S. INIAN Pass

rips

Strong currents

Pt. Lavinia

SOUND

Is.

INIAN

F

PENIN.

Elfin Cove
See detail
above.

CROSS

Three

Hill Is.

Althorp Rk.

58°10'N

Port
Althorp

To Lisianski
Inlet

PELICAN, LISIANSKI INLET and LISIANSKI STRAIT

The open Pacific Ocean lies beyond Cape Spencer and Cape Bingham at the entrance to Cross Sound. The direct, open sea route can be avoided by passing to the south of George Island and north of Three Hill Island to reach the entrance to Lisianski Inlet. This 21-mile long inlet extends southeasterly and is lined by pretty, snow-covered peaks. The first 6 miles lie between two very large islands, Chichagof Island on the east and Yakobi Island on the west.

The small port of **Pelican** lies about 11 miles inside Lisianski Inlet, on the northern shore. It is mainly a fishing town and in season hums with activity. Public floats operated by the city are in the center of town, about a half mile north of the Alaska Ferry dock. The harbormaster monitors VHF Ch. 16 or can be called at (907) 735-2212. A general store, post office and laundromat are along the boardwalk near the fuel dock where water is available. Rosies Bar is the center of activity in the evenings.

Lisianski Strait enters Lisianski Inlet about 4.5 miles northwest of Pelican (6.5 miles from the entrance). Miner Island, wooded and surrounded by kelp, lies off the northern point. A narrow passage separates the north point of Miner Island from Yakobi Island, but should not be attempted.

Southeast of Miner Island, and about a mile south is Junction Island, small, wooded, and marked by a quick flashing light. Between Miner and Junction Island (closer to the latter) there are rocky patches covered with only a few feet of water. For vessels that are not going to Pelican but are turning into Lisianski Strait the turn can be by staying about 300 m (1,000 feet) off Miner Island. There are tidal rips and swirls here, for the currents coming down Lisianski Inlet meet those coming through Lisianski Strait.

Almost as soon as one passes Miner Island the Strait begins to narrow. About a mile from the junction the channel passes between Yakobi Island and a shoal area with two small islands marked by a flashing red light at its southern end. Just beyond, a daybeacon marks a shoal near a small float and the buildings of a nickel exploration camp at Bohemia Creek. Four miles further on, the opening to Stag Bay is passed.

The opening to the ocean is encumbered with rocks on both sides, making the actual channel narrower than it appears. On the south side is Esther Island which has a flashing red light with a red triangular day mark. A course can be laid passing between the rocky patches at the entrance and south of the seasonal bell buoy off Star Rock. Swell, surge and breaking waves may be encountered, depending on the external sea conditions.

Sea otters are well established here and may be seen in the Strait or around the entrance.

EXIT FROM LISIANSKI STRAIT TO GULF OF ALASKA, VIEW N'WARD

CROSS SOUND

Three Hill Is.

To Inian Passes
& Elfin Cove

Pt. Lucan

Chart 17302

PELICAN
LISIANSKI INLET
& LISIANSKI STRAIT

Column Pt.

Cape Bingham

Bingham Cove

Approx. Scale n.m.
0   1   2   3   4   5 m

Not to be used for navigation

Mite Cove Fl.R.

LISIANSKI

Nᵒ

YAKOBI
ISLAND

Bn

Fl.G.

Shoal

Miner Is
Currents meet here.

58° 00'N

Nickel Expl.
Mining Camp Bn
(small float)

Fl.R.

Fl.R 2.5s

Junction Is. Qk.Fl.

PELICAN

F   See detail below

Light

LISIANSKI STRAIT

Stag Bay

GULF OF ALASKA

Numerous inlets, islets, rocks and shoals along the coast

Grid   Grid

Fuel Dock

Seaplane Float

Shoal

Boardwalk

Sea Otters observed here

Fl.6s
Pt. Theodore
Surge, swell and breakers
Star Rock

Esther Is.
Fl.R Daymak

Foul

Pt. Urey
Bn Urey Rocks

Grid

Detail –
Pelican Harbor

Ramp

Ferry Dock

Brenkwater

LISIANSKI STRAIT to KHAZ BAY

The west coast of Chichagof Island is full of interest and spectacular scenery. From Star Rock bell buoy set a course to clear Porcupine Rock, a prominent, bare offshore rock 3 miles south. In good weather Ilas Bay to the east can be entered and a route threaded carefully into **Porcupine Bay**, where anchorage is available in 8 fathoms, mud. From this location a visit can be made to the hot springs at White Sulphur Springs, first by boat to the west arm of Bertha Bay about a mile south, then over a half mile trail to the two buildings at the springs. Bertha Bay is full of rocks. Use US chart 17321 when entering.

From Porcupine Rock a course can be taken for 6 miles to enter Imperial Passage between Hill and Hogan Islands. Though there are many rocks and islands off the points on each side, the passage is wide and leads into the expanse of Portlock Harbor. South Passage is an equally good entrance. Within Portlock Harbor the effect of the swell and wind are not felt, and an inner route can be threaded through Surveyor and Ogden Passages. **Didrickson Bay**, on the east side of Portlock Harbor, has anchorage toward the head of the bay in sight of the waterfall in about 10 fathoms, soft mud. The bay shoals for some distance before the waterfall.

A more protected anchorage can be taken in **Kimshan Cove** at the junction of Surveyor and Ogden Passages (just before reaching the #3 green day beacon near Fitz Island). Enter in the middle of the opening to the cove, taking care to avoid the crab traps that are scattered about, and anchor on the east side. On the southern shore there are the pilings and ruins of a wharf as well as buildings belonging to a gold-mining venture on Dooth Mountain.

Leaving Kimshan Cove be careful to pass at least 90 m (300 feet) away from the green day beacon near Fitz Island to avoid the reef which extends south of the marker. Ogden Passage leads behind a screen of islands towards Smooth Channel, which is the best outlet to the sea through Khaz Bay.

Entry to the anchorages in **Klag Bay** is marked by a day beacon and an unlit range leading roughly northwesterly into The Gate. From The Gate the route passes through the scattered rocks of Elbow Passage, then past the east side of Klag Island to the head of Klag Bay. Anchorage can be found anywhere in the bay, or off the abandoned mining town of Chichagof near the head. This is grizzly bear country so make plenty of noise—a pop can with a few pebbles being rattled works well—and be watchful while exploring on land. Enter Klag Bay just at or past low water slack when the many rocks can be clearly seen and the currents are reduced. At springs the current can run to 4 knots.

Guide Rocks, which are bare and noticeable, and a lighted buoy mark the exit from Smooth Channel leading towards Khaz Breakers and the open sea. A lighted whistle buoy marks Khaz Breakers, but in almost any swell breakers can be seen over the rocks. There are many rocks and breakers, but as long as the buoys and Khaz Breakers are identified the route passes through deep, clear water. This is no place to attempt to enter or leave in bad weather or fog.

There are other anchorages along Slocum Arm in **Waterfall Cove** or in Ford Arm at **Elf Cove**, which are worth visiting if time permits. A short-cut sometimes used by local boats through Piehle Passage close westerly of Khaz Point should not be taken for it is very complicated and has many rocks.

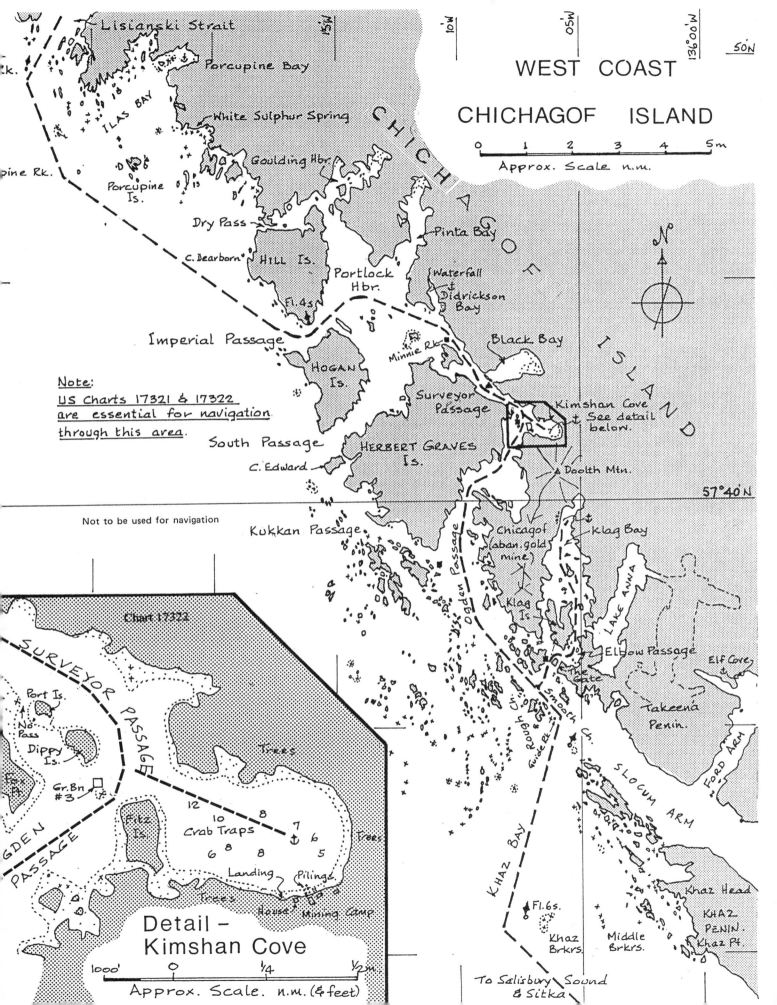

Lisianski Strait

Porcupine Bay

White Sulphur Spring

Goulding Hbr.

ILAS BAY

Porcupine Is.

pine Rk.

Dry Pass

C. Dearborn

HILL IS.

Fl. 4s

Portlock Hbr.

Pinta Bay

Waterfall

Didrickson Bay

Black Bay

CHICHAGOF ISLAND

WEST COAST
CHICHAGOF ISLAND

0 1 2 3 4 5m

Approx. Scale n.m.

N

Imperial Passage

HOGAN Is.

Minnie Rk.

Surveyor Passage

Kimshan Cove
† See detail below.

Note:
US Charts 17321 & 17322 are essential for navigation through this area.

South Passage

C. Edward

HERBERT GRAVES Is.

▲ Doolth Mtn.

57°40'N

Not to be used for navigation

Kukkan Passage

Chicagof (aban. gold mine)

Klag Bay

Klag Is.

LAKE ANNA

Ogden Passage

Elbow Passage

Elf Cove †

The Gate

Takeena Penin.

Smooth Ch.

Rough Ch.

Guide Rk.

Chart 17322

SURVEYOR PASSAGE

Port Is.

No Pass

Dippy Is.

Fox

Gr. Bn. #3

OGDEN PASSAGE

Trees

12   8   7
10   6
Crab Traps
6   8   8   5
Landing   Pilings
Trees
House   Mining Camp

Fitz Is.

Trees

Detail – Kimshan Cove

1000'   0   ¼   ½m

Approx. Scale. n.m. (& feet)

KHAZ BAY

SLOCUM ARM

FORD ARM

Fl. 6s

Khaz Brkrs.

Middle Brkrs.

Khaz Head

KHAZ PENIN.

Khaz Pt.

To Salisbury Sound & Sitka

PERIL STRAIT and the APPROACH to SITKA

The usual approach to Sitka is through Neva and Olga Straits. The straits are entered from the north, either via the offshore route into Salisbury Sound or via Peril Strait from the inside waters of Southeast Alaska. Salisbury Strait is open to the ocean on the west, while Peril Strait and Neva Strait lie on the western end of the sound. The straits are slightly protected while the sound is open to the prevailing wind and sea conditions.

The outer route leads south from Khaz Bay into Salisbury Sound. Make certain that the course is clear of the many rocks that lie off the coast, where heavy swell breaks to warn of danger. One such danger is Olga Rock which lies about 1.25 miles west of Klokachef Island. Once past Olga Rock and Klokachef Island the course can be altered to enter the sound. There are two anchorages that can be useful while waiting to enter Peril Strait.

Kalinin Bay is on the south side of Salisbury Sound and indents the north shore of Kruzof Island. The entrance is wide at first but the west side should be favored to avoid the rocks off Sinitsin Island. The inlet narrows and bends, and a mid-channel course should be followed from the bend. Rocks lie off the shores at the narrowest part of the bay but the opening is sufficiently large for small vessels. At half tide or less most rocks are visible; a float marks a submerged rock on the west side. The head of the bay offers a good anchorage.

Sukoi Inlet, at the entrance to Neva Strait, provides another anchorage, though you must go in about 3 miles. This inlet is actually a narrow strait between Kruzoff and Partofshikof Islands. The head of the inlet is shoal and very narrow. The sketch shows the position of the anchorage well out past the shoal area at the outlet of the small creek.

Peril Strait is the most frequented route to and from the inside waters and Sitka. It is about 39 miles from the entrance off Chatham Strait to Kakul Narrows and Salisbury Sound. The frequent twists in the channel and strong currents make it essential that proper navigational charts are used. Charts Nos. 17323 and 17324 cover Peril Strait, Neva, and Olga Straits for the route into Sitka. This passage is straightforward except for the short section at Whitestone Narrows where a range guides one through the dredged channel. The currents "meet" north of Olga Straits and south of Neva Straits. So the flood in Olga Strait runs north and the ebb in Neva Strait also runs north. To take advantage of these currents Sitka should be left two hours before high water slack. Many lights and markers lead past Starrigaran Bay (where the ferry terminal is located) and Sitka Rocks, and on to Sitka.

For an easterly passage through Peril Strait, enter Kakul Narrows slightly before low water slack to arrive at Sergius Narrows (about 3.5 miles along) just at or before slack water. Passage through the narrows is simple except for heavy traffic; good judgment and a sharp lookout are essential. If you lack current tables, the tide turns from south to north about 1.75 hours before low water at Sitka, and from north to south about 2 hours before high water at Sitka. Though Kakul Narrows has tidal swirls it is easier to traverse than Sergius Narrows.

Anchorages on the east side of Sergius Narrows can be found at **Deep Bay** and a less suitable one in **Bear Bay**. Enter Deep Bay between the green day mark on Grass Top Rock and a big island northeast of it, keeping closer to Big Island. Thereafter use mid-channel and anchor about a mile past the entry marker, staying clear of the shoal area that fills the head of the bay.

Chart 17323, 17324, 17325

0   1   2   3   4   5
Approx. Scale n.m.

PERIL STRAIT cont'd.

Poison Cove

Povorotini Is.

30'

34 shoal!

Reefs

12

6

1f

1f shoal

Dries
Stay off
100'

‡4

shoals

DETAIL
KALININ BAY

DETAIL
DEEP BAY

‡9

7

12

Grasstop Rk

Little Is

Big Is.

Little Rose Is

Big Rose Is.

Baby Bear Bay

Deep Bay
See detail
above

Big
Is.

See Chart 17323 for
navigational details.
SERGIUS NARROWS

Bear Bay

Schulze Cove
Log boom area.
Open to SE winds.
Piper Is.

25'

CHICHAGOF   ISLAND

Fortune Reefs

Iga
Rk.

KLOKACHEF Is.

Klokachef
Pt.

Pt. Leo

KAKUL NARROWS

From
Khaz Bay

SALISBURY SOUND

Not to be used for navigation

Morskoi Rk.
Sea Rk.

C. Georgiana

Eagle Rk.

Kalinin Bay
see detail
above

Scraggy
Is.

Sinistin
Cove

Kane Is.

Sukoi
Inlet

16

10

Slides

FISH BAY

BARANOF   57°20'N

ISLAND

St. John the Baptist
Bay

open to NW winds.
Confined area.

NEVA STRAIT

KRUZOF
ISLAND

PARTOFSHIKOF
ISLAND
No passage

Whitestone
Narrows.

To Sitka

55'

50'

45'

135° 40'

35

30

15'

SITKA

This is a great place to visit and it is also one of the busiest fishing ports in the US. Sitka has natural beauty, a historic background, friendly people and the best gift and specialty shops in the South East. It is no accident that the cruise ships have discovered Sitka.

Sitka can be approached from the north as described, or from offshore via Sitka Sound, between Biorka Island and Cape Edgecumbe. The cape is an easily recognized cliff of black lava 30 m (100 feet) high, with the prominent landmark of Mount Edgecumbe behind it. When it isn't raining this 1,000m (3,271 ft.) volcanic mountain can be seen both from seaward and from Sitka. Its isolated position, crater-formed flat top, conical shape and snow-streaked gullies make it a good landmark. After entering the harbor through the opening in the breakwater you are in a NO WAKE area which must be adhered to.

There are five small boat harbors in Sitka, and the northernmost (**New Thomsen Harbor**) is the designated transient harbor. After passing through the opening in the breakwater it is the first facility seen and is adjacent to the **Old Thomsen Harbor**. The City **ANB Harbor** (opposite the government docks) is off Katlian Street, just north of downtown. The other two small craft harbors are at **Sealing Cove** and **Crescent Harbor**, neither harbor has moorage for transient vessels. Clearance at the bridge is 16 m (52 feet).

The harbormaster controls both moorage locations; his office is located next to the Old Thomsen Harbor. Office hours are 7 a.m. to 6 p.m. daily. Vessels approaching Sitka should call the harbormaster on VHF Ch. 16 or phone (907) 747-3439 to obtain directions for moorage. In the event you are assigned a slip on a "hot berth" basis you must be ready to move on short notice. A supermarket, marine hardware, liquor store and sporting goods store are 200 yards from the harbor. An internet café is near the "Suds and Duds Laundromat." Moorage charges are very reasonable. Fueling is available at the Chevron station near the bridge and at the Texaco dock south of the Old Thomsen Harbor where propane is available.

This city offers many interesting things to see and do, all within easy walking distance. Tlingit artifacts and other Alaskan Indian, Inuit, and Aleut items can be seen at the Sheldon Jackson Museum as well as at the Visitor Center at the Sitka National Historic Park. At the latter there is a great collection of totem poles arranged along a lovely walk which leads to the site of the battle between the Tlingit and Russians. The Russian occupation period is featured in St. Michael's Cathedral, the Russian Bishop's House, the Russian cemetery, Castle Hill, and the Isabel Miller Museum in the Centennial Building.

Today's arts and crafts are well represented in shops, featuring native and Russian influences and modern artists; thus making this a fascinating place to explore. In June a chamber music festival and the All-Alaska Logging Championships are held, the conjunction well describing Sitka.

APPROACH TO SITKA FROM OLGA STRAIT. i.e. W. (Sitka still 10m. away)

SITKA

Chart 17324, 17327

Approx. Scale n.m.

0   1/4   1/2

T = Transient berthing
Water on the dock but
_No_ electricity

Pile

Pile

5

4

2f

3

2

6

7

8

9

10

Showers +
x Phones

Path

To downtown Sitka
via Katlian Street

Cafe

Harbormaster's Office

Park

Pump·out

F Fuel

(New) Thomsen Hbr. (Old) ↑

From
Olga Strait

BARANOF

Watson
Pt.

FIG4S

FIR2.5S

Channel Rk.

FIG!2.5s

Western
Anchorage

See detail

To ferry

◇ Laundromat / Showers

Supermarket

◇ TEXACO
(Propane)

JAPONSKI Is.

SITKA

Katlian St.

◇ FL.G

◇ FL.G

Halibut Point Rd.

See detail

St. Michaels
Cath.

Bishop's House

Grids

Katlian Street

City Floats   ANB

Mt. Edgecumbe
(town)

Sitka Int'l.
Airport

57°03'N

Harbor Dr.

Sealing
Cove Hbr.

135°20'W

F Fuel

P.O.

Shops

Castle Hill
Bridge
50' clearance

Crescent
Hbr.

Centennial Bldg
Visitor Inform.

Sawmill Cr. Rd
To Pulp Mill

Sheldon Jackson College
(Museum)

Sitka Nat. Hist Park
Visitor Center

Totem Pole Walk
Battleground

Eastern Anchorages

Not to be used for navigation

Bear totem at Sitka National Historic Park

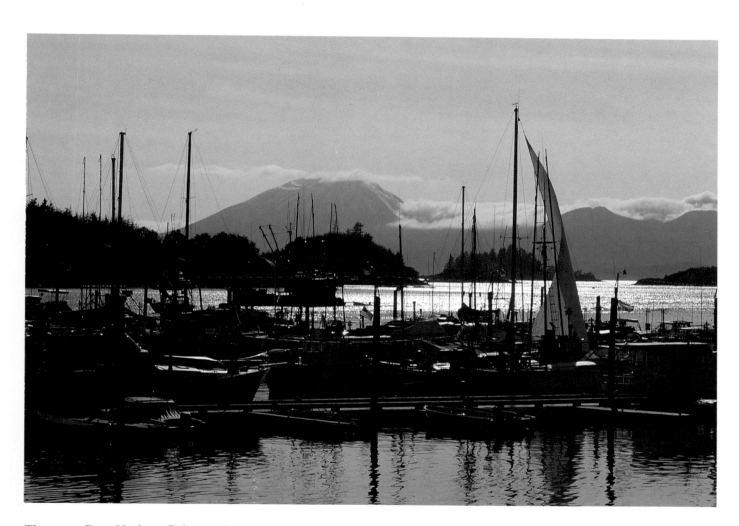

Thomsen Boat Harbor, Sitka, with Mount Edgecumbe

El Capitan Passage

135°

134°

ADMIRALTY Is.

210

Angoon

F

Hood Bay

Gambier Bay

Pybus Bay

STEPHEN'S PASSAGE

Hobart Bay

172

Port Houghton

Peril Str.

204

BARANOF Is.

206

206

F

Sitka

Kelp Bay

212

Takatz Bay

Baranof

Warm Spring Bay

214

KRUZOF Is.

Sitka Sound

Biorka Is.

Pt. Gardner

Keku Strait

Kake

FREDERICK SOUND

Portage Bay

168

KUPREANOF Is.

57°

Murder Cove

Kui'u Is.

Duncan Canal

Bay of Pillars

Whale Bay

CHATHAM STRAIT

216

Tebenkof Bay

220

Port Protection

SNOW PASS

GULF

218

Port Alexander

Cape Ommaney

SUMNER STRAIT

Shakan Bay

El Capitan Pass

222

OF

Cape Decision

56°

PRINCE

ALASKA

Spanish Is.

Coronation Is.

Warren Is.

Sea Otter Sd.

OF WALES Is.

224

Helm Pt.

Heceta Is.

Tuxekan Is.

Klawock

Noyes Is.

F

226

Craig

Joins page 163

Not to be used for navigation

135°

134°

Cape Addington

TENAKEE INLET and ANGOON

Tenakee Springs is a charming little village on the north shore of Tenakee Inlet, which enters the east side of Chichagof Island off Chatham Strait. It serves as a vacation home area for many of Juneau's residents, but is equally attractive for visiting cruisers because of its hot springs. A grassy track meanders along the shore, dotted with cabins along the way. Vehicles are not allowed except for oil and fuel trucks. The ferry dock is at the village where fuel is available. The state-maintained small craft basin is about .5 mile east of the village. The harbormaster monitors VHF Ch. 16 or can be reached at (907) 736-2211.

A store, cafe, laundromat and tavern are in the village. The green concrete bath house is the center of Tenakee and separate bathing hours are posted for men and women. Remove silver jewelry before entering the baths as there is sulfur in the water. The storage of gear on the floats and breakwater is prohibited.

Crab Bay is 4 miles to the southwest, on the south side of the inlet. There are mud shoals at the head of the bay and on the south side, but the north side is steep-to. Anchor in mid-bay in 5 - 10 fathoms, mud. A 2.5 fathom spot is east of the private mooring buoy.

Another spot is 3 miles northwest in **Saltery Bay** where good anchorage in the small inner basin can be taken in 5 - 10 fathoms, mud.

EAGLE
TOP OF CEREMONIAL STAFF
(Tlingit)

ANGOON

Angoon lies on the east side of Chatham Strait, about 20 miles south of Tenakee Inlet, and almost directly across from the exit of Peril Strait into Chatham Strait. This Tlinglit village, located in the Tongass National Forest, is the only permanent settlement in the wilderness of Admiralty Island. It lies on the narrow section of a peninsula behind which Kootznahoo Inlet enters Admiralty Island. Kootznahoo means, "Fortress of the Bears," a most appropriate name since Admiralty Island has the highest brown bear population of the Southeast, as well as the greatest number of bald eagles. A long pier extends into Chatham Strait. Fuel and water can be obtained at the dock but there is no moorage available for transients. There is a small store with limited supplies and local crafts are sold at Whaler's Cove Fishing Lodge.

The state-built, village-operated small craft floats are inside Kootznahoo Inlet in **Favorite Bay**. As the current is swift, and the passage is narrow, get local advice and information before entering at slack water if you want to stop at the small craft area. It is about 1 mile south of the main village. The state ferry docks are at Killisnoo Harbor, about 3 miles south of Angoon, facing Chatham Strait. For information phone (907) 788-3653.

Chart 17338, 17339

Trail - ½ mile to Tenakee
& hot springs

Wharf

Tidal
Grid

Transients

Concrete
Breakwater

Transients

Breakwater

Detail - Tenakee Springs

0   200'   400'   500'
Approx.   Scale - feet

TENAKEE SPRINGS

ANGOON

CHATHAM STRAIT

Not to be used for navigation

0   5   10   15   20 n.m.

Approx. Scale n.m.

To Icy Strait & Lynn Canal

See detail above

Seal Bay

TENAKEE   Tenakee   East Pt

INLET

Crab Bay

CHICHAGOF Is.

ADMIRALTY IS.

See detail
across

To Sitka

PERIL   57°30'N   STRAIT

Rodman B.

B. Saook B.

BARANOF

Kasnyku B.
Ell Cove

Takatz B.

Baranof
Warm Spring B.

Murder
Cove

To Petersburg

To C. Decision

CHATHAM   STRAIT

Fl. 6s.
Danger Pt.

Kootznahoo Head

Do not enter the Inner Hbr
without first getting local
information and the
time of slack water.

Turn Pt

Village Rk
Fl. R.4s

ANGOON

R.
#4

Angoon dock

O
Tower

Rose Rk.

R. #6

Kenasnow Rks

Inner Hbr
Public Floats

Detail - Angoon

1000'   0   ½   1 n.m.

Approx. Scale, n.m. & feet.

ANCHORAGES NORTH of WARM SPRINGS BAY

After passing out of Peril Strait into Chatham Strait there is a truly spectacular stretch of coast which can be followed southward along the west coast of Baranof Island. Several interesting anchorages can be found here.

The coast of Catherine Island must be passed for several miles before the first large bay opens. This is Kelp Bay, which divides into three long arms and a large basin behind Pond Island. As these arms are deep there are no recommended anchorages here, except in **Echo Cove** at the southeastern tip of Catherine Island which is open to the south and is useful only as a temporary anchorage. Kelp marks a submerged reef extending .6 mile south of Point Lull.

Cosmos Cove is about 2 miles south of Kelp Bay. One large and two small islands lie off the northern point of the cove, connected to it by shoals. Proceed well clear of their southern shores and enter the cove in mid-channel. The head and sides are shoal for some distance. Anchor about .5 mile in where there is good shelter, 4 to 6 fathoms, mud.

Kasnyku Bay is the next large opening. At the southern end is a magnificent waterfall that is visible from several miles away. This is Kasnyku Waterfall. Kasnyku Bay appears too open for shelter though there are several islands in it. At its western end are three islands and a Fish and Game Salmon Hatchery. A small anchorage can be explored above the northwest of the three islands. Here one can see another spectacular waterfall, Hidden Falls. The ruins of an old lumber operation are found here.

An especially intriguing anchorage can be found in the little reversed L-shaped cove south of Round Island, called **Ell Cove**. See US chart 17337. This little beauty spot is well protected, and as you approach it yet another waterfall will come into view when approximately due east of it. Ell Cove and Round Island can also be identified by the enormous semi-spherical bowl-like scoop in the rock face. The year-round snow-capped peaks and contorted rock faces with deeply water-cut gorges make travel along this coast most interesting.

Waterfall Cove, at Kasnyku Falls itself, appears too open and unprotected to be useful as an anchorage. Even if the southeast corner, the most protected part were used, the current from the waterfall would make it less than satisfactory.

About 4 miles further south is a large bay with several islands and arms—**Takatz Bay**. Entry is made around Point Turbot into the northern arm. Stay in mid-channel till past the outer rocks off the south point then favor the south side to pass the mid-channel rocks. Excellent anchorage in 6 - 8 fathoms, mud, is past the narrows then into the inner basin. Do not pass the largest islet .5 mile beyond the narrows, for shoals begin and reach to the head of the bay. It is only a few miles further to Baranof in Warm Springs Bay so Takatz Bay could be bypassed.

ARCTIC TERN

Chart 17337

VIEW LOOKING SSE TOWARDS WARM SPRINGS BAY, FROM NEAR ST. CATHERINE IS.

Not to be used for navigation

134° 50'W

COSMOS COVE

‡6

3½ m

BARANOF

North Pt.

KASNYKU BAY

Hidden Falls

ISLAND

Round Is

Waterfall
(Visible only when
roughly due east)

ELL COVE

57 12'N

WATERFALL
COVE

Kasnyku Falls →
(visible for many miles away)

134° 50'N

Anchorage can also be found in the
inner basin of Takatz Bay, about
4 miles south of Ell Cove.

Kasnyku Falls → Round Is 9 Kasnyku Bay Cosmos Cove

Ell Cove Kasnyku Bay To Cosmos Cove

APPROACH FROM NW TO COSMOS COVE, ETC. ANCH'S.

Kasnyku Falls Ell Cove Entrance Hidden Falls Round Is. Kasnyku Bay

APPROACH TO ELL COVE FROM N.W.

Kasnyku Falls To Ell Cove Falls

ELL COVE FROM APPROX. DUE EAST.

ANCHS. N. OF WARM

SPRINGS BAY

CHATHAM STRAIT

0   1   2

Approx. Scale n.m.

BARANOF, WARM SPRINGS BAY

A few miles south of Takatz Bay the steep slopes of the snow-capped mountains open to form the shores of Warm Springs Bay. A light is located on the southern point of the bay. Another identifying factor is the microwave reflector seen on the crest of the northern ridge.

A rock surrounded by kelp lies in the middle of the entrance. Pass on the southern side of this in deep water and proceed into the bay. The steep, green, forested slopes, the prominent white cascade at the head of the bay, the roofs of the few houses, and steam (sometimes trapped in the southern bights) give this place a special mood.

At the head of the bay the public floats lie east of a pier near the waterfall. Moorage can be taken on both sides of the 75 m (250-foot) float, but beware of the submerged rock close to shore on the northern side. Rafting may be necessary. The heavy current passing in front of the float should be taken into account when approaching it. The current affects the outer vessels of a raft more noticeably, so be certain that all vessels are well tied to the dock as well as to each other, preferably with extra lines to the dock. There is no fuel or electricity at the dock, only water. However, good fishing can be had right off the ends of the dock. Sometimes the cruise vessel, *Majestic Explorer*, comes in at night (all lit up) for a quick view of the falls—this is a cruise ship exploration trip!

If it hasn't become overgrown, a trail beyond the buildings leads to an interesting lookout over the falls and further on to Lake Baranof where the US Forest Service cabin is located at the south end of the lake.

If the wharf is full, anchorage may be taken in one of two coves on the south side of the bay, the westernmost being shallower at about 8 fathoms.

From Warm Springs Bay there are several routes that can be chosen. One route proceeds south along the west coast of Chatham Strait towards Port Armstrong and Port Alexander before crossing over to pass Cape Decision. A second route crosses Chatham Strait to anchorage at the Bay of Pillars or Tebenkof Bay before rounding Cape Decision. The third route turns at Point Gardner on Admiralty Island (7 miles southeast) to go up Frederick Sound. A light is situated on the westernmost of two rocks off Point Gardner. Pass between this light and a lighted buoy marking the rocky shoals around Yasha Island. Heavy tidal rips occur in this neighborhood, which is frequented by humpback whales.

On the eastern side of Point Gardner is **Surprise Harbor**; though not a good anchorage, it can be useful if strong winds are found in Chatham Strait. The next long indentation is **Murder Cove** (which got its name when a murder was witnessed here). It is best to enter at low water when the rocky hazards show clearly. Anchorage is fair off the ruins of an abandoned cannery about 1 mile into the cove.

BARANOF FLOATS

BARANOF
WARM SPRINGS BAY
CHATHAM STRAIT

Boardwalk to lake 2+ hotsprings

Tidal Grid

Sea plane Float

250' Float

Strong current from Waterfall

Under water rock

0   1   2

Approx. Scale n.m.

Not to be used for navigation

Baranof Floats

100   200

Scale – feet

Baranof

Hot Springs

← Lake

Waterfall

WARM SPRINGS BAY

CHATHAM STRAIT

Rock

12f

8f

Light Fl. 4s

57° 05'N

134° 50'W

N

Rock

APPROACHING WARM SPRINGS BAY FROM NNW, distant about 1 mile

TEBENKOF BAY

This large bay on the east side of Chatham Strait is the central feature of the Tebenkof Bay Wilderness Area of the Tongass National Forest. Located on the west side of Kuiu Island, it is 50 miles southwest of Petersburg. Extending 7 miles inland, the bay has a myriad of islands, islets, reefs, rocks and shoals within its boundaries and demands accurate navigation in order to reach safe anchorage. The low-lying islands are in stark contrast to the snow-covered peaks in the distance. The entrance to the bay is between Point Ellis on the north and Swaine Point on the South. An approach from the north is free of dangers. When entering from the south or leaving southbound care is needed to avoid Davis Rock and rocky patches and shoals to the southwest.

This is a cruiser's dream for there are numerous beautiful anchorages within the confines of the bay. In addition, Dungeness and Tanner crab, shrimp, herring and halibut are prolific in these waters. Wildlife often seen ashore includes black bears, wolves and foxes, plus many species of waterfowl including occasional sightings of trumpeter swans.

Happy Cove on the north shore of the bay is seven miles southeast of Point Ellis. Two islands (one bare, the other treed) identify the entrance to the bay. A narrow channel links the southern part of the bay to an inner cove, where anchorage may be taken with good protection. Several anchorages can be found in Elena Bay, the best one apparently having no name.

The southeast arm of the bay, **Petrof Bay**, is entered to port of the Tebenkof Bay Light, 2.1 m (14 ft.), located on a small island. A daybeacon is on a rock awash, 1.7 miles southeast of the light. There are several coves where secure, serene anchorage may be taken in 4 - 8 fathoms.

Thetis Bay, the southern arm of the bay, provides first-class anchorage well into the bay in 9 to 10 fathoms, good holding mud. Magnetic variations as much as 4° have been reported on the west shore of the bay.

Explorer Basin is part of a deep bay at the north end of Kuiu Island sheltered on the north by a phalanx of islands, rocks and shoals comprising Windfall and Troller Islands. Approach from the west where entry is between a rock (marked by breakers) off the southern Windfall Island and shoal water (identified by kelp) extendiing north of Swaine Point. Passable anchorage can be taken in coves to the south during southerly weather.

Gedney Harbor is about four miles south of the entrance to Explorer Basin. This harbor is popular with fishermen and cruisers since water, ice, fuel and limited provisions are available during the summer months at the scow anchored in the harbor. Care must be taken when entering. The entrance is on either side of a ledge .2 miles west of the island in the center of the bay. Rocky heads barely visible at high tide are on the NW and SE ends of the ledge. A mid-channel course on either side of the ledge leads into the bay. Anchorage can be taken anywhere in the harbor in 6 to 10 fathoms, good holding mud. Avoid shoal water indicated by kelp when moving in the area.

Tlingit Indians occupied this picturesque area in the past, and remains have been found of winter villages, seasonal fishing camps and gardens. In addition, vestiges of fur farms dating from the early part of the 20th century dot the shores of Kuiu Island as well as many other parts of the Southeast coast.

TEBENKOF BAY

Chart 17376

Approx. Scale n.m.

Pt. Ellis

Tebenkof Bay

Not to be used for navigation

Elena Bay

Happy Cove

Davis Rock

Troller Is.

Windfall Is.

Explorer Basin

Swaine Pt.

Gedney Harbor

Pt. Cosmos

Thetis Bay

Petrof Bay

134°15'   134°05'

56°30'

56°25'

PORT ALEXANDER

With the closing of Keku Strait a vessel proceeding from Chatham Strait to Sumner Strait has two choices. One is to go through Frederick Sound then down Wrangell Narrows, and on exiting turn westward into Sumner Strait. The other is to go down Chatham Strait and round Cape Decision into the entrance to Sumner Strait. If the latter route is chosen then Port Alexander is a suitable anchorage to await the best time to round Cape Decision This harbor lies about 5 miles north of Cape Ommaney at the southern tip of Baranof Island. The small community relies on fishing for its survival.

Two islands surrounded by shoals lie ENE of the entrance. Pass well south of them to approach from a little south of the lighthouse on the point. The entrance channel is 120 to 150 m (400 to 500 feet) wide. It lies between the lighthouse and a red buoy (N2) marking a shoal with rocks awash. A lighted range of 334° on two markers inside the harbor leads through the channel. A speed limit of 3 miles per hour is set for the harbor.

From well inside the entrance, turn northward up the harbor. Shoals occur well out from each side so stay roughly mid-channel. A fish receiving barge is permanently at anchor in the middle of the bay south of the ruins of a large wharf. North of these ruins are the main public floats on the east side, about .5 mile into the harbor. This float is 140 m (450 feet) long and vessels can moor on either side, 3 fathoms, open mooring. Rafting may be necessary. Another public float with a tidal grid attached is in the inner harbor about .25 miles further into the harbor where the minimum depth is 3.5 ft at spring low water. Across Chatham Strait there are several good alternative anchorages in the **Bay of Pillars** and in **Tebenkof Bay** on Kuiu Island. In these more remote anchorages there is a good chance that brown bear can be seen; great care should be taken if shore excursions are planned.

Cape Decision lies about 23 miles southeast across Chatham Strait. It is a low, bare, rocky point with a square white lighthouse at the tip. Decision Passage, the route into Sumner Strait, is 1 mile wide and lies between the Cape and a string of islands, the Spanish Islands. When making the passage stay well off Cape Decision before turning.

Strong tidal rips and currents can be encountered in the area off Cape Decision and the stronger winds and weather of the open ocean can be felt here. Since fog often occurs in summer it is best to wait for good, settled weather before attempting to round Cape Decision.

More adventurous sailors can take the longer route around Coronation Island which is south of Cape Decision. This will take the vessel past Helm Point, a unique and spectacular sight. It is a flat tableland ending in sheer cliffs over 300 m (1,000 feet) high, where thousands of seabirds nest. If there is any possibility of stormy weather or fog this trip should not be lightly undertaken.

From Cape Decision it is about 10 miles northeasterly to Shakan Bay and the entry through Shakan Strait to wonderful El Capitan Passage.

Light Fl.6s

To Warm Springs Bay
& Baranof

Ruins & Piling
(old whale & herring
reduction plant)

7m

Chart 17331

10
PORT ARMSTRONG

15

15

10

John Bay

PORT ALEXANDER

BARANOF ISLAND

0   17'   ½   1

Approx. Scale n.m.

Not to be used for navigation

N

Pt. Conclusion

16'

CONCLUSION

Ship Cove
Capt. Vancouver's anch.

.3f

.5f

Tidal Grid

3f

250' float

Seaplane Float

250' Float

The state of the
channel to the
Inner Harbor is
not known, but
it is shallow.

Port Alexander
Community

56°15'N

See Detail

3

PORT

Ruins

PORT ALEXANDER
Fish Processing Barge
Range lights

PORT

3

BARANOF IS.

Buoy R.#2

Channel 150'
Wide

Detail -
Outer Harbor State Float

Light Fl.4s

Entrance Range 334°

40'   134° 39'W   38' To Cape Decision

PORT PROTECTION

An alternative approach to Shakan Bay and El Capitan Passage is from the southern end of Wrangell Narrows, going west down Sumner Strait. Several isolated rocks marked by buoys act as mileposts along the way. The chart is the best guide. At Point Baker, the northwest tip of Prince of Wales Island, Sumner Strait changes to a north-south orientation. Across the strait to the north is the exit of Keku Strait which connects Sumner Strait to Frederick Sound, but all navigational aids have been removed to discourage any effort to transit this very challenging passage.

Point Baker, a small fishing community, has a state-operated small craft float in the harbor, which is in the gap between False Island and the northwest tip of Prince of Wales Island. Enter only from the north, between Point Baker light (with a red and white daybeacon to the west) and Point Baker anchorage daybeacon (on a smaller island to the east). Postal services, fuel, water, and provisions are available. Free moorage is found at the small dock on a first-come, first-served basis. A narrow, very shallow dinghy passage carries on behind False Island and Joe Mace Island to join Port Protection.

About .75 of a mile northwest of Point Baker is the bell buoy marking Helm Rock. The buoy is located about .25 mile north of the rock. At times there are heavy tidal rips and swirls around the rock. Small vessels would do well to avoid this rip by passing between the rock and Point Baker.

Port Protection is a large bay opening about 1.5 miles south of Point Baker. The same name is given to a small community in a well sheltered cove. The southern entrance point of the port is Protection Head which is a bold landmark visible from several miles. Port Protection light is on a red and white daymark on the point of an island on the north side of Wooden Wheel Cove. Note the detached reef with a daybeacon on it about .5 south of Joe Mace Island. Vessels can pass it on either side while giving the reef a wide berth.

Wooden Wheel Cove is boot-shaped, the toe of the boot facing southwest. Located behind Jackson Island, this small, well protected area has floats and some buildings. The 75 m (250-foot) public float is in the southern corner, unconnected to the shore. The southern end of the float is reserved for sea planes, but vessels can moor on either side of the remainder which has deep water alongside. There are no garbage collection facilities; vessels must retain garbage.

There are several private floats around the rim of the cove. The large log cabin at the end of the largest float contains a small store. This a very pretty and peaceful setting, especially if you have come in to avoid the slop outside in Sumner Strait. Protected anchorage is found in the cove or further down the bay of Port Protection on the east side behind the islands where log booms are moored.

Many places (including Port Protection) were named by Captain George Vancouver who surveyed this area in the summer of 1793. The port itself received its name because the *Discovery* and *Chatham* sheltered here from a severe storm in Sumner Strait.

APPROACHING PORT PROTECTION (WOODEN WHEEL COVE) FROM WNW
distant about 1 mile.

Chart 17378

WOODEN WHEEL COVE

Trees

Light Fl.6s

Jackson Is.

Trees

Kelp

21

10

10

7

6

Shoal

Kelp

Dries

Public Float

PORT PROTECTION

N

6

Seaplane

Trees

Private

Private float

Large log house/store

Tanks

Not to be used for navigation

133°40'W
Helm Rk.

133°35'W
Wrangell Narrows

Point Baker

Joe Mace Is.

PRINCE OF WALES IS.

56°20'N

SUMNER STRAIT

PORT PROTECTION

56°20'N

Wooden Wheel Cove

Cape Decision

Port Protection

Protection Head

LABOUCHERE BAY

PORT PROTECTION

SUMNER STRAIT

0   ⅛   ¼

Approx. Scale - n.m. (feet)

EL CAPITAN PASSAGE

The southern part of Sumner Strait is open to the Pacific and to southerly winds. However, with good weather one can reach over from Cape Decision, or run down from Port Protection to enter Shakan Strait on the east side of Sumner Strait. Enter in the center of the opening for there are many rocks and islands on each side, then steer for the south end of the largest island (Hamilton Island), where a daybeacon stands, and enter Shakan Strait.

At the end of Shakan Strait is an open bight to the east, where log booms are moored. El Capitan Passage leads off to the east with its entrance marked by a red beacon on a mid-channel rock. Anchorage can be taken a little further north in the bight in **Marble Creek**, or further on in **Calder Bay**.

El Capitan Passage is a little-known but fascinating part of Alaska. The passage follows a marked, narrow channel towards the east which is dredged to a controlling depth of 3 m (10 feet) and a minimum width of 21 m (70 feet). At Dry Pass the controlling depth is 2 m (7 feet) and it appears narrower than the width indicated on the chart. Chart #17387, with its enlargement of this part of El Capitan, should be used when negotiating the passage.

Before entering the narrows from either end call "Securite, Securite, Securite" on VHF Channel 16, to warn of your passage and to inquire of any vessel going the opposite direction. There are several wider spots where vessels can pass each other, but if a tug and boom are in the passage it is best to wait till they are through. There is no room to pass in the narrows. Currents of about 1 to 2 knots occur through the passage. Tidal change occurs at about the same time as at Sitka. Passage through is best near high water.

Beyond Dry Pass the passage widens, though it is still relatively shallow. Deadheads are hazards of shallow waters, resulting from use of the waterway by log booms, so it is wise to keep a sharp lookout at all times. After turning the bend, leave the small wooded island to the west. In the wider section that follows a logging camp is located on the small peninsula on the north side.

At Aneskett Point, the Passage turns southward and gradually begins to widen. About 3.5 miles south of this point the opening to Devilfish Bay is passed. A little further on, **Sarheen Cove** on the east, and an unnamed cove on the west (both about 2.5 miles further along) could be used as anchorages except during southerly weather. El Capitan Passage continues southward, widening, with beautiful vistas of low forested hills on either side and many islands. Five miles from Sarheen Cove is Burnt Island which has a light on it marking the main passage.

East of Burnt Island is **Sarkar Cove** where anchorage can be taken in about 6 fathoms, mud, near the head of the cove and off the ruins of Deweyville (once a gold-mining town). The main route continues directly south from Burnt Island, past the daybeacon at Hub Rock, then towards Tuxekan Narrows. Proceed around either end of El Capitan Island to visit the small community of Tokeen on the western side of the island where fuel and basic groceries may be available.

Calder
Bay

Use US Chart 17387 for this very interesting passage. The channel is dredged to a controlling depth of 7 feet × 70 feet width, and appears even narrower. Full of interest & beauty.

Marble
Creek

Old Marble
Quarries

PRINCE OF WALES ISLAND.

56°10'N

Middle
Is.

SHAKAN
BAY

Hamilton Is.

Dry Pass

Aneskett Pt.

RW Bn.

RW Bn.

Site of old
Shakan Cannery

See view below

Shakan   Strait

EL CAPITAN PASSAGE

DRY PASS FROM W.

KOSCIUSKO Is.

Devilfish Bay

Sarheen Cove

Bare

Old ramp

N

APPROACHING THE WEST ENTRANCE TO EL CAPITAN PASSAGE

Not to be used for navigation

133°30'W   Holbrook Arm

Tokeen Bay

Tenass
Is.

Rocky
Cove

Clam
Cove

Chart 17387

Fl.4s.
Burnt Is.

Brockman Is.

North Is.

Sarkar
Cove

EL CAPITAN PASSAGE

El
Capitan
Is.

Deweyville
(ruins)

PRINCE OF WALES IS.

Sarkar
Pt.

Hub
Rk.

0   1   2   3   4   5

Approx. Scale n.m.

To Tuxekan Narrows

TUXEKAN NARROWS to SAN CHRISTOVAL BAY

This "inside passage" through the waters south of E1 Capitan Passage continues the very interesting and scenic route southwards. The series of large and small islands screen off this route from Sea Otter Sound and the open sea beyond. US Charts 17403 and 17404 should be used for navigation.

Tuxekan Narrows has daybeacons on the main rocky reefs. Aikens Rock is passed on the east side, but Village Rock can be passed on either side. The route passes about 90 m (300 ft.) east of the rock, keeping well away from Kinani Point on the Prince of Wales shore. A vessel is then aiming right into the 180 m (600 ft.) opening of Tuxekan Narrows. Though narrow, it is deep, and currents are not extreme. Thus, this passage is preferred by most vessels. (It is also possible to go around the west side of Tuxekan Island into Sea Otter Sound to join the route south through Karheen Passage.)

At the southern end of Tuxekan Narrows there is a village and logging camp at Little Naukati Bay, but anchorage is not recommended. A little further south on Tuxekan Island is **Nichin Cove** where good anchorage may be taken within the cove for small craft. Larger craft can find less protected anchorage off the entrance in 6 to 8 fathoms, mud bottom. A ramp and float are on the west side of the cove.

Tuxekan Passage is wide and about 10 miles long. The current is not strong, and the route is unmistakable. At Kauda Point (the southern tip of Tuxekan Island), Tuxekan Passage, Karheen Passage and Tonowek Narrows meet in a large, square bay which is littered with islands and reefs. Careful examination of the chart is needed. Enter Tonowek Narrows in mid-channel leaving the green daybeacon to the west and the red buoy NNE of Point Swift rocky shoal area to the east. Known locally as Little Skookumchuck, passage through the narrows is usually trouble-free since the current reaches a maximum of 3 knots.

When passing the first island on the west side within Tonowek Narrows look well above on the shoreline, where two mortuary poles and a burial box can be seen. The location on the island in the pass amid the tall guardian-like trees creates an atmosphere that engenders respect for the personage buried here. Pass by and do not disturb the quietness of this burial spot.

From Tonowek Bay there are two routes southward. One may proceed along the outer route into the Gulf of Esquibel, clear Curacao Reef and the rocks off St. Philip Island to enter San Christoval Channel. This route is exposed to the swell and these dangers must be identified. The preferred (inner) route stays in the channel behind Harmony Islands and the string of islands that follows, then behind Culebra and St. Philip Islands before exiting north of Blanquizal Island. Most rocks are visible, except for the mid-channel reef east of the north end of St. Philip Island.

At the southern end, St. Philips Island is joined by a sandy spit to a small island to the south where middens of white sea shells are seen. This is **Bob's Place**, the site of an old village. Good anchorage in about 5 fathoms can be taken in mid-channel, protected by the islands. San Christoval Channel, just a few miles further, leads through a well buoyed pass into San Alberto Bay.

from El Capitan Passage

55° 55'

ORE Is.

Owl Is.

Hoot Is.

Cap Is.

EL CAPITAN PASSAGE

Tuxekan Narrows

Kinani Pt

Village

Jinhi Bay

(Shoal)

Little Naukati Bay

Village

An alternate route is to exit El Capitan Passage and re-enter via Karheen Passage.

SEA OTTER SOUND

Jum Pt.

Nichin Cove Village

TUXEKAN Is.

Kugun Pt.

Karheen Passage

Chapin Is.

Kauda Pt.

Winter Hbr.

HECETA Is.

Tuxekan Passage

PRINCE OF WALES Is.

Tonowek Narrows Burial Site

Pt. Swift

N

Anch

TONOWEK BAY

Anch

Nossuk Bay

Alternate outer route →

Harmony Is.

"Inner" route

Not to be used for navigation

Chart 17403, 17404

TUXEKAN PASSAGE

PRINCE OF WALES IS.

0   5   10

Culebra Is.

133° 20' W

To San Christoval Channel & Craig

Approx. Scale n.m.

CRAIG

The northern approach to Craig is through the San Christoval Channel into San Alberto Bay, then southeast across the bay to the well buoyed channel between Klawock Reef and Fish Egg Island. This channel leads into Klawock Inlet. On turning south the town of Craig is visible on Craig Island which is joined to Prince of Wales Island by a causeway. The mountains on the large islands are steep, though not high, and make this a picturesque area. The most prominent landmarks are a brown water tank and a microwave tower on the southeast side of the island. Craig may also be entered from the south through Bucareli Bay and Ulloa Channel.

Two coves are in the town, one on each side of the causeway. The fuel dock is on the small island with two tank that is passed when approaching from the north. The channel leading to **North Cove** passes a blue-roofed cannery just before the floating breakwater is seen. Docks and floats for fishing vessels and other craft are along the north waterfront. The 90 m (300 ft.) main float has four fingers at right angles. When approaching call the Harbormaster on VHF Ch. 16 or telephone (907) 826-3404 for dock assignment. He controls moorage in both coves and will direct you to a temporarily vacant dock if necessary, but transient moorage is usually available at the public floats in both North and South (Shelter) Coves. Daily moorage fees vary from $3 for vessels less than 6m (20 ft.) to $25 for vessels over 33m (110 ft.). The outermost finger, 50 m (175 ft.) long, has transient moorage along its north (outer) side. Water and power are available at the floats and a fuel dock is north of North Cove Harbor.

Shelter Cove (the docks in South Cove) can be reached by going west around Craig Island, then passing through the buoyed channel between Craig and Fish Egg Reef. A controlling depth of 2.4 m (8 feet) is in the channel and float area.

Craig is the largest community of Prince of Wales Island and is the economic center of the island. It is the service center and home port of a large commercial fishing fleet. In addition to marine services there are stores, a post office, banks and an ATM, laundromat, a library with internet service and a health care facility. Restrooms and showers are in the harbormaster's office in Shelter Cove. There are several wharves and structures connected with the canneries, a boat repair shop and garbage collection facilities. A magnificent collection of totem, memorial and mortuary poles are featured in the park above the harbor. Craig is 9 miles from the Klawock Airport.

The road across the causeway continues up the coast of Prince of Wales Island to **Klawock**, a Tlingit village towards the head of Klawock Inlet. Klawock can also be reached from Craig by boat by proceeding up the inlet, rounding Klawock Island, then through a marked channel. Public floats (max. 72 hours) are about .25 mile south of Klawock dock (the pier seen first). A small wooded peninsula resembling an island, projects out between the dock and the floats. Over 100 years ago this village was the site of the first cannery in Alaska

A number of caves have been discovered in the northwestern part of Prince of Wales Island and the Forest Service has daily tours to the most accessible cave, El Capitan.

Chart 17405

Craig beyond

Klawock Reef   Channel   Fish Egg Is.   Ballena Is.   Balandra Is.   San Juan Bautista Is.

APPROACHING CRAIG FROM W, i.e. from San Alberto Bay

Klawock Reef

KLAWOCK INLET

Road to Klawock

55°30'N

SAN ALBERTO BAY

FISH EGG Is.

F

Fuel

Crab Bay

Cannery

See detail

CRAIG

Microwave Twr

Ballenas Is.

andra Is.

Cape Suspiro

BUCARELI   BAY

133° 10'W

Not to be used for navigation

55°28'N

Floating Breakwater

Transient

phone

lf.

NORTH COVE

Tidal Grid

launch

Garbage and Waste Oil

Store

Telephone

Tidal Grid

D

C

B

Harbor Master

A

SOUTH (SHELTER) COVE

CRAIG

PRINCE OF WALES IS.

0   ½   1

Approx. Scale n.m.

Sunny Hay Mtn.

Fish Egg Is.   To Craig, N.Cove   South Cove   Cape Suspiro

APPROACHING CRAIG FROM S, i.e. from Bucareli Bay about 3 miles

BARRIER ISLANDS and CORDOVA BAY

It is a good day's run from Craig to the Barrier Islands in Cordova Bay, passing through Ulloa Channel, Tlevak Narrows and Strait and into and across Cordova Bay. There are several anchorages in this area.

The topography of Ulloa Channel—steep hillsides along a passage opening into a larger body of water—causes local fog to be trapped within, while the open water clears. White cottonwood fog banks at the entrances to the channels are a clear warning of these conditions. Navigation at these times needs care, even with the assistance of radar. Similar conditions can occur in other channels in this area.

Waterfall is an old cannery site on the Prince of Wales coast midway along Ulloa Channel. The cannery has been converted into a fishing resort, operating mainly during the summer with guests flown in from Ketchikan. Permission should be obtained for overnight tie-up at the dock. Some isolated pilings and an abandoned wharf create a hazard when it is foggy.

Tlevak Narrows is a short, narrow but deep passage opening into Tlevak Strait. Several islands and rocky groups occur on both sides of the narrows, but buoys and lights, and U.S. Chart 17407 are sufficient to navigate a vessel through. Currents are fairly strong inside the narrows where boils and swirls may be experienced, but the effect reduces rapidly with distance. Use this passage at or near slack water unless the strength of the current is low.

Once past the narrow section between Turn Point and Block Island Tlevak Strait is entered. Lively Islands are passed on their western side. If bound for **Hydaburg**, a principal village of the Haidas, stand to the ESE for Sukkwan Island and South Pass. There are public floats at Hydaburg.

If bound for Cordova Bay stand southeasterly down the Strait. Several deep coves indent the narrow length of Dall Island, though not all show evidence of being good anchorages. The mountainous backbone of the 40-mile-long island shows rugged, partially wooded peaks which appear to consist of marble. Ruins of canneries and/or logging camps are seen in some inlets.

There is a long reach across **Cordova Bay**. Wallace Rock, marked with a red buoy, lies to the north of the Barrier Islands and can be passed on either side. Once it is identified, the daymark at Guide Rocks to the ESE can be found. When nearing Guide Rocks the position of the Narrows leading to Eureka Channel becomes evident. A good anchorage can be found just past the Narrows in a small cove to the south. The sketch shows the anchorage. Another anchorage can be found behind the reefs west of the channel past the green daymark. Several similar anchorages could be discovered in the other passages of the Barrier Islands, though care should be taken because of the many rocks and reefs in the area.

Eureka Channel leads southward, past Mexico Point. There are many outlying rocks along the coast, and you should clear Nunez Rocks before attempting either to round Cape Chacon or to sail across Dixon Entrance to Prince Rupert.

Chart 17433

Hills on Prince of Wales Is. behind

Guide Rks.
Red Beacon.

From Wallace Rk.

The Narrows
Barrier Islands

APPROACH TO BARRIER IS. & EUREKA CHANNEL N. END FROM W
distant about 1½ miles.

ANCHS. IN THE BARRIER IS.

CORDOVA BAY

0   1   2   3

Approx. Scale – n.m.

Not to be used for navigation

Ebb Current   The Narrows   Fld

Trees

8
7
20   ‡6 m & r
8   6
7   5
8

10
5

Stony
beaches

Trees

Trees

DETAIL – ANCHORAGE

2°30'W   132°25'W   132°20'W   54°50'N

R.#2
Wallace Rk

CORDOVA   BAY

#4

The Narrows
‡See detail above.

NOTE:- Though complex in this small
scale the passage is not difficult
in clear weather. However, the many
rocks and shoals make it essential that
the large scale chart 17433 be used
when navigating this area

#3
G.Bn.

Center Is.

Middle
Is

PRINCE
OF
WALES
Is.

Rocky Pass

Egg Passage

‡

Eureka Channel

G.Bn.
#1

Hessa
Is.

ound Is.

BARRIER   IS.

Mexico
Pt.

DIXON   ENTRANCE beyond

54°45'N

ROUTES ACROSS DIXON ENTRANCE

It is necessary to stand out into Dixon Entrance when leaving Cordova Bay or the Barrier Islands for Prince Rupert. Several routes are available, the choice depending on wind, wave and weather conditions.

Going directly to Prince Rupert via Brown Passage is, harbor to harbor, about 90 nautical miles, of which 65 cross Dixon Entrance to Brown Passage. In good weather this can be a straightforward crossing, usually with quartering seas, and for sailors a good broad reach. Swells in Dixon Entrance are mostly from the west and southwest. Bad weather or fog should be waited out, and the crossing should be arranged to have daylight on the approach to Brown Passage. and Prince Rupert. An alternative destination for southbound travel is to turn southeast from Georgia Rock, enter Porpoise Channel and proceed to moorage facilities in Porpoise Harbour. This choice will save some distance as well as time otherwise spent maneuvering in Prince Rupert Harbour. For details on Porpoise Harbour and Prince Rupert see pages 140 and 142.

A shorter and slightly more protected route passes Cape Chacon crossing to Foggy Bay, about 65 miles, then on to Ketchikan or Prince Rupert. Shorter distances can be found to anchorages on Duke or Annette Islands. **Ryus Bay** is on the north side of Duke Islands, and it is an excellent, sheltered anchorage. **Tamgass Harbor** on Annette Island is also a good anchorage. If necessary, there are harbors and anchorages on the east side of Prince of Wales Island which are closer and in the lee of the land. If a cruise of the Queen Charlotte Islands is next on your itinerary it is just 50 miles across Dixon Entrance and a call to Canada Customs in Prince Rupert is all that is needed if you pre-registered and have a Canpass number. If you do not have a Canpass number you must first clear customs in Prince Rupert before approaching the Queen Charlotte Islands for Massett is not a Port of Entry.

Brundige Inlet on the north side of Dundas Island is another good anchorage which is also useful on the northward route.

ROUTES ACROSS DIXON ENTRANCE

Not to be used for navigation

NOTE: Only those few lights, rocks, and dangers near the passages described are shown. Proper navigational charts are essential for safe travel in these waters.

Depth contours are approximate, given to show the extent of shallow areas.

No Port of Entry in the Charlottes. Use this route if you have a CANPASS No.

To Ketchikan 45 miles via Revillagigedo Channel

55 miles Foggy Bay

65 miles to Foggy Bay

90 miles to Prince Rupert

50 miles to Queen Charlotte Is.

to Prince Rupert

Var. 25° 15' E (1985)

Chatham Sound

Portland Inlet

Foggy Bay

Lord Rk

C. Fox

Kla R.

Port Simpson

Tsimpsean Peninsula

Holiday Is.

Green Is.

Dundas Is.

Metlakatla Is.

Brundige Inlet

Edmanno Passage

Zayas Is.

East Devil Rk

West Devil Rk.

Barren Is.

Ray Anch. & Marie Cove

Duke Is.

Kyus Bay

Saleal Passage

Tamgass Hbr

PRINCE OF WALES IS.

Clarence Strait

Cape Chacon

Nunez Rks.

Barrier Is.

Round Is.

Cordova Bay

Wallace Bk

54° 30' N

54° 20' N

54° 00' N

Eureka Channel

DIXON ENTRANCE

Brown Passage

TreeNob Group

Lucy Is.

Petrel Rk

Porpoise Hbr

Prince Rupert

Venn Pass

Digby Is.

Malacca Passage

Hunt Inlet

Stephens Is.

PORCHER IS.

Hecate Strait

DogFish Bank

Breakers & Overfalls

Racon

Rose Spit

Massel Hbr

Entry Pt.

Wiah Pt.

C. Naden

Naden Hbr

C. Edensaw

Alexandria Narrows

GRAHAM ISLAND

Massel

Naden Harbour

10

3

132° 00'

131° 00'

20'

40'

APPENDIX I: CHARTS and PUBLICATIONS

Canadian Charts and Publications

3313	Strip charts of Gulf Islands
3311	Strip charts of Sunshine Coast
3312	Strip charts of Jervis Inlet and Desolation Sound
3462	Juan de Fuca Strait to Strait of Georgia
3463	Strait of Georgia - Southern Portion
3512	Strait of Georgia - Central Portion
3513	Strait of Georgia - Northern Portion
3538	Desolation Sound and Sutil Channel
3539	Discovery Passage and Seymour Narrows
3541	Approaches to Toba Inlet
3543	Cordero Channel (includes Green Point, Dent, and Yuculta Rapids)
3544	Johnstone Strait, Race Passage and Current Passage
3545	Johnstone Strait - Port Neville to Robson Bight
3546	Broughton Strait with plans for Port McNeill and Alert Bay
3547	Queen Charlotte Strait - Eastern Portion (including Stuart Narrows and Kenneth Passage
3548	Queen Charlotte Strait - Central Portion (including Blunden Harbour and Port Hardy
3549	Queen Charlotte Strait - Western Portion with detail of Bull Harbour
3550	Approaches to Seymour Inlet and Beliize Inlet
3605	Quatsino Sound to Queen Charlotte Strait, Scott Channel
3727	Cape Calvert to Goose Island including Fitz Hugh Sound
3779	Penrose Island
3921	Fifer Bay, Green Island Anchorages
3785	Namu Harbour to Dryad Point, Kliktsoatli Harbour, Namu Harbour
3720	Idol Point to Ocean Falls, Gunboat Passage, Troup Narrows
3728	Milbanke Sound and Approaches
3734	Jorkins Point to Sarah Island, Jackson Narrows
3738	Sarah Island to Swanson Bay, Hiekish Narrows
3739	Swanson Bay to Work Island, Butedale
3740	Work Island to Point Cumming
3742	Otter Passage to McKay Reach
3743	Douglas Channel to Kitimat
3745	Gardner Canal, The Kitlope
3772	Grenville Channel, Sainty Point to Baker Inlet
3773	Grenville Channel, Baker Inlet to Ogden Channel
3927	Bonilla Island to Edye Passage
3957	Approaches to Prince Rupert Harbour
3955	Prince Rupert Harbour, Detail of Venn Passage
3959	Hudson Bay Passage

Chart numbers are constantly changing as new charts are issued. The above list is intended merely to assist in choosing charts for the area covered.

APPENDIX I: CHARTS and PUBLICATIONS Cont'd.

B.C. Coast Pilot - Volume 1: South Portion (Juan de Fuca to Cape Caution)

B.C. Coast Pilot - Volume 2: North Portion (Cape Caution to Stewart)

Small Craft Guide - Volume 1: Port Alberni to Campbell River

Small Craft Guide - Volume 2: Boundary Bay to Cortes Island

List of Lights, Buoys, and Fog Signals - Pacific Coast

Canadian Tide and Current Tables - Volume 5: Juan de Fuca and Georgia Strait

Canadian Tide and Current Tables - Volume 6: Barkley Sound, DiscoveryPassage to Dixon Entrance

Radio Aids to Marine Navigation (Pacific)

A free brochure map, showing the extent and coverage of the charts can be obtained from the Canadian Hydrographic Service or any of its agents. It is useful for determining your own choice of charts.

United States Charts and Publications

17420	Hecate Strait to Etolin Island including Behm and Portland Canals
17360	Etolin Island to Midway Islands including Sumner Strait
17300	Stephens Passage to Cross Sound including Lynn Canal
17320	Coronation Island to Lisianski Strait
17434	Revillagigedo Channel
17430	Ketchikan Harbor
17385	Ernest Sound - Eastern Passage and Zimovia Strait
17382	Zarembo Island and Approaches
17367	Thomas, Farragut and Portage Bays
17363	Pybus Bay, Frederick Sound, Hobart and Windham Bays
17315	Gastineau Channel and Taku Inlet, Juneau Harbor
17316	Lynn Canal - Icy Strait to Point Sherman
17317	Lynn Canal - Point Sherman to Skagway
17302	Icy Strait and Cross Sound, Inian Cove and Elfin Cove
17318	Glacier Bay, Bartlett Cove
17303	Yakobi Island and Lisianski Inlet, Pelican Harbor
17321	Cape Edward to Lisianski Strait, Chichagof Island
17322	Khaz Bay, Chichagof Island, Elbow Pass
17323	Salisbury Sound, Peril Strait and Hoonah Sound
17324	Sitka Sound to Salisbury Sound
17338	Peril Strait - Hoonah Sound to Chatham Strait
17337	Harbors in Chatham Strait, Kelp Bay and Warm Springs Bay
17376	Tebenkof Bay
17375	Wrangell Narrows, Petersburg Harbor
17378	Port Protection, Prince of Wales Island
17386	Sumner Strait - Southern Part
17387	Shakan and Shipley Bays and part of El Capitan Passage

APPENDIX I: CHARTS and PUBLICATIONS Cont'd.

17408   Central Dall Island and Vicinity

17431   North end of Cordova Bay and Hetta Inlet

17433   Kendrick Bay to Shipwreck Point, Prince of Wales Island

17435   Harbors in Clarence Strait: Port Chester, Metlakatla Harbor and Tamgass Harbor

   U.S. Coast Pilot: Dixon Entrance to Cape Spencer (CURRENT EDITION)

   Tide Tables, West Coast, North & South America

   Tidal Current Tables, Pacific Coast of North America and Asia

   Light List, Pacific Coast and Pacific Islands (CURRENT EDITION)

   If you have difficulty in finding all the charts for a trip at a local chart outlet try the following: Captain's Nautical Supply, 1500 West 15th Avenue, Seattle, WA 98119, phone (800) 448-2278 or Nanaimo Maps and Charts, 8 Church Street, Nanaimo, BC V9R 5H4. Order by telephone at 1-800-665-2513 or Fax at 1-800-553-2313.

APPENDIX II: MARINE WEATHER SERVICES from ENVIRONMENT CANADA

MARINE WEATHER ONE-on-ONE

   Mariners can speak directly to an Environment Canada forecaster by calling 1-900-565-5555 when on land. The $2.99 per minute charge gets you detailed information on your specific area of interest.

WEATHER CALL ($5 for the first 3 minutes, $1.95 for each minute thereafter)

   When at sea, mariners can communicate with Environment Canada forecasters, by calling (604) 664-9072, or Fax (604) 664-9081 to set up an account.   Can this be charged to MC or VISA?

WEATHER MENU

   Extended marine forecasts can be obtained by calling 1-900-565-5000. The charge is $.95 per minute.

MARINE WEATHER PHONE

   This free service provides prerecorded marine forecasts from various locations in B.C.

Vancouver	(604) 664-9010	Comox	(250) 339-5044
Victoria	(250) 656-2714	Campbell River	(250) 286-3575
Victoria	(250) 656-2715	Port Hardy	(250) 949-7148
Nanaimo	(250) 245-8899	Prince Rupert	(250) 624-9009

MARINE REPORTING PROGRAM (MAREP) is a means whereby offshore vessels can report weather observations that are relayed to the Pacific Weather Centre and used to improve the accuracy of weather reports. MAREP operators can be reached on the MAREP VHF working channel 69, 10 and 78A or reported to any Coast Guard station on VHF Ch. 26 or 84 at any time.

TELEPHONE NUMBERS OF INTEREST:
RCMP Coastal Watch Program   - Toll free: 888-855-6655
EPIRB Registration – (800) 727-9414
Fisheries Violation Reporting Line – Toll free: (800) 465-4336
Coast Guard Emergency/Pollution Response Hotline - (800) 889-8852
Shellfish Information (including red tide updates) – (604) 666-2828
To report Marine Mammal activities and strandings - (250) 756-7253

APPENDIX III: MARINE WEATHER REPORTING STATIONS, WEATHER BUOYS, WEATHER REPORT CHANNELS and LOCATION OF MANNED LIGHTHOUSES

Coast Guard Call Channel: VHF Ch. 16
Coast Guard Working Channel: VHF Ch. 22A

☺ Manned Lighthouse

Marine Forecasts
(Local Times)
0400
1030
1600
2130

DIXON ENTRANCE EAST

Mount Dent (21B)

DIXON ENTRANCE WEST

Central Dixon Entrance 46145

West Dixon Entrance 46205

Dundas I. (WX2)
Grey Islet
Green Island
Triple I.
Lucy I.
Prince Rupert
Mt. Hayes (21B)

Langara I.
Rose Spit
Naden Hbr (WX2)
Holland Rock

Kitimat (21B)

DOUGLAS CHANNEL

Nanakwa Shoal

WEST COAST CHARLOTTES

N. Hecate Strait 46183

Kindakun Rocks
Sandspit
Van Inlet (WX1)
Cumshewa (WX3)
Cumshewa I.

Bonilla Is.

Mount Gil (WX2)

HECATE STRAIT

Barry Inlet (WX2)
Hoskins Islet
Scudder Pt.

West Moresby

S. Hecate Strait

Boat Bluff

Cape St. James

Klemtu (WX1)
McInnes I.
Ivory I.
Dryad Pt.
Bella Coola
Cathedral Pt.

CENTRAL COAST

QUEEN CHARLOTTE SOUND

West Sea Otter

Addenbroke

BOWIE

South Moresby

East Delwood

Calvert (WX2)

Egg I.

Pine I.

QUEEN CHARLOTTE STRAIT

Herbert I.
Scarlett Pt.

JOHNSTONE STRAIT

Sartine I.
Cape Scott
Pulteney Pt.
Alert Bay (WX1)
Helmcken I. (WX3)
Chatham Pt. (21B)
Fanny Island

STRAIT OF GEORGIA

Quatsino
Discovery Mtn. (21B)
Campbell R.
Cape Mudge

Solander I.

Sentry Shoal
Powell River
Grief Point

HOWE SOUND

WEST COAST VANCOUVER ISLAND NORTH

Eliza Dome (WX1)
South Brooks

Cape Lazo (WX1)
Comox
Sisters I.
Chrome I.
Ballenas I.

Merry I.
Pam Rocks
Bowen I (WX 3)
Pt. Atkinson
Jericho
Sand Heads
Tsawwassen
East Pt.

Nootka (WX2)
Estevan Pt.

Halibut Bank

Entrance I.
Nanaimo

EXPLORER

Lennard I.
Tofino
Amphitrite Pt.

Alberni (WX2)
Mt. Ozzard (21B)
Pachena Pt.
Carmanah Pt.
Cape Beale
Mount Park (21B)

La Perouse Bank

Mt. Helmcken (WX3)

Kelp Reef
Discovery I.
Smith I.
Trial Is.
Race Rocks

Sheringham Pt.

WEST COAST VANCOUVER ISLAND SOUTH

Cape Flattery

HARO STRAIT

WX1 - 162.55 MHZ
WX2 - 162.40 MHZ
WX3 - 162.475 MHZ
21B - 161.65 MHZ
Weatheradio Canada - 162.40 MHZ
Weatheradio Canada - 1260 Khz (am band)
Weatheradio Canada - 103.70 MHZ

APPENDIX IV U.S. WEATHER INFORMATION FOR SOUTHEAST ALASKA

NOAA WEATHER RADIO

Continuous VHF - FM radio broadcasts are available from the National Weather Service and the U.S. Coast Guard. Weather information may be found on seven VHF high-band FM frequencies between 162.400 and 162.550 megahertz; weather channels 1 through 7.

VOICE WEATHER BROADCASTS and MARINE OBSERVATION REPORTING

Voice weather broadcasts are provided on the upper sideband (USB) 4125 khz from the following stations at the times listed:

Annette	KGD58	0700 and 1540
Kodiak	KWL38	0800 and 1800
Yakutat	KDG91	0515 and 1930

FORECAST UPDATES

0400 hours and 1600 hours local time
Marine warnings and amendments are issued at any time.

SOURCES OF ADDITIONAL INFORMATION

National Weather Service Offices

Annette	(907) 886-3241	Valdez	(907) 835-4505
Juneau	(907) 790-6800	Yakutat	(907) 784-3322

Recorded Marine Forecasts

Juneau	(907) 586-3997	Wrangell	(907) 874-3232
Sitka	(907) 747-6011	Yakutat	(907) 784-3654

Alaska Weather Line

Recorded weather statewide menu within Alaska 800-472-0391
In Anchorage (907) 266-5145 In Juneau (907) 790-6850

Dial-a Buoy (907) 228-688-1948 or visit www.ndbc.noaa.gov

Marine weather information includes temperature, wind direction and speed, wave height, swell wave period and steepness. Use the station identification number to request the observation. Buoys are located at the following locations:

#46083 – Fairweather Grounds: 58°15'04"N, 137°59'56"W
#46084 – Cape Edgecumbe: 56°35'24"N, 136°09'36"W
#46184 -- North Nomad: 53°54'60"N, 138°50'60"W
#46205 – West Dixon Entrance: 54°09'60"N, 134°16'07"W
#46145 -- Central Dixon Entrance: 54°22'02"N, 132°26'60"W
#46183 -- North Hecate Strait: 53°37'60"N, 131°05'60"W

Internet site for Alaska: www.arh.noaa.gov

DESCRIPTIVE CRITERIA USED IN WEATHER FORECASTS

WIND SPEED	CANADA	U.S.
0 – 11 knots	Light winds	
12 – 19 knots	Moderate winds	
20 – 33 knots	Strong winds	Small craft advisory
34 – 47 knots	Gale force winds	Gale warning
48 – 63 knots	Storm force winds	Storm warning
64 knots or higher	Hurricane force winds	Hurricane force wind warning

APPENDIX V

Table of Distances

The intersection of columns between two places is the approximate distance in nautical miles. Distances can be added between sections. Use only for planning Measure the actual distances on your chart.

Example: Safety Cove is 222 miles from Prince Rupert, and 222 + 179 = 401 miles from Wrangell.

Northern section

Craig	144						156
	Sitka	148	162	159	170	224	314
		Glacier Bay	94	188	220	290	380
			Juneau	108	148	220	310
				Petersburg	40	112	200
					Wrangell	89	179
						Ketchikan	90
							Prince Rupert

Craig–Sitka (via Cape Decision & El Capitan); Craig–Prince Rupert = 156 (via Cordova Bay & Cape Chacon); Sitka–Prince Rupert (via Peril Strait)

Central coast section

Prince Rupert	100	138	180	222	277
	Butedale	66	80	122	177
		Klemtu	43	85	142
			Bella Bella	42	97
				Safety Cove	75
					Port Hardy

Port Hardy	26	108	140	161	183	207
	Alert Bay	83	114	136	158	182
		Campbell River	31	53	75	99
			Powell River	26	52	70
				Pender Harbour	30	48
					Nanaimo	34
						Vancouver*

Gulf Islands section

Vancouver*	27	40	50	73
	Silva Bay, Gabriola Pass	23	35	58
		Montague Harbor, Active Pass	17	39
			Sidney	24
				Victoria

(Via Gulf Islands)

Strait of Georgia / San Juan Islands section

Vancouver*	32	45	50	80
	Point Roberts	13	28	47
		Blaine	31	53
			Friday Harbor	27
				Victoria

(Via Strait of Georgia)   (Via San Juan Islands)

* At the entrance to Burrard Inlet

APPENDIX VI: SYMBOLS

- - - - - -	Recommended route	(symbol)	Lights in line on bearing
⚓	Anchorage	⚓	Reported anchorage
×	Rock or reef underwater	⊛	Dangerous rock or reef
(symbol)	Rocks exposed by tide	(symbol)	Shoal area exposed by tide
(symbol)	Steep rocky edges	(symbol)	Sand or pebble beach
(symbol)	Glacier	5 kn	Current velocity in knots
☼, ⚑	Lighthouse, navigation lights	△, ⊡ Bn	Beacons, not necessarily lit
_3_	Depth contour in fathoms	→	Flood current
4 , 4f	Depth in fathoms	←	Ebb current
S	Sand bottom	↺, ↻	Eddies or whirlpools
m	Mud bottom	∿∿∿	Rips and/or overfalls
r	Rock bottom	▽P	Pump-out facility
F	Fuel	AR	Artificial reef

NOTE: All depths are given in fathoms, except where specifically mentioned in feet. Approximately 2 meters = 1 fathom and exactly 1.8 meters = 1 fathom.

INDEX

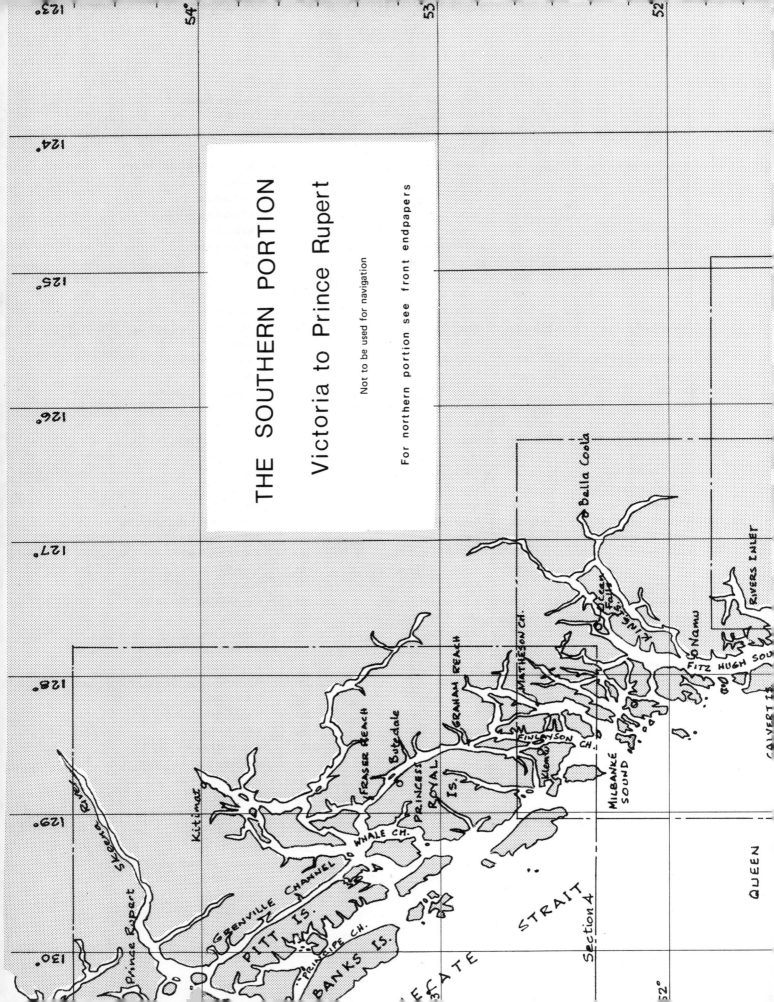

THE SOUTHERN PORTION

Victoria to Prince Rupert

Not to be used for navigation

For northern portion see front endpapers